Economic Literacy

Basic Economics with an Attitude

Second Edition

FREDERICK S. WEAVER

ROWMAN & LITTLEFIELD PUBLISHERS, INC.
Lanham • Boulder • New York • Toronto • Plymouth, UK

For MADELINE, DAMIEN, TORSTEN, and EVA Q.

ROWMAN & LITTLEFIELD PUBLISHERS, INC.

Published in the United States of America
by Rowman & Littlefield Publishers, Inc.
A wholly owned subsidiary of The Rowman & Littlefield Publishing Group, Inc.
4501 Forbes Boulevard, Suite 200, Lanham, Maryland 20706
www.rowmanlittlefield.com

Estover Road
Plymouth PL6 7PY
United Kingdom

British Library Cataloguing in Publication Information Available

Library of Congress Cataloging-in-Publication Data
Weaver, Frederick Stirton, 1939–
  Economic literacy : basic economics with an attitude / Frederick S. Weaver. — 2nd ed.
    p. cm.
  Includes bibliographical references and indexes.
  ISBN-13: 978-0-7425-5429-0 (cloth : alk. paper)
  ISBN-10: 0-7425-5429-5 (cloth : alk. paper)
  ISBN-13: 978-0-7425-5430-6 (pbk. : alk. paper)
  ISBN-10: 0-7425-5430-9 (pbk. : alk. paper)
  1. Economics. I. Title.
  HB171.5.W3 2006
  330—dc22   2006020252

Printed in the United States of America

♾ ™ The paper used in this publication meets the minimum requirements of American
National Standard for Information Sciences—Permanence of Paper for Printed Library
Materials, ANSI/NISO Z39.48-1992.

Contents

2 The Theory of the Firm, Market Structures, Factor Markets, and the Distribution of Income

II MACROECONOMICS

3 The Economy as a Whole: Definitions and Analyses

4 Fiscal Policy, Monetary Policy, Recession, and Inflation

III INTERNATIONAL ECONOMICS AND NATIONAL ECONOMIES

5 International Economics and Comparative Advantage

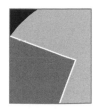

Figures

Tables

Preface

T he principal goal of this book is to convey the basic concepts and language of economic theory at a level necessary for understanding current affairs and for reading some of the professional economics literature. This goal also requires describing the economy and the principal economic institutions, and in doing so, I highlight the important changes in the U.S. economy over the past three decades. This is important stuff. A familiarity with formal economics is essential for sorting out key processes in contemporary society and for understanding and participating in debates about public issues, which are increasingly cast in the language of economics. Acknowledging this situation, advanced courses in the social sciences often depend on an ability to work with economic concepts.

There are a lot of books out there with goals that sound similar to mine. These range from business-oriented books that promise insight into the workings of the economy in order to make money to those that strive to show how the rationality and logic of economic analysis can dispel sloppy thinking about everyday life. Then there are the books that are the most like mine, books that directly attempt to explicate the workings of the economy for "non-economists." While some of these books are better than others, what they all have in common is that they claim to achieve their purposes without using the "arcane jargon" and "technical analyses" of economics. This is very different from my endeavor. My book deliberately confronts and explains the jargon, analyses, and fundamental ideas of academic economics as a necessary step for readers to move beyond being passive consumers of other people's conclusions.

This takes us to the foremost category of books on economics: standard textbooks designed for college and university courses in introductory economics. This is a major industry in its own right, and publishers have paid millions of dollars in advances to authors for a marketable textbook. These books do introduce readers to the interior workings of economic analysis, but they also tend to be encyclopedic in scope and size, frequently cost $70 or more for six-color graphs and other expensive trimmings, and devote substantial space to the complex (and easily forgotten) analytics for students going on to advanced courses in economics. I have written this book for those who do not need the theoretical constructions of advanced economics but desire to achieve a workable level of economic literacy, whether or not they are veterans of a course in introductory economics.

My major dissatisfaction with these standard introductory textbooks, however, is not their bulk, expense, and comprehensiveness. First of all, I believe that the way that textbooks portray economics is one of the reasons that the introductory economics course has such a terrible reputation among students. With depressingly few exceptions, textbook authors, deliberately or not, set themselves up as smug wizards who reveal truths to the reader. In addition to being distasteful to students, this stance discourages critical thinking. All textbooks present examples to show how economic thinking cuts through muddled common sense to arrive at correct and often amazingly counter-intuitive conclusions, but this is just the wizard again.

By representing economic theory as seamless, satisfactorily nailed down, and indistinguishable from the subject matter (processes of production and distribution), these textbooks give no space for skepticism and thereby assure students that critically scrutinizing economics itself is a waste of time. No matter how many interactive electronic gizmos come with the textbooks to promote "active learning," as long as the texts present the discipline of economics as a self-contained body of knowledge with universal applicability, they are encouraging intellectual passivity.

Finally, these books repeatedly drive home the superiority of a supposedly unbiased "positive science" over subjective "value judgments" and thus deliberately empty economics of social and political content and detach it from general currents of liberal thought. I believe that removing moral and political issues from the realm of legitimate economic inquiry further contributes to students' resistance to the subject, and I make the connections that I believe are important and interesting.

In order to avoid these problems of representation, it is imperative to distinguish between explaining "economics"—an academic discipline—and explaining "the economy"—the processes of producing and distributing goods and services. These two dimensions of explanation are not the same. The discipline of economics provides one way to view the organization and operation of economy, and it is extremely important to grasp this mode of analysis. This is what the book is about. Nevertheless, academic economics is not the only lens through which one can view economic practices, and like all intellectual constructs, academic economics contains definite limits as well as buried presuppositions that affect conclusions. So while this book focuses on conventional economics, it also expresses my conviction that true economic literacy requires the ability to think critically about the particular viewpoint proposed by the discipline of economics, which has come to dominate political discourse. This is one of the key differences between my book and other seemingly comparable books.

But this book is neither a critique of economics nor a treatise on social theory. It is an introduction to the basic ideas of mainstream economics and to economists' distinctive brand of linear logic and worldview. My decisions about what is worth including and what is not are based on my forty years of teaching introductory economics. While some of my presentations are quite conventional, many of them are my own particular approaches that I have honed on numerous cohorts of students. I use some graphs (mostly in the first chapter) as a supplement to written descriptions, and I use tables to present information and to introduce students to the most important and easily accessible sources of economic data. In all of this, however, the book contains nothing that goes beyond good ol' fashioned arithmetic.

The second edition has allowed me to bring the tables and discussions of economic trends up to date and to include some additional material.

The most extensive new discussions concern the Social Security crisis, tax reform, surging petroleum prices, and two topics essential for understanding the global economy: the 1980s international debt crisis and the rise of China as a world economic power. I have also incorporated into the second edition some reflections on the shifts in market power from producers to retailers, patterns of corporate dishonesty and malfeasance, and the economic effects of the war in Iraq and of the devastation from Hurricane Katrina.

Working on the second edition also gave me the opportunity to revise and clarify some of the prose and to insert a couple more one-liners. After all, like the first edition, the book is serious, but it is not grim. It is introductory economics with an attitude.

Acknowledgments

In a sense, I began writing this book when I first taught introductory economics in the fall of 1961 as a teaching assistant at the University of Washington. Or maybe better, it was the fall of 1962 when, as a senior teaching assistant at Cornell University, I first taught introductory economics with full course responsibility. The actual starting point is not all that important, but what is important is that despite the number of years that I have been teaching this stuff, my students continue to make it enjoyable. Not always, but usually, and I acknowledge them with real appreciation.

In the actual period in which I sat down and wrote the first edition of the book, I incurred a number of debts to people who read earlier drafts and helped me make it a better book. And it really was a better book than when they saw it, in good part due to their comments and criticisms. Harold Barnett, Michael Edelstein, Laurie Nisonoff, and Nancy Wiegersma read the manuscript in various stages of development and were generous with their time and experience in pointing out problems, suggesting better formulations, and forcing me to rethink the selection of topics and issues appropriate for such a book. And Soren Johnson did a great job on the figures.

My greatest debt, however, is to my colleague Stanley Warner. Stan and I began the book together, and we wrote some of the first chapters together.

Although he had to drop out because of scheduling problems (or was it to protect his reputation?), he continued to read drafts and help me. He has left an indelible and positive mark on the book, and I am deeply grateful.

My wife, Sharon Hartman Strom, was less directly involved in this book than in my more historically oriented projects. Nevertheless, even though she was finishing yet another book of her own, she read some of the manuscript, made good suggestions, and always came through with encouragement and wonderful companionship.

Finally, I have had the good fortune to work with an outstanding group of people at (and through) Rowman & Littlefield. I am especially appreciative of the professionalism and humor of Jennifer Knerr, Jehanne Schweitzer, Mary Bearden, Renée Legatt, Erin McGarvey, and Brigitte Scott. Niels Aaboe became the editor of the second edition after the preliminary revisions and timetables had already been set, and although the situation must have been difficult for him, he embodied the spirit, competence, and patience of the Rowman & Littlefield staff that I value so highly.

Thank you all very much.

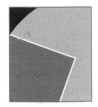

Introduction

I n the primal stirrings of human history, as the morning mist lifted from the velvet valley floor, a thunderous voice from the mountains to the east roared: I Demand!!!

And—with scarcely a pause—a valiant voice from the mountains to the west resounded: I will Supply!!!

Much later, in the seventeenth, eighteenth, and nineteenth centuries, the founders of a fledgling science—economics (though not yet so named)—sought to uncover the natural laws that govern the ways humans produce and exchange the goods and services of life. In 1776 Adam Smith, occupying a chair in moral philosophy at the University of Glasgow, published *An Inquiry into the Nature and Causes of the Wealth of Nations*. In it he articulated the most famous and paradoxical principle of economics: People who engage in the production and sale of goods are motivated by a quest for personal gain, but the operation of the competitive market leads them "as if by an invisible hand" to accomplish the greater social good. What was that good? It was the allocation of a society's resources to make the combination of products most prized by consumers, with each item produced in the most efficient manner and sold at the lowest price possible.

While Adam Smith offered many a wise caution about the ways markets could go astray—not the least of which was the tendency of competition to give way to monopoly—his discovery that competitive markets advance the public good while being driven by private profit-seeking behavior was so captivating in its esthetic beauty that most economists still haven't gotten over it. So producers compete fiercely with one another, consumers and producers seem to have opposing interests, and struggles over shares of income and claims of price gouging are rampant. All the same, the strong conclusion is that these apparent conflicts add up to a social system that is, in its essence, characterized by harmony.[1] Any serious inquiry, therefore, into the question of whether our social system is one of fundamental social harmony or fundamental social conflict must be informed by an understanding of the principles of economics. This is the purpose of this book.

Markets, of course, had been around for a long time before the rise of capitalism. The ancient trucking and bartering of the village marketplace gradually expanded within feudal and slave societies, and exploration and conquest created new or more secure trade routes. Before European contact, nearly every indigenous group on the North American continent used tobacco, obtained largely through trade, as part of its medical and social practices. But it is under capitalism that markets have become such dominant institutions. Even at that, the predominance of markets is historically quite recent.

In 1900, over 120 years after Smith first celebrated the market, the most developed economies still produced over half of their national output outside the market within the household. (The original Greek meaning of "economy" was household economy.) Now, at the beginning of the twenty-first century, the trenchant march of the monetization and commodification of every corner of human life brings "advanced" societies to the point where we transact to have our hair cut and set, our bodies exercised, our psyches probed and realigned, our children watched over, our gardens groomed, our pets spayed or neutered and trained, our lunches manufactured at McDonald's, and our health insured. And in the quintessential expression of the principle "nothing is free," we push a quarter into the slot of a meter to purchase fifteen minutes of curbside time to park the machine that got us there. It is not simply the marvels of technological change that have been transforming—as spectacular as they are. The larger revolution is the incorporation of so many dimensions of human existence into market-driven processes of production and exchange.

There were no primal voices from the mountains across the valley floor. There are no "natural laws" of supply and demand. There is only the explosion in very recent human history of a system called capitalism. Slave systems, feudalism, and communes have all wrestled with issues of production, scarcity, efficiency, distribution, and credit, but it is the special domain of capitalism to structure these matters around an elaborate web of markets. Not the least of these markets is the labor market, in which the vast majority of adults sell their labor time for a wage or salary. The defining feature of capitalism is not the effort to seek a profit or surplus. Slavery and feudalism had their ways for doing that as well. It is the pervasive use of labor markets, in conjunction with product markets and financial markets, that determines the character of economic activity and forms the defining feature of capitalism.

Markets are the principal subject of economics, and a common definition of economics is that it is the study of how markets operate to organize the production and distribution of material goods and services, allocating scarce resources among competing ends to meet unlimited wants and needs. The assumption that wants and desires are unlimited means that the (finite) capacity to produce goods and services will always fall short of fully satisfying everybody's (infinite) desire for more. Although not necessarily implying material deprivation, scarcity is posited as a constant condition. This notion of scarcity means that the basic productive resources (e.g., land, labor, and capital) used to produce a particular set of goods and services could always be employed making something different. That is, productive resources always have alternative uses, and every economic decision necessarily involves a trade-off. Economists call the value of those alternatives, or trade-offs, **opportunity costs.**[2] The principle of efficiency, then, requires that the value of any particular use of a productive resource should have opportunity costs less than its current employment.

The idea that everything has an opportunity cost lies behind the familiar mantra of economics: "There ain't no such thing as a free lunch." When a corporation uses its own funds to build a new plant, the opportunity cost to the corporation is the earnings that could have been made from an alternative use of those funds, such as the purchase of interest-bearing government bonds. At the level of national policy, do we use our resources to occupy Iraq or to fight a war against terrorists? At a more mundane level, when Joe buys a snowboard, he has forgone the enjoyment of having bought skis instead, to say nothing of a trombone or an economics textbook.

The particular way in which social relationships are structured around production and distribution is the "social" side of economics as a social science. More than any other social science, however, economics aspires to be a *science*, capable of standing alongside physics in its methods of inquiry, its use of quantitative data, its criteria for confirming or disproving hypotheses, its universal relevance, and its claim to being "objective" or value free (i.e., without political predispositions). The aspiration to be a "real" science has led to a definite abstractness. ("To economists, the real world is a special case.") Thus human and nonhuman entities are treated as having parallel importance or standing: "labor," "land," and "capital" are coequally inputs to production (or "factors" of production); prices, quantities, and markets are given independent identities; and human behavior is reduced to rational (maximizing) decisions carried out in the role of either producer or consumer. These comments are not a criticism of the need to abstract in order to construct a theory that emphasizes some variables to the exclusion of others. They are simply to remind everyone that abstraction entails choices about emphases, and those choices have very definite implications that go beyond the immediate field of inquiry. Moreover, as I show in chapter 2, the goal of being a value-neutral science struggles against a set of substantial ethical judgments that are embedded so deeply in the economics discipline that they are all but invisible as value judgments.

Despite the discipline's scientific goals, divergent political opinions among economists do color their professional work, but even so, there are large areas of substantial agreement that follow from the analytical principles that define the academic discipline. The results from a survey of economists' beliefs in the 1990s, presented in table I.1, counter all the jokes about economists' never agreeing ("Lay all the economists end on end, and you'll reach no conclusion.").[3] This survey, along with my own experience, is the basis for my frequently making statements like "Economists generally agree that . . . ;" or "Most economists believe that. . . ." I'm not just making it up.

Before I describe the organization of the book, there is one more important piece of introductory information. The U.S. economy is large and complex, and a myriad of goods and services are produced and sold every year. Table I.2 lists the range of goods and services arranged in very large categories arrayed by the number of employees working in the sector. The purpose of this table is to give you some sense of the relative (and changing) importance of different economic activities.

Two of the most striking changes shown by the table are the sharp reduction of employment in agriculture and the more general increase in the employment in all sorts of services at the expense of material goods, including manufacturing. Some of this shift toward services has to do with the previously mentioned increase of market production for what had previously been produced in the household outside the market. This in turn reflects the substantial expansion of married women working for pay as well as changes in lifestyles that prosperity has made affordable to many.

TABLE I.1 Examples of Economists' Consensus in the 1990s	
Statements pertaining to chapters 1 and 2	**Percentage of Economists in Substantial Agreement**
A ceiling on rents reduces the quantity and quality of housing available.	92.9
A minimum wage increases unemployment among young and unskilled workers.	78.9
Cash payments increase the welfare of recipients to a greater degree than do transfers-in-kind of equal cash value.	83.9
The redistribution of income within the U.S. is a legitimate role for government.	81.9
Statements pertaining to chapters 3 and 4	
Fiscal policy (e.g., tax cut and/or expenditure increase) has a significant stimulative impact on a less than fully employed economy.	89.9
Wage-price controls are a useful policy option in the control of inflation.	26.1
Statements pertaining to chapters 5 and 6	
Tariffs and import quotas usually reduce general economic welfare.	92.6
Flexible and floating exchange rates offer an effective international monetary arrangement.	89.6

Source: Richard Alston, J. R. Earl, and Michael B. Vaughan, "Is There a Consensus among Economists in the 1990s?" *American Economic Review* (May 1992): 203–9.

Note: The survey also revealed areas of strong disagreement. Some of the most notable included the self-correcting nature of economic recessions, the desirability of the former Soviet Union's going so rapidly into a market system, the causes of inflation, the need to reduce the level of government expenditures, the existence of a "natural rate" of unemployment, the negative effects of large balance-of-trade deficits, the efficacy of several government policies—antitrust, consumer protection, decreasing tax rates (including capital gains taxes), and retaliation against nations engaging in unfair trade practices.

TABLE I.2	Employment by Major Industries (percentages of total employment)		
	1950	1980	2004
Goods Production	**51.8**	**31.2**	**17.8**
Agriculture	18.0	3.9	1.5
Mining, Forestry, Fishing	1.6	1.1	0.4
Construction	4.3	4.6	5.2
Manufacturing	27.6	21.6	10.7
Service Production	**48.3**	**68.8**	**82.0**
Transportation & Public Utilities	7.3	5.5	4.4
Wholesale Trade	4.8	5.6	3.4
Retail Trade	12.2	16.0	11.2
Finance, Insurance, Real Estate	3.4	5.5	6.0
Other Services	9.7	19.0	40.8
Federal Government	3.5	3.0	2.0
State & Local Government	7.4	14.2	14.2
Total (percentages)	100.0	100.0	100.0
Total (1,000 people)	55,123	94,105	134,315

Sources: Economic Report of the President, 2000, p. 358; Economic Report of the President, 2001, pp. 318, 326–29; Survey of Current Business (May 2000), p. D-34; Economic Report of the President, 2005, table B-46.

Notes on subcategories for 2004:

Oil and gas extraction workers made up 12 percent of "Mining, Forestry, and Fishing."

Transport workers were 80 percent of the "Transportation and Public Utilities" category.

In the "Finance, Insurance, and Real Estate" category, employees in banks and real estate comprised roughly a third each, insurance a quarter, and stock brokers, mutual funds, and so on make up the rest.

In the heterogeneous "Other Services" subcategory, health services are more than a quarter of the subcategory, business services (lawyers, accountants, security, janitors, and so on) are over a fifth, while education and leisure-hospitality (including zoos and museums as well as hotels and restaurants) each make up a fifth. The remainder of the subcategory is made up of membership organizations (churches, Sierra Club, NAACP, unions), auto repair, car washes, beauticians, morticians, laundries, and other disparate miscellaneous groupings.

"Federal Government" does not include men and women in the military.

Education is about half of "State and Local Government" employment.

The move away from material production to services is substantial, but there is a way in which the table exaggerates the size of the change. As large corporations have reorganized themselves ("restructured" or "downsized"), they have tended to contract out for a range of services that they had previously done in-house, by their own employees. For example, when an automobile firm hired people directly to work in security, accounting, cleaning, hauling, and advertising, those people were counted as working in the automobile manufacturing sector. When the firm fires all of those folks and contracts for the services with independent specialized firms, however, workers performing the same functions are counted as services. In any case, look over the table and pay attention to the notes to get a preliminary idea of what is out there.

The Organization of the Book

This book, while a bit irreverent around the edges, is above all about mainstream, consensus economic analysis. Nevertheless, I do not hesitate to remark on some areas of real dispute in the profession and indicate other areas in which I believe there should be more dispute.

I have organized the book into three parts with two chapters in each. The first part is on **microeconomics**, sometimes called neoclassical economics, which is the branch of economic analysis that studies the workings of individual markets. In this part I discuss how prices are set, the consequences of different degrees of competition, how resources are allocated among various uses, how changes reverberate throughout the economy, how income is distributed, and in general, the anatomy of the invisible hand. Microeconomics is the heart of economic theory, and although it involves the workings of individual markets, its approach has profound implications for social organization and government policies.

Part II focuses on **macroeconomics**, sometimes called Keynesian economics. As "macro" suggests, this is a level of analysis that looks at the performance of the economy as a whole—the big picture—with particular attention to business cycles, inflation, unemployment, and growth. Moreover, the theory is designed to guide government demand management policies. By showing the effects of changes in taxation, expenditure, and interest rates on the level of aggregate demand, macroeconomic theory enabled the federal government to be deliberate in its effort to stimulate or retard the general level of economic activity in order to promote economic stability and growth. There is definitely some tension between microeconomics and macroeconomics, and the desirability and feasibility of government intervention in the economy are not the least of their differences.

The third part focuses on international economics and the international economy. In chapter 5, I describe the theory of international trade, adjustment mechanisms for trade imbalances, and the roles of exchange rates and international investment. The final chapter stands apart from the others in that it draws on many of the principal points made in the first five chapters in order to discuss the effects of recent increases in international trade and investment and greater economic interdependence among nations—"globalization," to use that unlovely word. Although I focus on the organization of international trade and finance, these are increasingly the most important contextual factors for understanding the functioning of the domestic U.S. economy. The most effective way to develop this context is through describing the international realm's post–World War II evolution, emphasizing the manner in which it has changed and developed new stress points. This includes describing some of the principal international economic institutions, such as the International Monetary Fund, the World Bank, and the World Trade Organization, as well as some of the watershed events that transformed the international trade and payments systems.

While it is different, the sixth chapter's difference can be seen to have simply extended the organizational pattern of the rest of the book. In a rough sort of way, the first chapter of each part is more about economic analysis and the second is more about the U.S. economy. But don't hold me to that.

Notes

1. This apparent contradiction has been celebrated by the aphorism that capitalism is the only social system in which elites' status and wealth depend directly on their satisfying the demands of the masses.

2. Terms in bold typeface are especially important and can be found in the index.

3. You may not yet understand a good number of the terms and ideas used in the table, but after all, that's why you're reading this book.

Microeconomics and the Theory of Markets

Demand and Supply

A t the very core of modern economies is a system of markets that regulates the production of goods and services, determines the wages and incomes of the citizenry, and serves as both cause and cure for economic instability. One factor above all others—price—is singled out as the key arbiter of the complex set of forces that shapes market behavior.

The terms supply and demand represent the view that the many factors determining price can be divided into two largely independent sets: those that determine the willingness of sellers to produce and sell (the supply side) and those that determine the willingness of purchasers to buy (the demand side). While the explanation of how markets function is not the only task of economics, it is the main starting point.

Demand

Other things held equal, people buy (demand) more of a commodity if the price is lowered, and they buy (demand) less if the price is raised. This modest observation, found true with rare exception, can be illustrated with the simple graphs in figure 1.1. In addition to the downward (negative) slope, demand curves are usually drawn as straight lines, although they still are called curves (or functions). Nevertheless, they may meander downward in any fashion as long as they do not bend back. Finally, the usual direction of causation is from price to quantity demanded; that is, price is the determining variable.

The first graph in figure 1.1 (A) is the demand curve for coffee purchases, with the price of coffee on the vertical axis and the quantity (pounds in this case) on the horizontal axis, and the second (B) is for fresh strawberries, both in Northampton, Massachusetts. If the price of coffee were to rise from $4.00 a pound to $6.00 a pound, the people of Northampton would buy fewer pounds of coffee. In a similar manner, if strawberry prices rise from $1.50 a pint to $2.50 a pint, people buy fewer

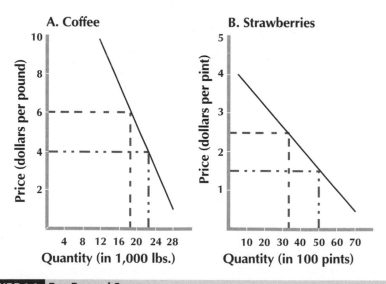

FIGURE 1.1 Two Demand Curves

pints of strawberries. The equal and opposite relationship holds for prices declining, which would stimulate increased purchases of each product.

There is, however, a noticeable difference between the two demand curves, apart from the units in which their quantities are calibrated. Northampton folks *really* like coffee, and as a result, the quantity of coffee demanded does not change as much in response to a change in price as does the quantity demanded of strawberries. Why might that be? Availability of good substitutes? Coffee shops as a good place to meet people? Addiction?

As important as what the graphs display (the relationship between quantity demanded and price) is what the graphs hide. Everything that influences quantity demanded except price is not shown, and in addition, those other influences are assumed to be held constant in order to focus on the effects of price changes. What are these other influences?

Income and Wealth

Income is how much money one receives, usually in wages, salaries, interest, profits, and rent, over a period of time (e.g., a year) and therefore is called a **flow variable**. Wealth, on the other hand, is the value of how much one *owns* at a particular point in time (e.g., his or her total assets such as houses, cars, bank deposits, and cash in pockets at midnight on December 31, 2006) and is called a **stock variable**. Higher levels of income and wealth lead people to buy more of most goods (called "normal" goods). On the other hand, hamburger or used cars may be examples of "inferior goods," which people buy less of when their incomes rise. Some goods are normal over some range of incomes and inferior at higher incomes: tourist class airline tickets, rat poison, and picket fences, for example.

Prices of Other Goods

Some goods are substitutes for each other. If the price of chicken declines, it probably reduces the quantity of beef purchased at any given price as people switch to the cheaper meat. Other goods are complements to one another. A decline in the price of sports utility vehicles leading to the purchase of more SUVs requires an increase in the amount of gasoline sold.

Tastes

"I hate turnips." "I buy only union label." "I'm a vegetarian." "I like both kinds of music, country *and* western." All the mysteries of consumer psychology are bundled together in the one variable, taste. Changes in taste (which in other people we call fads) that affect a significant number of consumers at one time increase or decrease the quantity of a product that is demanded at any given price.

Expectations

"I expect the future price of this commodity will be higher, so I'll buy more now." "I'll wait for the post-holiday sale."

All the factors listed here affect the quantity demanded of a particular commodity, but on the graph only the relationship between price and quantity demanded is noted. This means that a change in income, tastes, and whatever lead to a change in the relationship between price and quantity demanded. In geometric terms, the effect of, say, a change in income will be registered as a shift in the price-quantity line, so it is no surprise to learn that these factors are called **shift variables**. For example, a rise in consumers' incomes leads to a rightward shift in the demand curve that relates price to quantity demanded. That outward shift means that with higher incomes, people will buy more of the commodity at each price.

You have to be careful, then, about what is affecting the quantity demanded. Changes in demand conditions, of the demand curve, or of the demand function are different ways to say that there has been a shift in the curve, altering the relationship between price and the quantity demanded. On the other hand, a "change in quantity demanded" refers to a movement *along* the existing demand curve in response to a change in supply conditions that affected price.

Supply

Now let's examine the concept of supply in the same terms I used for demand. Other things held equal, a firm will supply a larger quantity of its product as the price rises and will supply smaller amounts if the price falls. In figure 1.2, you see the relationship between prices and quantities supplied as typically drawn.

Just as in the case of the demand function, price is thought to determine the quantity that firms are willing to produce and sell, but it is a *positive* relationship—higher prices lead to more goods and services supplied, and lower prices lead to fewer supplied. Again like the demand curve, the relationship between price and quantity supplied is affected by a number of shift factors.

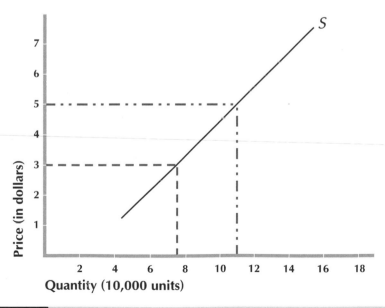

FIGURE 1.2 Supply Curve

Prices of Inputs

The prices of raw materials, labor, energy, capital equipment, land, and so on affect costs of production and therefore the quantity of a good that producers are willing to supply at any particular price.

Technology

This is a catchall category that refers to the efficiency by which inputs are combined and converted into output, thus affecting production costs. New kinds of manufacturing processes and improved forms of organizational coordination are two of the many possible ways of improving efficiency and lowering costs of production.

Expectations

How might anticipations of future events alter the decision about how much to produce today? Parallel to demand analysis, a "change in quantity supplied" means a movement along the supply curve induced by a change in price. On the other hand, a change in any of the supply curve's shift factors ("a change in supply conditions") causes the entire relationship between price and quantity supplied to alter, and in geometrical terms, it means a shift in the entire supply curve.

Shifts in the supply curve can be tricky. For example, a *decrease* in supply conditions causes the curve to shift inward, or to the left, indicating that for reasons of higher production costs or whatever, producers are willing to supply fewer goods at any given price than they had previously been willing to supply. Looking at the supply curve in figure 1.3, this can appear to be an increase in supply because the eye interprets the change as a vertical shift upward. In general, it is better to think about changes in both demand and supply curves in terms of shifts to the left or the right rather than up or down. Look at figure 1.3 to remind yourself that a shift left, or inward, shows a decline in the quantity produced

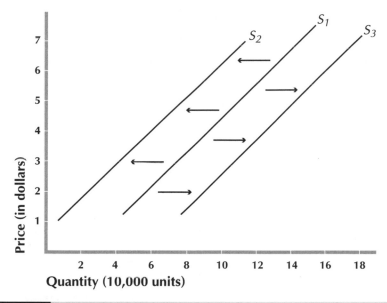

FIGURE 1.3 Supply Curve Shifts

and sold at each price, and a shift right shows an increase in production and sales at each price.

Why do supply curves rise from left to right, indicating firms produce a greater quantity only if the price is higher? To sort out the answer I need to distinguish between what economists call the **short run** and the long run. In the short run—a time span too short for adjusting plant capacity—some of the costs of production must be paid no matter how much is produced; these are **fixed costs**. Usually these are costs associated with the land, buildings, and capital equipment that establish the maximum output a firm is capable of producing, but they also include other overhead costs, which frequently are contracted costs such as insurance, interest on loans, telephone hookups, and Internet access. **Variable costs** are those that vary or change as the firm's level of output changes. These costs are usually dominated by labor and raw material costs. Another aspect of the short run is that the total number of firms producing in that particular industry is assumed to be fixed.

Total costs in the short run therefore equal variable costs plus fixed costs, and it follows that average total costs (AC)—per-unit costs—are total costs divided by the number of units produced. AC are equal to the sum of average variable costs (AVC) plus average fixed costs (AFC). So let's get specific. Veronica's Vermont Maple Syrup is a small firm in Brattleboro, Vermont, that supplies six- and eight-ounce jugs of maple sugar to souvenir stores throughout Vermont. She buys the rustic-looking jugs, complete with Vermont motifs, from China, the corks from Spain, and the maple syrup from a wholesaler who says (but won't put in writing) that the maple syrup comes mostly from Vermont. Her fixed costs are mostly the wear and tear (depreciation) on her capital equipment—the plant (a converted garage), a computer for record keeping, some tables, and seven steel frames to hold the large casks while decanting the syrup into small jugs. In addition, there are real estate taxes, interest on borrowed money, liability insurance, and expensive gifts to two members of the local zoning board. She has to pay these expenses no matter how many of the small jugs of syrup she "produces." Her variable costs include the syrup, the small jugs, the corks, the boxes in which she ships her output, and the wages she pays the high school kids who do the work. Figure 1.4 shows what the firm's short run cost structure looks like, and you see that AC is equal to the sum (added up vertically) of AVC and AFC.

Note that as output increases, total fixed costs ($600 a month) are spread over more and more units of production and AFC decline steadily as output increases. Total fixed costs (AFC times Quantity) always equal $600. This means that the AFC curve is a rectangular hyperbola—remember plane geometry? If you don't, it doesn't matter.

The steadily declining AFC helps to pull down average total costs (AC), so as output expands to 1,100 jugs a month, the average cost of producing each unit of output declines. In other kinds of production, this downward trend in average costs may prevail over long stretches of output, because high levels of output may offer **economies of scale** in

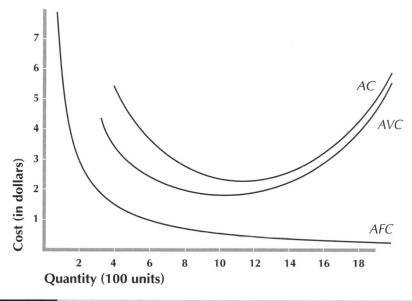

FIGURE 1.4 Average Cost Curves

which the cost per unit is lower if mass production designs can be implemented. For example, the most efficient auto assembly plants achieve
lowest average cost at about 250,000 cars per year, while the most efficient level of production for automobile engines is around 450,000 per
year. Consequently, it is not unusual to find one engine plant serving two
assembly plants. Some activities within the modern firm are particularly
subject to economies of scale. These include financial management,
inventory control, dealership or franchise coordination, packaging and
transportation, research and development, and not the least, advertising
and marketing.

But at some point the cost of producing a unit begins to rise, as the
firm begins to encounter the limits of its production facilities and higher
input costs. If Alcoa Aluminum seeks to expand output, it may have to
pay more for the very high levels of electricity needed to manufacture aluminum because it and other firms have already bought up all the cheap,
off-peak power produced by utilities.

This point of rising average total costs for Veronica, as you can see from figure 1.4, is around 1,100 units. The teenage workers need to be paid overtime premiums for additional hours, equipment maintenance may become more expensive, controls over quality may deteriorate, material wastage (spillage) increases, and so forth.

A more general idea related to this tendency for average costs to rise as output increases is captured by the term **diminishing returns**. This is the assumption that more of the same beyond a certain point generates positive but diminishing rewards. Extra people added to cultivating a field may increase output, and for a while experience **increasing returns** as each new person adds greater amounts to total output. At some point, however, with a fixed amount of land and other inputs, the increases will be successively smaller. Additional machines increase output in a factory, but given the size of the factory and the workforce, the additions soon lead to diminishing returns. The possibility that beyond yet another point, returns could actually be negative, is consistent with this. Workers become so congested on the land that they trample seedlings, and machines become so crowded on the factory floor that accidents happen.[1]

Returning now to the example in figure 1.4, when rising costs are taken into account for the industry as a whole, it is reasonable to conclude that short run supply curves rise to the right. Firms would be willing to produce more only if the higher costs of production can be covered by a higher price.

Long run supply curves have a different character. The long run is defined as the time span in which all costs are open to change, including the costs of expanding or closing existing plants, building new facilities, or reshaping the organizational structure of the firm. Wal-Mart can add new stores, McDonald's can expand franchises, BMW can build a new plant in South Carolina, and Nike can contract for more production in China. All costs are variable; none is fixed. The firm seeks to expand production in the least costly way. Another aspect of the long run is that it also represents the time when new firms may enter the industry or old firms may exit.

In my previous graph of the short run, 1,100 units was the point of the lowest per-unit cost of production for that production facility. If Veronica wished to double its output in the long run, she could simply build an identical plant and operate each of them at the 1,100 level, rather than incurring the higher costs of operating one plant at a higher level. For this reason, the long run supply curves are considerably flatter than are short run supply curves. Nevertheless, they usually do have some positive, upward slope to them, because even in the long run, a firm may run into **diseconomies of scale**—a version of diminishing returns. For example, as Wal-Mart or Staples expands into markets of lower population density or greater competition from rival firms, the efficiency (dollars of revenue per square foot of retail space) of the additional outlets may decline. Similarly, as a single enterprise becomes larger and larger, bureaucratic and coordinating problems could reduce efficiency, even with electronic communications.

Long run supply curves can be slippery. All of the shift factors that have been held constant in order to draw the relation between the quantities of an item supplied to the market and the item's price tend to change over any extended period. Therefore, we work with mostly short run demand and supply curves, which I believe are the most useful at this stage.

Market Equilibrium

And now for the anticlimax. When the forces of consumer demand, embodied in the demand curve, and the forces of producer supply, represented by the supply curve, are joined together in a graph, the conclusion fairly leaps off the page: the market finds its equilibrium price and output levels where the two curves intersect. The notion of equilibrium is simply a point of balance among the variables included in the analysis—price, quantity demanded, and quantity supplied in this case. Figure 1.5 illustrates this by looking at a generic set of demand and supply curves without cute examples. At a price of $4.00 and with 10,000 units demanded and

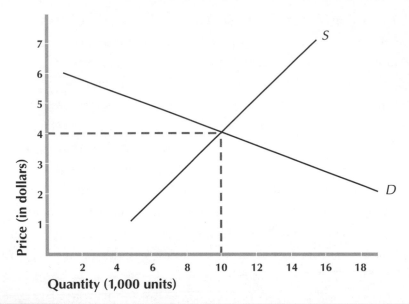

FIGURE 1.5 Equilibrium of Demand and Supply

supplied, there is nothing in the relationships among these three variables that would change their size.

The beauty of this simple apparatus lies not only in the conclusion that an equilibrium price and quantity exists. What should really bowl you over is the further claim that if an individual market should happen to be out of equilibrium, it is self-correcting. Look at figure 1.6.

Suppose that a change in a shift variable, say, declining incomes, moves the demand curve to the left, and as a result, the previous equilibrium price of $4.00 is above the new equilibrium price. Tracing along the dotted line at that old equilibrium price, firms continue to produce 10,000 units (as the supply curve informs us) but consumers buy only 7,000 (as the new demand curve tells us). The rest of the stuff—the 3,000 units that are the difference between the quantities supplied and demanded—is not sold and piles up in the stores as unwanted inventories. But no worries, mate. Retailers cut prices to sell excess inventories, and as prices come down, consumers increase the amount they buy, moving down the demand curve.

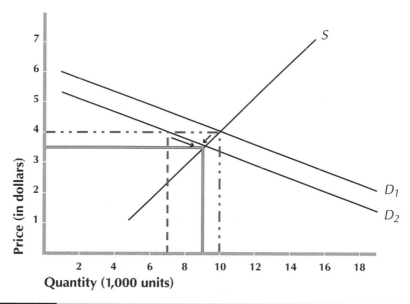

FIGURE 1.6 From Disequilibrium to a New Equilibrium

On the other side of the market, as prices decline, producers cut back their output, moving back down the supply curve toward the new equilibrium. As the arrows suggest, these dual forces—increased consumers' purchases and declining production—reestablish market equilibrium at $3.50 and 9,000 units. (You can check your understanding by drawing a figure like figure 1.6 but with a price that is too low. How much is produced and sold at that price and why will equilibrium be restored?)

The workhorse duty of supply and demand analysis is to explain how the full range of possible changes in a market can produce new and different equilibrium outcomes. A review of the supply and demand shift variables listed earlier will remind you of the different variables that might lead to such a change. In most instances, the intent is to determine the *direction* of change in market equilibrium.

To hone your skills in applying supply and demand analysis let's explore four case situations. In each case a three-step process should guide your thinking:

1. Does the initial source of change alter the conditions of supply or the conditions of demand?

2. Does the appropriate curve increase (shift to the right) or decrease (shift to the left)?

3. How does the new equilibrium compare with the old?

Case 1

Suppose the initial source of change is a shift in dietary preference in favor of chicken over beef. (Come on, you vegetarians, don't sit this one out.) The demand for chicken increases and the new equilibrium in the chicken market shows that the direction of change is toward a higher equilibrium quantity and a higher equilibrium price. (See figure 1.7.) ■

Case 2

Now let's consider a situation in which most of the action takes place on the supply side. The quantity of gasoline supplied to the U.S.

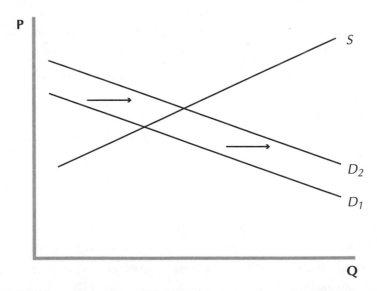

FIGURE 1.7 Changed Demand for Chicken

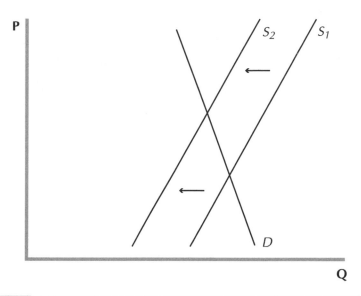

FIGURE 1.8 Changed Supply of Petroleum

market is sensitive to decisions by the Organization of Petroleum Exporting Countries (OPEC), which is a cartel of a dozen or so nations that possess over 70 percent of the world's petroleum reserves. If OPEC decides to reduce production in order to drive up the price for petroleum, as it did most recently beginning in late 1999, the supply curves shift to the left, shown in figure 1.8. As a result, the quantity supplied and demanded is less, and the price is higher. (Recent petroleum price spikes are due to demand changes rather than to producers' manipulation of supply.) ■

Case 3

Over the past fifteen to twenty years, the technology, materials, and ideas about combining materials have led to significant reductions in the costs of production of electronic products, including computers, audio equipment, televisions, cellular telephones, and so on. This has led to a substantial outward shift of the supply curve for electronic products, and

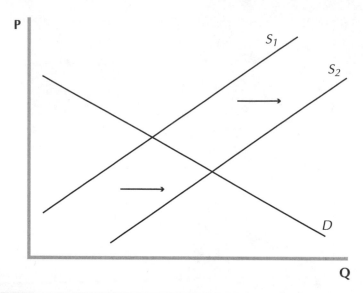

FIGURE 1.9 Changed Supply of Electronic Goodies

the quantities purchased have risen while prices have continued to decline. This is shown in figure 1.9. ■

Case 4

The first case was an example of changes that generated higher quantities demanded and sold at higher prices, the second led to lower quantities demanded and sold at higher prices, and the third meant higher quantities demanded at lower prices. So what is an example of the fourth possibility? Work it through on a piece of paper. ■

In thinking about these four cases, let's relax the restrictions of the short-term model and think in the long term. So here are some considerations that should be kept in mind. First, both demand and supply curves move in and out over time due to changes in shift variables. So what we actually observe in an individual market is the interaction between these continuing changes. From case 1, as the long run demand for (and prices of) chicken increases, we would expect some new entrants into the chicken industry and/or expansion of some current firms. The resulting outward shift in the supply curve for chickens would offset to some extent the rise in prices for chickens. But if the original locations of the chicken processing plants had been optimal in terms of input and transportation costs and (lax) pollution restrictions, one would expect that the newer plants would not be able to operate as inexpensively as the older ones. The long run equilibrium price, therefore, would still be higher than the initial price, and the result is that between the shifts in demand and supply, the shifts in demand predominated and led to higher prices and outputs.

In a similar vein, in case 2 the rise in gasoline prices due to OPEC decisions may induce a leftward shift of the demand curve from the use of more fuel-efficient autos. Still, the rise of gasoline prices indicates that shifts in the supply curve have overwhelmed any shifts in the demand curve that might have offset the price rise. Finally, price declines in computers and other electronic goods show that even though computers are becoming more popular, even necessary, shifts in the demand curve are not fully countering the effects of supply curve changes, which prevailed over any changes in demand. How about the fourth case, which was yours?

These four cases illustrate the powerful arguments in favor of a free market economy. Prices act as signaling devices for producers and as rationing devices among consumers, and flexible markets adjust demand and supply in accordance with new conditions, such as changes in production costs or changes in consumers' preferences. Or you might say that consumers come to the market with dollar "votes" for the mix of products they desire, and when they change their minds (more chicken, less beef), producers automatically adjust their production to give the people what they want. Of course, these signaling and rationing functions are deeply affected by the fact that some consumers have many more dollar votes than others do—and thus disproportionately determine what is produced. Still, the moral of the story is clear: since individual markets are self-correcting, the heavy hand of government can stay in its pocket and not interfere with the invisible hand.

A HISTORICAL NOTE

If it seems simple and self-evident that price is determined by the interaction of supply and demand, it wasn't always so. In the first two-thirds of the nineteenth century, most thinkers in the field called political economy held that price was normally determined by the cost of production. Since labor cost was usually a large part of total cost, it was an easy step to suggest that shoes cost more than bread in proportion to the amount of labor necessary to produce each. It wasn't just Karl Marx who advanced a labor theory of value; Adam Smith, David Ricardo, John Stuart Mill, and others developed their own versions. Then, in the 1870s, the diametrically opposite view was advanced that demand, in the form of the utility of a good to the buyer, was the central determiner of price. As the century came to a close, Alfred Marshall, the great English economist, was instrumental in shaping a synthesis and introducing supply and demand curves to portray the result. To ask, said Marshall, whether supply or demand determines price is like asking which blade of the scissors does the cutting.

His legacy in these matters does have one flaw. Marshall was less a mathematician than an economist. When he first constructed supply and demand curves, he failed to heed the mathematical convention that the independent variable is placed on the horizontal axis and the dependent variable is plotted on the vertical axis. Thus quantity demanded should have been on the vertical axis and price on the horizontal axis. Only mathematical types who dabble in economics seem to have a problem with this.

The political implications are evident when demand and supply analysis is applied to situations in which the government directly interferes with this automatic market adjustment process. For this, we first look at the labor market and the effects of minimum wage legislation. To do this, we can set up a supply and demand model for the low-wage segment of the labor market, often in retail trades, affected by minimum wage legislation. In figure 1.10, the wage rate on the vertical axis is the price of labor, while the hours demanded and supplied are on the horizontal axis. The demand curve for labor shows the willingness of employers to hire various hours of labor (quantities) at different wage rates (prices), and the supply curve shows the number of hours people are willing to work at different wage rates.

In figure 1.10, $4.50 an hour was the market equilibrium wage before the introduction of a minimum wage and 6,500 hours of work was demanded by employers and supplied by employees. But there is a minimum wage—a legally imposed floor below which the wage paid cannot fall. It is shown on the graph as a horizontal dotted line at $5.15, the federal minimum wage since 1997. Reading across that line to the demand curve reveals that the quantity of labor hours that firms are willing to hire at that minimum wage is 500 fewer than at $4.50, and the number of hours workers would like to work is 1,500 more than at $4.50. The difference between the number of hours demanded and supplied (2,000) is the number of hours that people are willing to work at the minimum wage but cannot. That is, it's unemployment, and the minimum wage

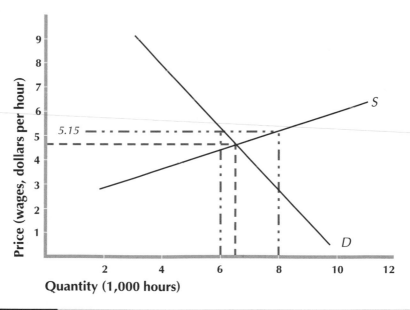

FIGURE 1.10 Effect of a Minimum Wage

CORPORATE LEADERS GATHER IN A FIELD OUTSIDE DARIEN, CONNECTICUT, WHERE ONE OF THEM CLAIMS TO HAVE SEEN THE INVISIBLE HAND OF THE MARKETPLACE.

law prevents the market from returning to its equilibrium with lower wages and no unemployment.

It is obvious that the way in which I draw the curves affects the magnitude of the effect. Nevertheless, if we stop the analysis right here, the conclusion is compelling that minimum wage laws are against the best interest of workers because they increase unemployment. The argument against minimum wage legislation is further advanced by pointing out that employers—given enough time to adjust—may find that higher minimum wages are incentives to substitute capital (machinery or equipment) for labor or to take the whole operation to Mexico. Both of these actions would shift the demand curve for U.S. labor to the left and increase the unemployment effects even more (not shown in figure 1.10). An analysis identical to this has led to the claim that unions are against worker interests because they impose a wage above the "natural" equilibrium wage, thereby leading to higher unemployment.

Empirical studies have had trouble demonstrating what seems to be obvious from the logic of demand and supply, and those studies suggest that dynamic factors such as economic growth are more important in determining levels of employment than the static demand and supply relationships. Moreover, it is worth noting that although states have a variety of minimum wages, the federal minimum wage ($5.15 an hour) has 25 percent less purchasing power than the minimum wage in 1968. Congress would have to raise it by more than $1.70 to have the same "real value" (purchasing power) as the 1968 rate. Still, the minimum wage is really a good example of demand and supply analysis and is hard to resist.

The second illustration along these lines is rent control. When a municipal government decrees a maximum rent, it will have no effect unless it is below the equuilibrium rent (price). Figure 1.11 shows the demand for and supply of rental housing related to the price of rental housing.

The equilibrium price would have been $600, but the maximum (ceiling) price set by local authorities is $450. (These examples simply stand for

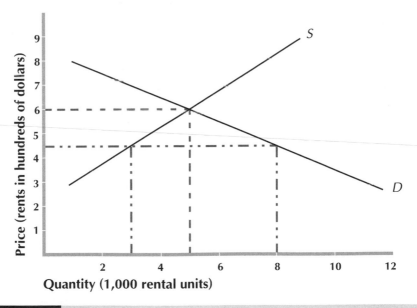

FIGURE 1.11 Rent Control

a range of rents.) Compared to equilibrium price and quantities, the rent ceiling reduced the number of housing units available on the rental market by 1,000 and increased the quantity demanded by 1,500. As a result, rent control created a shortage of 2,500 rental units where there had been none when the market was able to operate free from government encumbrances and to have flexible prices equilibrate the quantities of rental housing demanded and supplied.

In this example, the very special way in which economists use the notion of "shortage" is worth noting. When demand equals supply at a price that clears the market, there is no shortage, even if large numbers of people are living in the streets. If these people have no way to participate in the housing market by registering their demand with money votes, they are outside the market and their unmet needs do not represent a shortage in terms of the market.

So why might rent control reduce the number of available rental units? Some people are simply renting out rooms in their homes, and at the lower price, they do not consider it worth the bother to have a renter living with them. And in the longer run, an apartment building owner, facing low rent limits, can turn the apartment house into a condominium and sell the individual units. Why would there be greater demand? One example is young people who are living with their parents or many roommates but would like to get a place of their own, and this would be feasible only at the lower, controlled rents.

Once again, demand and supply analysis demonstrates the desirability of free markets. The story, however, does not end here. One conclusion from this analysis is that social policy to relieve the plight of the working poor, as in the minimum wage policy, or to reduce the cost of housing for low-income folks is more properly done through direct subsidies to low-income workers and low-income renters. Direct subsidies do not have to be in cash. If authorities do not trust recipients to spend their subsidies in approved ways, the subsidy may be in the form of a voucher that can be redeemed only for rent payments. Food stamps and education vouchers are the obvious models. The principal idea is that through direct subsidies, social ends can be achieved without distorting the operation of the market mechanism for labor or for rental housing.

Direct subsidies can also be more precise in delivering benefits to the target groups. For instance, although the minimum wage affects mostly workers over twenty years old, it also helps middle-class teenagers who work in order to buy a better car than the one that their parents have already given them. While I have nothing against middle-class teenagers, having raised a rather nice couple of them, they are not the population for whom social policies like minimum wages have been designed. And the same is true for the truly wealthy in New York City living in rent-controlled housing.

There are, however, other considerations. Apart from enforcement costs, mandated minimum and maximum prices (wages and rents, respectively) do not require government expenditures and increased taxes, while direct subsidies do. These increased expenditures along with higher administrative costs definitely affect the political character of the debate and the likelihood of implementing such policies.

Elasticity

Thus far I have used supply and demand analysis to predict the *direction* of changes (higher or lower prices and quantities). A more sophisticated analysis would recognize that the quantity demanded of some products is more sensitive to price changes than others. How can the *degree* of sensitivity be expressed or measured?

One intuitive indicator of the greater price sensitivity of a demand curve is its slope. The difficulty with using the slope as a measure of sensitivity to price changes is that I can change the slope of any demand curve simply by changing the units of measurement on either axis. If the demand for wheat is measured in bushels, the demand curve appears much flatter than if the same demand information is presented in tons. We need a measurement of the sensitivity that is independent of the units of measurement and the scale of the graph.

Toward the end of the nineteenth century Alfred Marshall devised such a measure of the sensitivity or responsiveness of one variable to another, and in the classic style of all academic disciplines he gave it a peculiar name: **elasticity**. The most general definition of elasticity is:

$$E = \frac{\text{percentage change in something}}{\text{percentage change in something else}}$$

By taking the ratio of the percentage change in one variable to the percentage change in another, the problem of units of measurement disappears. The percentage change is the same whether wheat is measured in bushels or tons, even though the slope of the demand function would be altered.

Elasticity can be used in a variety of circumstances, depending on which two variables we want to associate.

$$\text{Price Elasticity of Demand} = E_d = \frac{\%\ \text{change in Quantity Demanded}}{\%\ \text{change in Price}}$$

$$\text{Price Elasticity of Supply} = E_s = \frac{\%\ \text{change in Quantity Supplied}}{\%\ \text{change in Price}}$$

$$\textit{Income}\ \text{Elasticity of Demand} = E_I = \frac{\%\ \text{change in Quantity Demanded}}{\%\ \text{change in Income}}$$

In the first two equations the ratios relate the same two variables, Price and Quantity. However, the numbers that would be entered would come from the demand curve in the first case and from the supply curve in the second. The third formula, for the income elasticity of demand, is for what I have called a shift variable.

We know from the "law of demand" that price and quantity are inversely related: when one goes up, the other goes down. Thus some people place a negative sign in front of the E_d value, but I just use the absolute value without a sign. Remember when calculating E_d and E_s

that the percentage change in *price* goes in the denominator (below the line), and the percentage change in quantity in the numerator (above the line); price is thought to be the determinant. Reversing the order is a frequent mistake.

Figure 1.12 allows us to explore how elasticity is different from the slope of the demand curve. Curves D_1 and D_2 in figure 1.12 are alternative (and hypothetical) demand curves for Garth Brooks's CDs. They are parallel and therefore have the same slope.

Beginning with demand curve D_1, a $10 price for a Garth Brooks CD brings in sales of 20,000 CDs, and lowering the price to $9 causes the quantity demanded to increase to 24,000. The percentage decrease in price is 10 percent, and it has induced a change in the quantity demanded of 20 percent. Thus the ratio of the two percentages—the elasticity—is $\frac{20\%}{10\%} = 2$.

The alternative demand curve (D_2) for Brooks's CDs has different properties. The quantity demanded at $10 is now 50,000, and when the

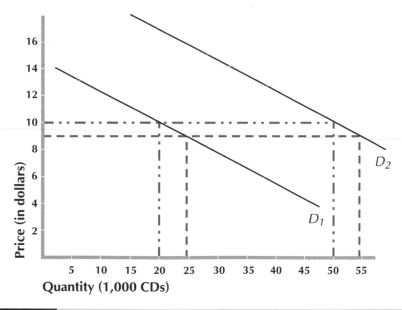

FIGURE 1.12 Two Demand Curves for Garth Brooks's CDs

price goes down to $9, the increase in demand is an additional 4,000 CDs, just as with demand curve D_1. After all, the curves do have the same slopes. But now look at the difference in the ratios of the percentage changes. A 10 percent decline in price has induced the same absolute increase in demand, but the increase of 4,000 CDs is only an 8 percent difference. The coefficient of elasticity, then, is $\frac{8\%}{10\%} = 0.8$.

So why is it worth knowing that the valve of elasticity cannot be easily eyeballed from the slope of a demand curve? Well, one interesting aspect (at least to Brooks) has to do with the amount spent on Brooks's CDs. In demand curve D_1, the $10 price sold 20,000 CDs, and since total expenditure is price times quantity sold, the total expenditures were $200,000. By dropping the price by $1, total sales went to 24,000 CDs, earning $216,000 ($9 times 24,000). How did this happen when the price went down? Aha! It must have to do with the proportional changes in prices and quantities! *Elasticity*! You're right; the elasticity of this portion of demand curve D_1 is greater than one, which is called elastic. That is, the percentage increase in sales was more than the percentage decrease in price; in fact it was double. Remember the ratio of percentages? It was 2.0. Therefore, the negative effect of the price drop on total expenditures was more than compensated by the increased number of CDs sold. This simply means that the negative effect on consumers' expenditures (and therefore, Brooks's revenues) from lowering the price was more than made up by increased CD sales.

In demand curve D_2, the drop in price from $10 to $9 again led to a 4,000 increase in CD sales, but the change in total expenditures was negative. It went from $10 times 50,000 equals $500,000 to $9 times 54,000, which equals $486,000, a reduction of $14,000. Once again, it is a matter of the elasticity of that portion of the demand curve. In this instance the elasticity was less than one (0.8), which meant that the negative percentage change in price was greater than the positive percentage change in induced demand. This is defined as an **inelastic demand.** Since we have no information on costs, we cannot say anything about profits, but this information is still worth knowing if you are promoting Brooks's CDs.

This characteristic of an inelastic demand curve also is important if the point is to raise price. First of all, how might a demand curve for a particular good become more inelastic (or better, less elastic)? One way is through the impact of advertising. One expectation of the makers of Coca-Cola is that advertising will *shift* the entire demand curve for Coke outward, increasing consumption at every price. But another hope is that advertising will also increase customers' brand loyalty to Coke and make the demand curve less elastic. This would allow Coca-Cola to raise the price and experience a loss of fewer customers (a smaller percentage change in quantity) to other brands of cola.

Making demand curves less elastic through advertising is big business, and it is nowhere more evident than in over-the-counter medications. Visit a national discount drugstore such as CVS, Walgreens, or Rite-Aid and compare the prices of Bayer Aspirin, NyQuil, or Imodium A-D with the prices of their chemically identical generic counterparts.

Armed with this new insight, we can now see that when elasticity of demand is less than 1, total expenditures by purchasers (which equal total revenues by sellers) decline if price goes down and go up when price rises. (Work it out.) The bottom line is that an inelastic demand means that the quantity demanded of a commodity is not very responsive to changes in price. This suggests that the commodity has few satisfactory substitutes, is something very important (heating oil) or perhaps something that is so small a part of consumers' budgets (black pepper) that consumers just do not pay much attention to price changes. On the other hand, when the demand for a commodity is elastic, a price rise reduces total expenditures on that commodity, and when price declines, expenditures rise. (Work it out.) A highly elastic demand curve suggests that the commodity has many close substitutes to which consumers will switch if this commodity's price rises and from which they will switch if its price falls.

For the end points of possibilities, a vertical demand curve or a vertical supply curve has zero elasticity (no change in quantities induced by changes in price), and a horizontal demand or supply curve is said to have infinite elasticity. Finally, to touch all bases, when a demand or supply curve in which the proportional changes in price induce equal proportional changes in quantities demanded or supplied, that curve is said to have **unitary elasticity**, because the ratio of the same percentage changes in price and in quantity equals 1. The total expenditures or revenues from price changes along a unity elasticity demand curve do not change—the proportional change in prices is equal to percentage changes in quantities demanded. Just to review your grip on this idea, work out for yourself why a straight-line demand curve is more elastic toward the top and less elastic toward the bottom.

Why all this arcane definition of terms and arithmetic relationships? Because it does help in understanding certain processes. For instance, would OPEC ever restrict petroleum production unless it was quite certain that the demand for petroleum, at least in the short run, was inelastic? If the demand for petroleum were elastic, restricting levels of production would reduce the amount of petroleum available, raise its price, but reduce the total receipts from the sale of petroleum. If OPEC were principally interested in resource conservation, this would have been a reasonable move. But there is no evidence that OPEC is interested in much other than maximizing receipts, and that requires an *inelastic* demand curve.

The OPEC cartel is still vulnerable, however, to conservation efforts and use of alternative energy sources that reduce the demand for petroleum. Also in the longer run, the higher price for oil affects non-OPEC producers and stimulates exploration, drilling, and increased production from higher-priced sites, such as the North Sea, Alaska, and off the California coast. Although producing petroleum from all three places is more expensive than drilling in the sands of Saudi Arabia or in Venezuela's Maracaibo basin, bringing in more petroleum from them will partially offset the initial price rise. A final problem for OPEC is cheating by its members. The best situation for one member of a cartel is to have all other cartel members restrict output to raise price while that one sneaky member goes ahead and violates the agreement by selling as much as possible at that higher price. Price-fixing agreements are inherently unstable for this reason.

Returning, however, to the justification for inflicting the idea of elasticity on you, let's look at U.S. agricultural policy. The farm sector is made up of a large number of production units that individually are too small relative to the size of the market to affect price by their own decisions. Even if the largest of the corporate farms were to cease production altogether, it would not appreciably affect the price of, say, wheat. The weather is an important determinant of yields (bushels per acre) in any particular year, and the irony is that when there are terrific wheat harvests, farmers have a bad year. Since the demand curve for wheat is inelastic, bumper crops and record yields mean that the receipts for wheat farmers as a whole are worse than in years of small harvests. Yet all that farmers can do is to maximize output, because their individual production does not affect price. Over time, the farmers' plight from an inelastic demand curve for wheat is an excellent example of the **fallacy of composition**: when individual units work rationally for individual maximization, the result is losses by the whole group. You might regard this as the opposite of the invisible hand—the invisible boot?

So individual farmers work hard to increase yields, and their efforts result in reduced receipts for the sector as a whole. And there is another problem. Given the weather, the supply of wheat in a particular growing season has been determined by months of already sunk costs, so only when the price is so low as not to cover the costs of harvesting and transporting the wheat, the amount of the crop is pretty much set. In the terms that I have been using, this means that the short run supply curve has virtually zero elasticity, and even slight shifts of the two inelastic curves generate wide swings in prices. The combination of highly volatile prices with the longer-run problem of declining revenues for the sector as a whole was the "farm problem," and the political weight of the agricultural sector in national politics led to a series of government policies to stabilize prices and aid the farm sector.

The particular approach chosen by the federal government offers a tailor-made example for economists trying to convince people of the usefulness of demand and supply analysis. Instead of supporting farmers' incomes directly, federal policy took the tack of supporting farm produce prices at levels above what the market would have generated. Although this type of policy goes back to the administration of President Herbert Hoover in the 1920s, it was refined and expanded until the 1960s. Look at figure 1.13, which shows a rather inelastic demand curve for wheat and a perfectly inelastic supply curve over the relevant range.

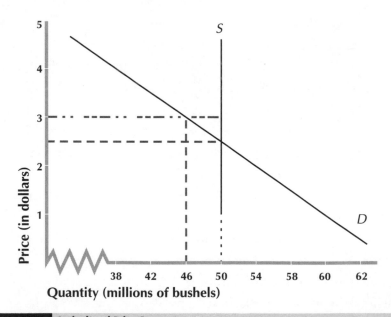

FIGURE 1.13 Agricultural Price Support

With no government program, the equilibrium price for wheat would have been $2.50 a bushel. This is the price at which the demand for wheat by producers of bread, pizza, pasta, and whatever would have bought all 50 million bushels of available wheat (i.e., cleared the market), generating receipts for the farmers of $125 million ($2.50 times 50 million). In this example, however, the federal government price support program has declared its willingness to buy any amount of wheat at $3.00 a bushel, which means that this will be the prevailing price. Why would anyone sell for less?[2] As you can read off the figure, the support price leads to 46 million bushels bought by the private market and a 4 million bushel surplus purchased by the federal government in order to sustain the support price. The total receipts of the wheat growers is $150 million ($3.00 times 50 million bushels), of which $12 million ($3.00 times 4 million bushels) comes from the federal government's purchase of the surplus.

Although this $12 million is what is recorded in the government budget as the subsidy, it is only part of the true subsidy. From the example here, the free market would have generated $125 million in revenue for the farm, and the government program generated a total of $150 million for the sector. So by this measure, the subsidy to the farm sector is actually $25 million ($150 million minus $125 million). We know that the government is directly contributing $12 million, but the other measure indicates $25 million, so where did the additional $13 million subsidy come from?

It came from the final consumers of the wheat products, who paid an extra $13 million more for 4 million fewer bushels of wheat in their bread, pizza, pasta, and whatever. This means that more than half of the actual subsidy was financed by the higher prices of wheat products, a taxing device that no doubt hits poorer people harder than the general federal tax system that financed the government's direct cost of $12 million.

This is pretty confusing; take a look at table 1.1 and figure it out. Now that you have figured out the magnitude of the subsidy, how is it distributed? As a price support, the subsidy is distributed according to

TABLE 1.1	A Hypothetical Price Support for Wheat		
	Price (dollars)	**Quantity (millions of bushels)**	**Total Revenue (millions of dollars)**
No price support	2.50	50	125
Price support	3.00	50	150
Private purchases		46	138
Government purchases		4	12

how many bushels each farm produces. Despite considerable rhetoric about saving the family farm, this program subsidizes most heavily the largest corporate farms.

As a couple of final indictments, the price support program required high tariffs against the importation of foreign wheat, because it is obvious that Canadian, Australian, and Argentinean wheat producers would have loved to sell their wheat at the supported price in the United States. And there was no way to export wheat; after all, the program generated surpluses that could not be sold at the support price. So some of the costs of the program were for storing the surplus in huge silos in the Middle West, stimulating the growth of the rat population. Much of the surplus wheat was eventually either given away or sold at concessionary prices to poor countries through Public Law 480—Food for Peace. The cheap food policy helped to feed the urban populations of poor countries and discouraged the expansion of the recipient countries' own agricultural sectors.

In the form that has been described here, the U.S. agricultural program for wheat is history, having been supplanted by export subsidies. It does live on, however, in support programs for other crops, and its spirit survives in efforts to revive the Northeast Milk Compact. Similar programs in Europe (especially France) continue to be a problem for the economic integration of the European Union (EU) and for the EU's engagement with other nations. In any case, the old-time agricultural price support program is too marvelous an example of how far one can get with demand and supply not to include it here.

Sales Taxes

One last example of elasticity takes us into the realm of the impact of taxes. When taxes are imposed on goods or services, they are usually in the form of general sales taxes or taxes on goods that have been especially targeted, such as gasoline and cigarettes. Figure 1.14 explores the question, who actually bears the burden of a tax on goods, consumers or producers? That is, the actual **incidence** of the taxes—who bears the actual burden—is not always obvious. The person who writes the check to the tax authorities may be able to pass the actual cost of the tax onto someone else.

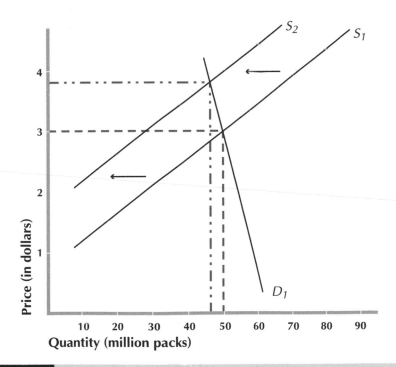

FIGURE 1.14 An Increase in Cigarette Taxes

One's first instinct is to say that the full amount of the tax is paid by consumers, since sales taxes, gasoline taxes, and cigarette taxes are added to the retail price paid. But to untangle the true impact we need to compare the market equilibrium price before the tax with the market equilibrium price after the tax.

Case 5

Let's use the tired but true example of a new cigarette tax. In figure 1.14, D_1 and S_1 represent the before-tax demand and supply curves, and $3.00 a pack and 50 million packs a week was the initial equilibrium of price and quantities demanded and supplied. If the government puts a new tax of $1.00 per pack on cigarettes, then the supply curve is vertically increased by $1.00 (although in effect the curve shifts to the left). The sellers must now cover the previous costs of production plus collect the new tax and send it to the government. The tax is a $1.00 wedge between expenditures and receipts, reducing by $1.00 what the cigarette producers actually get of the market price, and therefore they are willing to supply fewer cigarettes at each market price. This new supply function is labeled S_2. The new equilibrium is found at a price of $3.80 and a quantity of 45 million packs a week.

From figure 1.14 you can see that the inelasticity of the demand curve for cigarettes and the comparatively elastic supply curve means that in this case, consumers pay $0.80 more and sellers receive $0.20 less per pack. Consumers do indeed pay for most of the tax. And not only do they pay most of the tax, the inelastic demand curve causes the yield on the cigarette tax to be considerable. ■

Revenue versus Regulation   Taxes have historically been used for two purposes: revenue and regulation, and the two purposes conflict. The revenue function is fairly obvious, but the stated intention of some taxes, most notably the so-called sin taxes on tobacco and liquor, has been to discourage consumers from buying the items. And the taxes produce lots of revenue. If the item in disfavor has a very elastic demand curve, the tax sharply reduces the item's purchases and yields very little revenue. On the other hand, if the taxed item has an inelastic demand curve, the tax does little to discourage purchases and therefore generates considerable tax revenues. In the late 1990s, the Clinton administration proposed a sizable federal cigarette tax increase to discourage smoking and then immediately began wrangling with Congress over what should be done with the greatly expanded tax revenues that they expected. It's enough to make one wonder. (Maybe the elasticity of demand for cigarettes is much greater for young smokers and the rise in cigarette prices discourages them more than others?)

The results of case 5 are not all that surprising, but it is important that you understand the general principle: whichever side of the market, demand or supply, has the less elastic schedule is the side of the market that ends up bearing most of the burden of the tax. This stands to reason in that the more elastic a demand or supply schedule, the more willing are the consumers or producers behind that schedule to choose alternatives and duck the tax.

Case 6

So now you all work out another example. Let's say that the government puts a luxury (sales) tax on the super-rich when they buy very expensive handcrafted jewelry, yachts, and fur coats. After all, these are the people who can afford to bear an extra tax, and a nice by-product would be to discourage the vulgar ostentation that emphasizes class differences with undesirable political fallout. In working through the example, note that the super-rich have lots of alternative ways to spend their money and enjoy themselves, and each and any of the taxed items could easily be substituted by the purchase of travel, a golf course, additional kinds of personal services, and other hedonistic pleasures. On the supply side, let's say that the people who make these super-expensive items for the super-rich are highly skilled craftspeople, many of whom are the third- or fourth-generation artisans with skills difficult to transfer satisfactorily to other endeavors. Under these conditions, what is the incidence of the luxury tax? Tariffs (taxes on imported goods and services), taxes on polluting activities, and any other tax levied on each unit of output can be analyzed in a manner parallel to sales taxes. ■

Now that we have had fun and games with demand and supply, the next chapter continues with the microeconomic level of analysis but looks at two important aspects of markets: the different degrees of competitiveness in various markets; and the markets for labor and other productive services and the resulting distribution of income.

Notes

1. The notion of diminishing enjoyment in consumption is parallel to that of diminishing returns in production. The sixth ice cream cone on a warm afternoon is still enjoyable but not as enjoyable as the first five; the twelfth ice cream cone requires your stomach to be pumped.

2. The actual agricultural price support program was much more complex in its operation, and it included acreage restrictions. Nevertheless, this simplified description captures the essence of the program sufficiently well.

The Theory of the Firm, Market Structures, Factor Markets, and the Distribution of Income

Businesses are organized as individual proprietorships, partnerships, or corporations. **Proprietorships** are firms owned by a single individual, and **partnerships** are firms owned by two or more individuals. The difference between proprietorships and partnerships is not as substantial as between them and corporations. A corporation is owned by the holders of the corporation's stocks—certificates of equity (that is, of ownership). Stocks are very different from corporate bonds; bonds are no more than IOUs for money that the corporations borrowed. Bondholders do not have any equity in the enterprise; they are creditors. Corporations are juridical entities in their own right and enjoy a legal status called limited liability.[1] This means that the stockholders—the owners of the corporation— can lose no more than the money they have invested in the stock even if the corporation goes belly up with huge debts remaining. For a sense of perspective, table 2.1 lists firm sales by organization and size. When I talk about the business sector, I am talking about a large number of very different kinds of enterprises. But at the core of that sector, the largest corporations make up about one tenth of 1 percent of all firms, and their sales account for more than 60 percent of the value of total sales in the national economy. A more inclusive figure is that the largest 3.7 percent of firms accounted for more than 80 percent of total sales.

Corporations issue stocks in order to raise money for expansion and whatever, and this is an alternative to borrowing money through selling bonds. Once these stocks are issued, however, they take on a life of their own. The largest corporations' stocks are traded on secondary markets, which means that most purchases and sales of stocks occur among people who did not buy these stocks when they were first issued by the

TABLE 2.1 Number and Sales of Firms by Size and Type, 2001			
	Number of Enterprises (1,000)	**Total Sales (billions of dollars)**	**Total Sales (percentages)**
Nonfarm Proprietorships	18,338	1,017	4.4
Partnerships	2,132	2,569	11.2
Corporations			
With sales of less than $1 million	4,154	866	3.7
With sales between $1 million and $49.9 million	956	4,384	19.1
With sales over $50 million	26	14,058	61.4
Totals	25,606	22,894	100.0

Source: Statistical Abstract of the United States, 2000–2005, pp. 483, 489.

corporations. Nevertheless, the new owners of a corporation's stocks still get their cut of the corporation's profits (paid out as dividends) and hope eventually to sell the stock at a price higher than they paid for it (that is, receive **capital gains**). The corporations do not receive any money from the secondary transactions, but they do benefit from a rise in the price of their stocks, because it means that they might be able to issue some more new stock on favorable terms. When a corporation does get its act together and issue stock for sale to the general public, it is called an Initial Public Offering (IPO), and despite the recent hype and speculative bubble around technology stocks, IPOs are a small portion of overall stock market activity.

There are a number of stock exchanges in the United States, and the New York Stock Exchange (NYSE), the American Stock Exchange, and the NASDAQ (National Association of Securities Dealers Automated Quotations) are the most important. Despite the rather dramatic movements of the NASDAQ, which lists the stocks of many information technology ("new economy") businesses, the NYSE still dwarfs the others in importance.

The NYSE lists stocks of around 3,000 corporations, and the Dow Jones Industrials index ("average") is the most frequently quoted index of stock performance on the NYSE.[2] The Dow Jones index is made up of thirty stocks, around 1 percent of the stocks listed on the NYSE but accounting for about 25 percent of the total value of those stocks. The index is the sum of the thirty stocks' unweighted price changes for a day, adjusted for such modifications as stock splits. A one dollar increase in one stock boosts the index by about four points, and a one dollar increase in all thirty stocks raises the index about 120 points. Moreover, the Dow Jones folks occasionally change the list of stocks, substituting more active, high-performance stocks for stocks with weaker recent records. From the Dow Jones index, one can indeed say that all stocks are above average, and it is very likely that an undergraduate student who constructed an index like this for a statistics class would have to take the class again.[3]

Although economists have some interest in the legal organization and size of firms, their principal analytical categories are oriented toward distinguishing different patterns of competition among firms operating in product markets. In order to do this, economists usually identify four distinct market structures, by which they mean the particular types of competitive relationships among the firms in a specific market. Firms in different competitive environments face distinctive demand conditions that affect their behavior, and the four categories of these environments are perfect competition, monopoly, monopolistic competition, and oligopoly. The last three types of markets represent degrees of less-than-perfect competitiveness and are accordingly known as forms of imperfect competition.

The perfectly competitive market, with a large number of producers in a market, and the completely monopolized market, with one seller in a market, are polar forms that define the end points of a continuum of possible market structures. **Monopolistic competition**, characterized by a large number of producers with differentiated products, is closer to the perfectly competitive side, while **oligopoly** markets, with a few, interdependent producers, tends more toward the monopoly end of the continuum. Both oligopoly and monopolistic competition are somewhat more realistic descriptions of actual market situations than the polar, ideal types of perfect competition and monopoly, but the resulting loss of theoretical precision makes them less favored among economists.

Before delving into the various market structures, it is important to note a couple of analytical features that hold for all firms in all kinds of market structures. The first is how the cost curves are drawn. No matter whether it is a perfectly competitive firm or the more malignant monopoly, the cost curves are drawn very much the same as in figure 1.4. The reason to distinguish among different market structures is on the demand side, and the cost conditions of production are considered to have a very similar bowl-shaped average cost curve. The feature common to all types of firms is that they are assumed to strive to maximize profits, and that is *total* profits, not average profits or any other kind of profits.

Total Profits = Total Revenues (TR) – Total Costs (TC)

Although I do not believe that it is worthwhile to inflict the full, conventional geometry on you, you ought to know that the point of output at which firms do maximize total profits is where marginal costs equal marginal revenues.

Whoops, I need to back up a bit. First of all, whenever economists use the word "marginal," they are not referring to the blank areas at the sides of pages. But the idea does concern an edge in the sense that marginal refers to increment, addition, extra, added, further and any other synonym. **Marginal cost,** then, is the *additional* cost associated with the production of one more unit of output. In a similar manner, **marginal revenue** is the *additional* revenue associated with the sale of one more unit. Marginal costs are thought generally to rise as output increases, and marginal revenue is either constant or falling as output and sales increase.

As long as the firm's increased output and sales generate additional revenues (marginal revenues) greater than the associated increased costs (marginal costs), total profits rise. On the down side, as soon as marginal costs (the addition to total costs) are greater than marginal revenue (addition to total revenues), total profits decline. This decision criterion, then, leads to a reformulation of the previous formula; since marginal revenue (MR) is considered to stay the same or decline and marginal costs (MC) are assumed to rise, maximum profits occur when MR = MC. Get it? This profit-maximizing principle of marginal costs equaling marginal revenues, like the shape of the cost curves, pertains for all market structures. Now let's take a look at the various types of market structures.

Perfect Competition

The market structure of **perfect competition** is the centerpiece of market theory, the reference point for all other types, and it is often casually referred to as "natural." As already described, a perfectly competitive market is composed of a large number of firms that are so small relative to the size of their market that they cannot influence price. That is, if several of them were to shut down completely or, conversely, to double their output, the changes in supply would be insufficient to affect price. In addition, this is a market with a rather undifferentiated product for which there are no significant obstacles to the entry of new firms and the exit of existing firms.

In this situation, all firms are price takers—the price of the product is set by the forces of demand and supply for the entire market and has to be accepted as a parameter over which individual firms have no control. A firm's principal decision, therefore, is the output level that maximizes profits. In figure 2.1, graph (A) shows the general demand and supply curves for the entire weekly market for inexpensive cowboy boots. In contrast, graph (B) shows the average cost (*AC*) curve of a typical firm making cowboy boots. The price set in the market as a whole is $50 (I did say that this was the low end of the market), and that is the price faced by every cowboy boot producer. The horizontal price line, therefore, functions as the demand curve for the individual firm, because it shows the price at which the individual producer can sell its product. In the case of

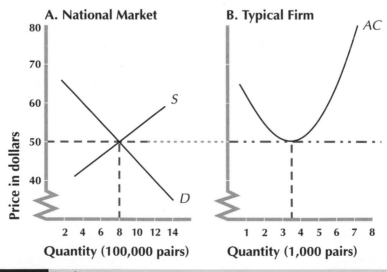

FIGURE 2.1 Cowboy Boots

perfect competition, the firm can sell at the same price as many pairs of boots as it can produce, since the size of its output is so small relative to the size of the market that it cannot affect price. As figure 2.1 shows, the price line/demand curve is tangent to (touches) the AC curve at its lowest point, where production cost per unit of output is the least.

This is all well and good, but it does mean that for that typical firm, there are zero profits. After all, total revenue (price times number of units produced and sold in a week, $50 \times 3,500 = \$175,000$) is exactly equal to total costs (average cost times number of units produced and sold, $175,000). This takes us to one of the tricky aspects of cost curves in economics textbooks. As you might expect, economists draw the cost curves to include all the costs one normally associates with producing a good or service—wages and salaries, costs of materials (plastic, leather, and glue), insurance, interest costs on borrowed money, depreciation, indirect business taxes, and so on. What you might not expect, however, is that these textbook cost curves also contain an average rate of return (profit) for the owners on their investments and risk. Including average rates of return in the cost curves, then, means that zero **economic profits** are sufficient to keep all producers interested (covering opportunity costs) but do not encourage new entries. Positive **accounting profits**, which is revenue minus conventionally defined costs, compiled by bookkeepers to show the Internal Revenue Service and other interested parties, are necessary for the zero economic profits on the graph.

Now that we have a good grip on this, we are off and running (in cowboy boots?). Let's say that in this perfectly competitive boot market, the proprietor of one of the firms, Damien's Dynamite Boots of Austin, Texas, figures out a new, cost-saving method to produce boots and thereby lowers the firm's AC curves 12 percent ($6 per pair at the bottom of the curve) to AC^*, as shown in figure 2.2. At the prevailing price of the product, Damien begins to haul in positive *economic* profits (i.e., above-average rates of return). These above-average profits are depicted by the length of the line between AC^* and price, multiplied by the number of units produced and sold ($6 $\times 3,500 = \$21,000$).[4]

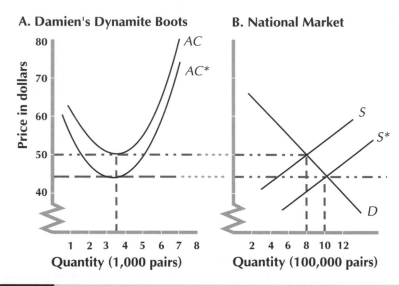

FIGURE 2.2 Innovation in Cowboy Boots

Alas, Damien's extra profits do not last. Two former CIA agents now working in industrial espionage soon ferret out the secret of his new cost-saving production process. Even if none of the other firms in the market wants to risk adopting the more efficient forms of production to get those higher returns, the promise of above-average returns attracts new entrants to the market to get some of the action for themselves. Some of these new entrants are aided by venture capitalists who underwrite either the establishment of new firms or the takeover of existing (but stolid) firms and install the more efficient production methods.

What this means for the market as a whole is that the supply curve shifts to the right, to S^*, indicating that there is a new willingness to produce more at any given price. This moves the price from $50 to $44, and all firms in the market have to either adopt the lower-cost methods or be driven from the market.

This apocryphal story contains powerful messages. The competitive regime gives firms the incentives to innovate, but their rewards for innovating, even if substantial, are only temporary. The eagerness of others, both insiders and new entrants, to use the new production method for higher profits soon causes the higher profits to go back to normal. In the process, less efficient firms are forced out of business. So competition forces all firms to use the most efficient production methods if they are to stay in the race. In addition, competition forces all firms to produce at output levels that are optimum (highest efficiency and lowest average cost) for their factories.

The new equilibrium for the overall boot market is a higher output at a lower price. Although Damien's firm, which led the innovation, did benefit for a while, the lower product prices mean that the long run benefits from the increased efficiency are diffused widely among all boot purchasers. Moreover, the innovation that reduced average costs means that workers' productivity $\left(\frac{\text{number of units produced}}{\text{hours of work}}\right)$ has risen. This is the meaning of material progress—increased productivity of human labor. This process is what both Adam Smith and Karl Marx recognized as the innately progressive nature of competitive capitalism. Marx did not, however, share in Smith's optimism about the widespread distribution of the benefits through the invisible hand.

So the upshot is that the competitive market system is a flexible signaling device that allocates resources among alternative uses in response to the vicissitudes of consumer demand and encourages firms to innovate. Furthermore, if firms do not use the most efficient (lowest cost) production methods and operate their plants at their optimal levels of production, they are driven out of business. Finally, the operation of the competitive market generates a vigorous **trickle-down effect**: the benefits of lower production costs are dispersed widely to customers through lower prices and to workers through increased employment and the potential for higher wages because of increases in output and productivity.

Now don't just rush by these conclusions; sit and savor them a bit. These mechanisms are a large part of the argument for free market capitalism. If individual consumers are free to choose what they want to buy, and entrepreneurs are free to enter or leave the production of a good or service, the result is freedom, efficiency, lowest possible prices, greatest scope of consumer choice, and so on. Later in this chapter you will see that the theory about the distribution of income further bolsters these conclusions.

Market Failure

There are some caveats to this celebration of the free market even when governments do not interfere with its operation. The inability of free markets to deliver these expected benefits, a situation called **market failure**, refers exclusively to the failure of markets to perform in their own terms—efficiency, flexibility, and so forth. It does not include market outcomes that may be undesirable in terms of equity, cultural effects, and so on. As mentioned in the earlier example of the housing market, when the price of housing moves to make the demand for housing and the supply of housing equal, the market is doing well. The fact that there may be a large number of people who have no access to housing because they cannot afford it is not an example of market failure. The conventional take on market failure is that it stems from problems of four kinds: public goods, external costs, macroeconomic stability, and natural monopoly.

Public Goods   **Public goods** are those goods and often services that do not lend themselves to production by private, profit-oriented enterprises. Their consumption by one person does not diminish their value to others, and there are serious problems in excluding those who do not pay— the **free rider problem**. The argument is that if such services as national defense, the eradication of cholera, and the protection of clean air are provided to anyone, they are available to all residents, whether or not a particular individual had paid the private firm that provided the service. They could therefore ride free, because there is no feasible way to exclude non-payers from benefiting from the service. Have you ever heard a public radio station guilt-tripping its listeners in order to convince them to "become a member" and contribute to the station? National Public Radio estimates that nine out of ten listeners do not contribute and are riding free in this example of a public good.

There is, of course, considerable disagreement about the actual number of truly public goods that are infeasible to be produced and distributed by profit-seeking firms and about which ones they are. The current debate about education is an illustration. Does having an educated citizenry yield general, social benefits that go beyond the private returns to the educated individuals? And if so, should education be delivered principally through locally controlled public schools? On a darker note, the tragic events of 11 September 2001 made it clear that the public goods aspects of airline security are critical and that it is unwise to regulate airline security so loosely that it is governed primarily by the market.

External Costs When some of the burdens and costs from production or consumption are borne by people not otherwise involved in the production and consumption of a good or service, the private market is not working properly. Water and air pollution (including second-hand smoke), greenhouse gases, agricultural pesticides, and traffic congestion are among the most frequently cited examples. In such instances, government regulation may (1) ban the activity (DDT, fluorocarbons, asbestos), (2) tax the activity so that it becomes a cost that is internal to the firm, or (3) limit the total amount of negative activity and allow firms to buy and sell the rights to pollute up to a mandated limit (known as "marketable permits").

Macroeconomic Stability In order for a market system to perform its miracles, the economy cannot be undergoing severe inflation or unemployment. Both conditions—rapidly rising prices or high unemployment and business failure rates—cause price irregularities that distort market signals and undermine the markets' ability to deliver the general social benefits promised in the model. Markets' inability to sustain the conditions necessary for their adequate functioning was especially (and painfully) evident in the Great Depression of the 1930s but was also implicated in the periodic downturns ("recessions") and bursts of inflation in the post–World War II years. Although seldom included in lists of market failure, inflation and recession should be regarded as other types of market failure that require some government intervention to ensure overall production at levels that fully (or very nearly) utilize the capacity of firms' plant and equipment and of the labor force. This problem area belongs to the field of *macro*economic analysis, which I deal with in part II of this book.

Natural Monopoly   If markets are not adequately competitive, the market system's capacity to activate the invisible hand and produce great and good social benefits is seriously impaired. Therefore, all kinds of enduring imperfect competition can be regarded as sources of market failure. Nevertheless, only one—natural monopolies—is usually included in such discussions, and I will adhere to that convention. After describing the properties of imperfectly competitive markets in the next three sections, however, I will return to this broader issue under the heading "Deregulation."

Natural monopolies are situations in which overwhelming economies of scale mean that a single firm could more efficiently produce a good or service than a number of competitive firms. Under these conditions, public authorities have chosen either to supply the services by publicly owned facilities, as is common with municipal water and sewage treatment, or to regulate a private monopoly to avoid its exercising its market power, which used to be the case with electrical power and telephone service.

In good part due to technological advances, much of this landscape has changed over the past couple of decades. As a result, the case for many activities being natural monopolies, such as telephone service, electrical power, and natural gas, now appears to be less compelling. Although consumers are being given more choices among a range of telephone, electricity, and gas suppliers, this new competitiveness does not include the delivery of these services through wires and pipes. This aspect of the services still has many of the characteristics of a traditional natural monopoly and is regulated. Let's consider some of the aspects of a monopoly.

Monopoly

Monopoly is the antithesis of perfect competition, and having only one seller in a particular market negates every one of the wonderful outcomes of perfect competition. The single seller is in a position to exercise **market power**—the ability to withhold some supply in order to charge a higher price. Competitive forces neither drive profits down to an average rate of return nor do they require producing at the most efficient level of output. Monopolists can slow down the introduction of innovations and wait until it is convenient, perhaps until old equipment wears out. In addition, most if not all of the greater profits from an innovation can be kept by those within the firm and often shared, albeit not evenly, among owners, managers, and workers.

Extensive market power requires effective barriers against the entry of competitive firms. In addition to the conditions of natural monopoly mentioned above, a number of other factors can constitute effective barriers to entry. The exclusive control of a natural resource, as in the case of the De Beers (near-)monopoly of diamonds, illustrates one kind of barrier. Another is a firm's predatory manipulation of processing, transportation, and selling prices to drive out or discourage competition. These were the strategies employed by John D. Rockefeller's Standard Oil Company in order to monopolize the market for petroleum products. Another deliberate anti-competitive activity was for a group of large firms to agree among themselves to certain market shares and to coordinate pricing (i.e., to form a "trust") in order to achieve the market power of a monopoly.

Legislation in the United States—most notably federal laws such as the Sherman Antitrust Act (1890) and the Clayton Antitrust Act (1914)—is designed to discourage anti-competitive behavior and to create more competition.[5] Anti-trust judgments broke Standard Oil into thirty-four firms in 1911. In the same era, the U.S. Justice Department successfully prosecuted the American Tobacco Company, which was broken up into three firms, as well as U.S. Rubber and International Harvester. A similar attempt to break up the U.S. Steel Corporation was unsuccessful. It is important, however, not to view these actions as some pure struggle between populist forces and big business. You have to remember that concentrated market power works to the disadvantage not only of individual consumers but also of firms, and often powerful firms, that buy from or sell to a monopoly.

Vigilance about anti-competitive behavior has waxed and waned, and some presidents were notorious for reducing the budget and personnel of anti-trust units to the point of effectively repealing anti-trust legislation. In the mid-1990s, however, the Justice Department became more active in limiting some anti-competitive market behavior. Although it approved some breathtaking mergers, it also blocked some, and the prosecution of Microsoft was the most dramatic episode of recent initiatives. President George W. Bush and his administration are profoundly skeptical about the need for vigorously enforcing anti-trust laws, so the level of anti-trust scrutiny is declining, with the possible exception of enforcing illegal price-fixing agreements among firms.

Government policy is a third source of the barriers to entry necessary to maintain market power. Patents and copyrights encourage research and creativity by guaranteeing a monopoly to holders of the patent or copyright for specified periods of time in order to make it worth the time and expense of coming up with something new. Debates about patent policies have become more complex with the practice of granting patents for live organisms created by genetic engineering. Finally, tariffs on imported goods, licensing provisions, some health and safety regulations, and the allocation of defense contracts can also reduce the competitiveness of domestic markets.

Price Discrimination

If you have a sweet little monopoly (or even some market power), the best of all possible worlds would be if you could charge different prices to different buyers, depending on how much they were willing to pay. As an imperfect competitor, you have some control over price, which means that your demand curve slopes downward. If you are selling your product at a single equilibrium price, you keep looking wistfully at the portion of the demand curve above that price. The existence of that part of the demand curve means that there are folks who are willing to pay more for the product. So how might you be able to sell to them at a higher price without losing the customers willing to pay only the lower price?

The trick is to be able to identify distinct markets for the product, and a market that can be segmented to the extent that those buying at lower prices cannot resell to those buying at higher prices. How about selling airline seats to those staying over a Saturday night for considerably lower prices than the same seats for those not willing or able to stay over a Saturday? This is an outstanding method of separating pleasure travelers from business travelers, whose demand for air travel is much less elastic. The tickets that movie theaters routinely sell to children, students, seniors, and those attending afternoon shows are cheaper than the tickets they sell to people who presumably have more money and less flexible schedules.

The practice of charging different prices for the same product is called **price discrimination**, and these two examples of price discrimination are relatively benign and are legal. There are, however, blatant examples of predatory practices that have triggered government intervention. Let's say that in the late 1870s, we had two railroads that competed for freight traffic between Chicago and Denver. One railroad, however, went a more northerly route and passed through Des Moines, and the other railroad's more southerly route went through Topeka. So the railroads competed fiercely for business between Chicago and Denver, but each railroad had a monopoly of rail transport in its intermediate stops. In those days, before the advent of trucking and air cargo, railroads were a type of natural monopoly, and pricing policies expressed their market power. You could find ton-per-mile costs of shipping from or to one of those monopolized intermediate points that was four or more times higher than the ton-per-mile cost of shipping between Chicago and Denver, where competition held down prices. The elimination of this kind of price discrimination (and some other unpleasant practices) was the reason to establish the federal Interstate Commerce Commission (ICC) in 1887, making it the first independent federal regulatory agency.

In a slightly less blatant current example, pharmaceutical companies routinely charge different prices for their patented medicines in different countries, and they charge the highest prices in (you guessed it) the United States. For example, U.S. drug companies sell some of their prescription medicines in Canada, where the government regulates medicine prices, for one-eighth of the price charged across its southern border.

Monopolistic Competition

Monopolistic competition and oligopoly are two models of market structure that lie between the polar extremes of perfect competition and monopoly and are more realistic. The model of monopolistic competition has many of the key characteristics of perfect competition: a large number of small firms compared to the size of the market and ease of entry and exit. Unlike perfectly competitive markets, however, monopolistically competitive firms produce goods and services that are differentiated, however slightly. This means that if one of its firms were to raise its price, it would not lose all of its customers, because the product is sufficiently distinct from those of competitors, so some people would still buy its product.

Just to give you some real world examples on which to hang the concept, think about restaurants. In any locale, there are a variety of restaurants offering different menus, prices, quality, atmosphere, service, location, and likelihood of food poisoning. Each restaurant's individual character means that there are some clientele, even if only passing through town, who would continue to patronize the establishment if it were to raise prices. On the other hand, if one were to hit the market suddenly with something unique and attractive, it would make economic profits for a while until competitors moved in.

Erin and Janet open up their Tahiti Tavern on a corner of a major thoroughfare in Santa Rosa (north of San Francisco), and the ambience and ersatz exotica bring in crowds and substantial economic profits. But in six months, Kevin and Joe open up their Polynesian Paradise on the other side of town. Although the décor is a bit more obviously plastic (especially the Easter Island heads and waitresses' grass skirts), the Paradise's Tropical Tornado is $1.00 less than the identical Hula Hurricane at the Tahiti Tavern. As a result, the new restaurant draws off some of the Tavern's patrons, and through its advertisements, it brings in new customers interested in something different from other eateries in town. And so profits at both places approach the average, maybe one older restaurant has to go under, and this part of the story is similar to that of perfect competition.

Nonetheless, the restaurants are different from each other, and they advertise and compete in a number of dimensions (e.g., price, quality, and location). After initial adjustments to the new restaurants, profits return to normal for all of them, but their (slight) differences mean that their individual demand curves are not completely elastic and have some slope. Look at figure 2.3, which shows the demand and cost conditions for a monopolistically competitive firm. As in the case of perfect competition, competition drives down individual restaurants' demand curves so that the equilibrium points for all the surviving restaurants are tangent to (touching) the average cost curve. This means zero economic profits that include enough in the way of returns to keep people interested in doing what they are doing. But unlike the perfectly competitive firms, the monopolistic firms' ability to differentiate their product enough to have some effect on price means that the equilibrium is at a point to the left of minimum costs. Translating the geometry into business terms, it means

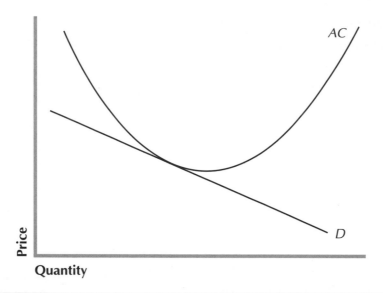

FIGURE 2.3 A Typical Firm in a Monopolistically Competitive Market

that while the restaurants continue to earn normal, adequate profits, they chronically operate at less than full capacity.

The model therefore helps in understanding why considerable turnover by firms, substantial advertising, price competition, normal profits, and excess capacity characterize firms in monopolistically competitive markets. Not too bad for a model. It is a reasonably accurate portrayal of most retail operations, such as restaurants, gas stations, grocery stores, clothiers, jewelers, convenience stores, or any other retail market in which there is easy entry but some significant forms of differentiation among them, even if that difference is nothing more than where it is located.

Oligopoly

The second intermediate market organization is the one with the funny name. The name is really not all that odd, however, when you realize that it is constructed in the same way as "monopoly"—one seller. Oligopoly is a market with a few sellers and corresponds to the more familiar political term, "oligarchy," or rule by a few. After you use the word for a while, it will not seem so awkward.[6]

So think about a market dominated by three, four, or five firms—the situation of many of the most important and prosperous U.S. industrial sectors in the post–World War II decades. Oligopoly market organizations prevailed in standardized consumer durables such as automobiles and electrical appliances, mass-produced nondurable consumer goods such as pharmaceuticals, cosmetics, detergents, cigarettes, gasoline, and processed foods and beverages, and intermediate and capital goods such as steel and other metals, fuels, plastics, glass, rubber, chemicals, and some machinery. As in the discussion of monopoly, an oligopolistic market requires significant barriers to entry into the market by other firms, whether those barriers are the large scale of output needed for efficient production, the high cost of the advertising required to overcome consumers' brand loyalties and habits, or other factors.

If these few firms could get together and act in concert, they could reap the benefits of being a monopoly. This kind of collusion, while certainly not unknown, is discouraged by law, and when it occurs, it has to be subtle and in many ways tacit. This is a somewhat delicate situation, because the principal feature of an oligopoly market is the clear and present interdependence among the major players. Unlike perfect competition, any change in production or price policies by one firm directly and immediately affects the market environment for all other firms.

When oligopoly firms cannot collude effectively, they are in a somewhat anomalous position. Their market strategies have to take into account the actions and reactions of their three or four major competitors. For instance, if one of them were to raise the price of its product, there is the strong possibility that the other firms would not follow. If indeed the other firms do not follow the cue, the first firm would have to rescind its price hike quickly in order to avoid losing big market shares to its competitors. One ploy has been for one of the firms to become the price leader, and while that role was necessarily informal, others tacitly agreed to follow the leadership. When this pattern in steel, cement, and tobacco was successfully challenged in courts, oligopolies were left with the less satisfactory device of one firm tentatively testing the waters with a price hike, with a lack of response leading to a quick reversal.

A price rise initiative is most likely to be successful when there have been cost increases that affect all firms in the particular market. For instance, if the United Auto Workers signed a new contract with one of the Big Three automobile producers—Chrysler, Ford, and General Motors—the other two firms could anticipate similar contracts with their workers. The higher labor costs would then be an industry-wide signal to raise prices to maintain (or increase) profits. This same logic held for any industry-wide cost increases, which would enable the oligopolistic firms to use their market power and raise prices to retain and even increase profits when they could depend on the others to act in a similar manner.

This is one of the reasons that labor unions in companies selling in oligopoly markets tended to be industry-wide unions—United Auto Workers, United Steel Workers, and so on. Not only did this form of labor organization enable firms to raise prices in a coordinated way, it also meant that labor costs were rather uniform for all of the firms in the market. This was equally important, because it meant that in labor costs, no one firm would have a cost advantage over its three or four competitors and be tempted to cut prices. If one firm were to cut prices, it could very easily degenerate into the oligopolist's nightmare: a price war in which only consumers would benefit. It is clear that this situation had to be avoided at all costs.

So here we have a situation in which each oligopoly firm generally is hesitant to raise prices because if other firms do not follow, it would lose customers to the other firms. On the price reduction side, however, the problem is not that the other firms might not follow but that they *would* follow. If one firm lowered prices to gain more customers, the resulting price competition would end up with each firm having roughly the same market share but receiving lower prices.

Since price competition clearly was not advantageous for companies in oligopolistic markets, they engaged in "co-respective" non-price competition through advertising, product differentiation, credit, and distribution and product services. Their protection from price competition by existing and newly entering firms enabled oligopolies to reap substantial economic profits. Some economists saw these behavioral patterns to be evidence of complacency, and the professional economics literature in the 1950s and 1960s contained frequent assertions that aggressive profit maximizing had been supplanted by other corporate goals, such as maximizing the size of the firm, levels of managerial pay, or simply "satisficing" for the easy life.

Without vigorous price competition, there was no mechanism to force oligopolies to operate at the most efficient levels of output and to utilize the most efficient methods of production. Nevertheless, oligopolies' size and prosperity enabled them to invest in research and development to a far greater extent than smaller and more competitive firms. This led some economists to argue that even though oligopoly firms were inefficient in static terms, they might be more efficient and materially progressive than perfectly competitive firms in dynamic terms because of their ability to invest in long-term research and development. Others counter that most of the research and development undertaken by oligopoly firms is better understood to be simply another dimension of advertising and marketing with only trivial (if any) effects on general welfare.

Without price competition, the firms' market power enabled them to capture and retain much more of the fruits of cost reductions within the enterprises than would have been possible in a competitive market. Whether the cost reductions stemmed from labor productivity, innovation, or materials prices, these increased earnings were distributed, albeit not evenly, among corporate employees and owners. Compared to competitive markets, oligopolistic market structures therefore impeded the benefits of productivity increases from being so widely diffused throughout the economy and society by means of lower product prices and increased output. This sharply curtailed the trickle-down effect expected in competitive market theory.

The End of Oligopoly?

At the very time that the oligopoly model was being refined and its implications debated, increased international competition was transforming the U.S. economic landscape. The foreign penetration of U.S. manufacturing markets by imports began in the 1960s and increased quickly, facilitated by cost-reducing advances in communications and transportation and by increasingly integrated international financial markets. The big news was that imports from foreign firms were successfully competing with U.S. producers not only in such branches as textiles, apparel, and toys in which U.S. production had been on the defensive in respect to international competition for some time. The new foreign competition was successfully competing in markets at the heart of U.S. manufacturing, including automobiles, steel, chemicals, electronics, and other products in which U.S. oligopolies had been virtually unchallenged since the end of World War II.

Imports and exports were not the only sources for changing the competitive conditions of U.S. oligopoly markets. Foreign-made components could be shipped into the United States with fewer restrictions than on finished products, and soon television receivers and automobiles with high proportions of foreign-made parts were being assembled in the United States. Some of this movement of foreign firms into the United States was in cooperation with U.S. firms (e.g., the GM–Toyota and Ford–Mazda joint ventures), but in any case, the threat from without had, to a goodly degree, moved to within. Already by 1990, foreign firms domiciled in the United States accounted for almost 15 percent of U.S. manufactured output *in addition to* imports of the same products.[7] Such "transplant" production and the extensive use of imported components and foreign assembling by "authentic" U.S. firms soon emptied the "Buy American" slogan of meaning.

U.S. markets are more competitive than they were a few decades ago, and whether the standard oligopoly model is still useful is an open question. Some have argued that the increased number of competitors in each market, their willingness to engage in at least circumspect price competition, and their heterogeneity by nationality and corporate culture may have transformed market dynamics in a way that requires new analytical tools. Others contend that it is not that firms in these markets have gotten smaller, that their profit rates have sunk to an average that includes family-owned restaurants, laundries, and funeral parlors, or that advertising and product differentiation are no longer major elements of competitive strategy. Internationally integrated markets dominated by very large players may require some modifications of the model to accommodate the global arena in which oligopolies are now operating, but it may well be that the central elements of the oligopoly model are still useful. This is what I mean by an open question.

Before letting go of this subject, I want to describe something that is new. In the old days (the 1950s and 1960s), the big oligopolies in automobiles, electrical appliances, laundry products, cigarettes, and so on dominated their respective markets, and in the process, dominated retailers. Not everybody was allowed to sell Chevrolets, and if you were granted a Chevrolet franchise, you certainly could not also sell Fords. This has changed significantly, and big retailers like Wal-Mart and Target dictate terms to producers. Pundits suggest that the merger of Gillette with Procter and Gamble was in part to offset the power of the big retailers. The frequency of store brands is another indication of this shift in power from producers to retailers. Sears and A & P grocery stores have had store brands for years, but their explosion is an indication that for consumers of some items, producers' brand names have become secondary to other considerations (such as price).

Deregulation

Having marched through the four conventional kinds of market organization, it is worth reflecting on a broader issue. It is not too simplistic to state that economists are generally divided between two very different sets of expectations about the innate tendencies of competitive markets.

One group contends that the force of competition is so powerful that it will quickly destroy the exercise of market power to reap above-average profits. Remember the example of Damien's Dynamite Cowboy Boots, where adoption of the new technique by competitors within the industry and entrepreneurs entering the market from outside the industry soon reduced boot prices and his extra profits. The conviction is that any exploitation of market power yielding high returns will quickly attract hungry new competitors whose presence will destroy the market power that was the source of the higher returns.

The second position is that competitive conditions in many markets are inherently fragile, because the very process of competition will soon produce some winners who will drive out less successful firms and create imperfect competition and market power that they can sustain against the threat of new entrants. That is, concentrated market power is the expected consequence of competitive forces in some industries. The conclusion, then, is that active public policy should either regulate an imperfectly competitive industry, such as a natural monopoly, in order to limit the exercise of firms' market power, or in situations where there is no natural monopoly, policy should force additional competition by breaking up existing firms, subsidizing new entrants, or some other device.

Although I have stated these alternative opinions rather starkly, they are recognizable descriptions of real points of view. And it is clear that in the past thirty years, the weight of opinion by both the economics profession and politicians in the United States has been shifting toward the first view. Greater international competition in virtually all markets along with technological changes, as in telecommunications, have made this position more plausible, at least in regard to the robustness of competition in national markets and the declining significance of natural monopolies. But even if markets do seem rather competitive, there still is the specter of market failure. Those who advocate a radical cessation of government regulation of private enterprise (**deregulation**) also have to dismiss the importance of genuine public goods along with the dangers of external costs such as health hazards and deleterious environmental effects.

The greater faith in the market has contributed to chronic anti-government sentiments that run deep in our history, and the process of systematic deregulation began with airlines and financial institutions during the Carter administration in the 1970s. Deregulation accelerated in the 1980s and slowed down a bit in the 1990s. President G. W. Bush intended to accelerate deregulation again in the early 2000s, but he was frustrated in this by two factors. The war on terrorism diverted attention away from deregulation, and the Enron collapse and continuing exposures of high-level business swindling reduced public support for letting the managers of large corporations do whatever they want to do.

Enron was not an isolated case, and it seems as though every week we hear of new instances of massive fraud in such major corporations as WorldCom, Tyco, Federal Home Loan Mortgage Association (Freddie Mac), HealthSouth, Westar, Federal National Mortgage Association (Fannie Mae), Nortel Networks, and Refco. The largest investment banks, such as Citicorp, Morgan Stanley, Credit Suisse, and Goldman Sachs, were complicit with one or more of the above or in serious trouble about cheating in some of their Initial Public Offerings. Major accounting firms were making big money as "consultants" to the same firms that they were supposed to audit for good accounting practices, and at the same time, these accounting firms were peddling illegal tax shelters for the very rich. Meanwhile, stock analysts for brokerage and investment banking firms were found to be lying to their clients in order to win contracts for the investment banking side of their companies, mutual funds traders were caught in unethical trading, and one of the largest insurance companies was rigging bids. This is a wide variety of misdeeds, but they all had one thing in common: they were not the actions of the economically marginal who were bending rules in order to hang on. These were and are transgressions conducted by very prominent and wealthy businesspeople.

The ability of the competitive market to discipline such unbecoming behavior is limited, and it did not take a subtle mind to realize that it was not a good time to weaken business regulation. In moves that were not empty gestures, the Bush administration replaced their first appointee as head of the Securities and Exchange Commission (SEC) with a person who took the job seriously, and they allowed the passage of the Sarbanes-Oxley law that turns many unethical practices by auditors and corporate managers into federal crimes.

In any case, the record of deregulation is not without some severe glitches. The deregulation of the savings and loan associations in the 1980s allowed poor judgment and good ol' fashioned criminal intent to ruin hundreds of savings and loan associations and to threaten the savings of all of their depositors. The U.S. Congress and the administration of George H. W. Bush, in a controversial decision, bailed out the institutions and their depositors at a cost to taxpayers of around $500 billion.

The airline industry has certainly not thrived in the deregulated environment, and railroads have experienced a set of mergers and acquisitions that have sharply reduced the number of firm. The direction of change in other deregulated markets, such as media and banking, looks similar. Moreover, the deregulation of the electrical power industry in California, led by the electrical power utilities and then-Governor Pete Wilson, has proved to be a disaster for customers and been disadvantageous for some of the utilities that helped design the deregulation process.

There are other horror stories and there are some more successful ventures into deregulation. Advocates of deregulation, in a mantra familiar from all reformers, argue that the horror stories were the result of poorly planned deregulations that just did not go far enough or fast enough to allow the competitive market to function.

As a final point, the word deregulation is a misnomer. Markets are always regulated if they are to work at all, and the choice is not regulation versus deregulation but rather is among the sources of regulation. The argument against government regulation is that the competitive market is powerful enough to regulate and discipline the behavior of economic actors, forcing them to work indirectly for the public good through the invisible hand. If the competitive market does not prove sufficiently powerful in all cases, then deregulation is simply a matter of shifting regulatory power from the bureaucrats and policies of government to the bureaucrats and policies of concentrated private economic power.[8]

The Theory of Factor Pricing

The standard list of **factors of production**—basic economic resources that combine to produce goods and services—is land, labor, and capital. These three factors of production are the essential elements in the production of consumer goods and services, intermediate products such as steel, glass, and chemicals (inputs into further production), and capital goods such as plant, equipment, and machinery. Sometimes an author includes a fourth factor of production, usually entrepreneurship (ideas, initiative, and risk taking) or technology (knowledge about better ways to combine the other factors). Nevertheless, I believe that the traditional triad is adequate for us to do what we need to do. The income from ("the returns to") land is called rent, the returns to labor are called wages and salaries, and the returns to capital are a bit more complicated.

We'll begin by looking at rent. As so often in economics, it has a meaning that goes beyond, say, the monthly fee for your apartment. It is the return to unimproved land and has a rather dubious economic function. The land (including subsoil resources such as oil, diamonds, and lead) is *there*, and so no matter what price (rent) it can command, its availability is not affected. For all intents and purposes, the supply curve for land is perfectly inelastic. The returns to improvements on the land, whether irrigation, drainage, mines, wells, or your apartment building, are returns to capital, not to land. The unique characteristic of land—that its price does not affect how much is available for production—has led economists to use "rent" as a metaphor for any return to a factor of production that is unnecessary to bring that factor into productive use.

For example, how much rent is involved in the salary of the U.S. president? I bet that for the status, power, attention, and "privilege to serve one's nation," all post–World War II presidents would have been willing to serve with *no* salary. This puts the economic rent component of the president's salary at 100 percent, assuming that poor people are effectively disqualified from being president.

The notion of wages and salaries as the return for labor is relatively clear, but there is a strong analytical parallel with land. Economists often try to distinguish how much of workers' income is attributable to an "unimproved" worker and how much is the return on improvements. These improvements are called **human capital**, and they include education, experience, training, and other productivity-enhancing activities. This enables economists to think about people investing in themselves using the same framework as a plant manager deciding whether to buy an additional drill press. The individual is thought to choose, in the sense of opportunity costs, between the option of earning current income from employment and the option of forgoing that current income and incurring other costs in order to pursue additional education that will bring more income in the future.

Turning now to the third factor of production—capital—I distinguish between financial capital (assets such as money, bonds, and other financial instruments) and real capital (produced means of production, such as plant and equipment). The return to financial capital is interest on lent funds, and I describe the determination of the interest rate as the relation between the demand for and supply of loanable funds in the next chapter.

Profit, the income from real capital, is the return to ownership of produced means of production. Although stocks in corporations are technically financial instruments, they are unlike bonds, because they are certificates of ownership of corporate assets and derive their value through the profits from corporations' production. Now you can see why I do not include entrepreneurship or technology as factors of production. In a world where large corporations produce such high proportions of goods

WE GET HIGH INCOMES BECAUSE WE'RE GOOD

John Isbister, in his thoughtful book, *Capitalism and Justice* (2001), cautions us against overemphasizing individuals' contributions to the value of output and at the same time underemphasizing the general social character of production and income. Consider the observation that carpenters, taxicab drivers, college professors, leaders of organizations, and just about everyone else in the United States earn *many* times more than people in the same occupations in, say, Ecuador. Does this mean that U.S. workers are that much more skillful, decent, hardworking, and generally effective than the corresponding workers in Ecuador? Even the most nationalist xenophobe would consider that a stretch. The principal differences are that U.S. workers work in a context of general prosperity and opportunity that enhances the value of their work. In a comparative perspective, it is not principally, and certainly not exclusively, differences in individual merit that account for these differentials in earnings.

and services, the entrepreneurial function of ideas, initiative, and risk taking is not the role of those who own the corporation—the stockholders. It is the responsibility of salaried managers, including chief executive officers (CEOs), chief operating officers (COOs), chief financial officers (CFOs), and the bureaucracies they supervise. In a similar vein, the development and application of technology are in the purview of employees. These functions of initiative, innovation, and risk, therefore, are performed by hired hands whose jobs and incomes are supposed to depend on their delivering satisfactory profits that are distributed to the owners in the form of dividends and the appreciation of the value of the corporation's stock (capital gains). One of the principal issues in corporate governance, however, is how to prevent upper-level management from packing the boards of directors with folks who will let managers pursue their own interests (for example, excessive salaries) rather than the interests of the owners/investors.

Rent, wages and salaries, interest, and profits are income flows, and at the same time, they are prices—prices for land, for labor, and for the two kinds of capital. As with prices in product markets, factor prices are governed by the interaction of demand and supply in their individual markets. But in considering the demand for these factors, it is imperative to understand that the demand for them is a **derived demand**, that is, they are in demand because, and only because, they contribute to the production of a good or service that has a market value. Their demand is thus derived from the demand for the products that they produce.

You walk into an attractive shop in an up-market neighborhood and are appalled at the prices of the items on display. The proprietor of the shop explains that her prices are so high because of the exorbitant rent that she has to pay. For her, that is true, but the concept of derived demand reveals to you that the prices are high not because the rent is high but rather that the rent is high because a wide range of different kinds of shops in this desirable location would be able to get away with high prices. In other words, the rent is high because the location is so prime that it is feasible for the shop to charge high retail prices. Or in the terms that I have been using, the high rent for the location is *derived* from the prospective income that could be garnered from selling something (almost anything?) at that spot.[9] In a parallel manner, the wages of auto workers are derived from the demand for the automobiles that they are making, and the price of land is derived from the value of the wheat or shopping mall planted there.

In thinking about the demand for factors of production, we are back to the profit maximization rule introduced earlier in the chapter. Increasing output is profitable as long as (and no longer than) marginal costs associated with the production and sale of additional units are less than the marginal revenue from their sale. The only difference is that in looking at factors of production, we have to include engineering aspects of production in order to figure out how much additional physical output would result from hiring one more worker, constructing one more check-out line, acquiring one more acre of land, or whatever. A manager of a firm will employ more productive factors (or a bundle of associated, complementary factors) if doing so increases profits, and there are three steps in this determination.

1. What does the addition of one more unit or bundle of productive factors (land, labor, or capital) add to total output? Or in the parlance of economics, what is the **marginal physical product** (MPP) from adding another unit of productive factor? In accordance with the idea of diminishing returns, when the other factors of production are held constant, the successive MPPs of a particular factor of production are thought to be positive but generally declining throughout the relevant range.

2. What is the addition to total revenue (marginal revenue [MR]) from the sale of the marginal physical product (MPP) produced by the additional unit of productive factor? This is called the **marginal revenue product** (MRP) and is derived by the simple multiplication of the two marginal quantities: MPP × MR = MRP. Since the MPP is declining as more and more units of a productive factor are employed or bought, the MRP also declines because marginal revenue (MR) is either constant or declining.

3. When the manager compares the MRP with the cost of the additional unit of the factor of production, the decision is clear. When the MRP, which is the marginal revenue from the sale of that additional physical product produced by the additional factor of production, is greater than the cost of hiring the additional factor, total profits increase and he or she will do it.

Each factor's MRP schedule is the demand curve for that productive factor. That demand curve, then, might shift if, for instance, the factor became more productive (the MPP component of MRP rose) or the demand curve for the product itself rose (meaning that the MR component rose).

Each factor has its individual supply curve, and the intersection of the supply curve and the demand curve (MRP curve) determines the market equilibrium for the price of the factor and the quantity of that factor that will be purchased. Again, this is logically parallel to the product market, and Nobel laureate Paul Samuelson dramatically illustrated the force of this idea when he wrote: "Remember that in a perfectly competitive market it really doesn't matter who hires whom."[10] That is, it does not matter whether capitalists hire workers or workers hire capitalists, because impersonal competitive factor markets ensure that factor returns are equal to their respective MRPs.

Some Reflections   Before rushing on, let's think a bit more about the central importance of the marginal revenue product theory of factor pricing and income distribution. The distributive pattern of wages, profits, interest, and rent (and therefore the distribution of income) is seen to be fair by the ethical precepts of economics. That is, the moral message is that there is a strong correspondence between what people get paid and what they and their resources contribute to the value of output, which is justice in the sense of quid pro quo. In addition, the economics discipline, with its roots in classical libertarian thought, values the unrestrained market freedoms of individuals and regards efforts to create a more equal society through political mechanisms as restrictions that violate individual freedoms, distort markets, and reduce efficiency. These are strong ethical statements from a discipline that denies harboring any value judgments. Moral tenets are embedded so deeply in the economics discipline that they are all but invisible as value judgments.

Deeply buried political commitments do not render MRP theory worthless. But while it makes sense in limited cases, its usefulness is considerably more uncertain when applied to more general issues. For example, in the 1960s and 1970s, there was a major debate among economists about how one even counts the value of total real capital (plant and equipment) in order to assess its contribution to total output. Among other issues, the fact that plant and equipment have different ages ("vintages") and therefore different productive capacities complicates these calculations. The debate was called the "Cambridge controversies" because, by and large, the debate pitted English economists at Cambridge University against Cambridge, Massachusetts, economists at the Massachusetts Institute of Technology and Harvard University. The debate reached no conclusion.

The aggregation of different kinds of capital is not the only source of problems, however, and in discussing the MRP theory, I'll focus on labor, with the understanding that the analyses for land and capital are sufficiently similar. So should one more person be added to a firm's workforce? In situations in which individuals' unique contributions to output are direct and easily identifiable, it is plausible to calculate a prospective employee's MRP in order to make such a decision. It is conceivable to calculate the costs and benefits of one more caller for a telemarketing firm, one more cashier in a discount department store, or even one more waiter along with six more tables at a restaurant.

This is not so, however, when production is organized in a highly interdependent manner, as on an assembly line, or when work is separated from production by layers of bureaucracy, as with a General Motors' vice president for human resources. In both cases, it is difficult to speak of individual contributions to the value of output with any precision. In addition, it is difficult even to identify the productivity of many service occupations, since the "product" is often simply the time spent with the customer (a half-hour appointment with a doctor, a professor's lectures and examinations, an hour with a sex worker). Finally, the assumption that workers are completely interchangeable, distinguished only by the amount and type of embodied human capital, can be distorting. This is especially so at the upper end of the professions when the employee must demonstrate qualities of leadership and creativity that are unusual and often uniquely individual. This includes the CEO of a large corporation, the designer of an advertising campaign, professional athletes and other entertainers, software researchers, and so on.

As soon as one gets away from simplistic examples like the fifth or sixth worker cultivating a plot of land, the empirical status of MRP is shaky, and the elegant precision and logic of the analysis can take on a mythical, even mystical, character. It is all too easy to fall into the tautological trap of deducing difficult-to-observe MRPs from actual wages and salaries rather than respecting the theoretical line of causation, which runs from MRP to wages and salaries. For an example of this fallacy, how did we know that, say, in 2001, the annual MRPs of the CEOs of Apple Computers, Citigroup, Oracle, Tyco International, and General Electric were between $140 million and $775 million? It was easy, because that was what the *New York Times* (1 April 2001) reported these CEOs' annual salaries to be, and it was not an April fool's joke. These extravagant salaries have moderated somewhat since then, and in 2005, executives in petroleum and financial firms were leading the pack.

Nevertheless, MRP is a reasonable starting point for organizing our discussion of changes in factor prices and the distribution of income, although I have to rely also on a coarser type of analysis based on relative bargaining power. In this, who hires whom is important.

The Distribution of Income

There are a number of dimensions along which to study the distribution of income. One of them is regional, and table 2.2 records the continuing shift of economic activity from the northern and middle Atlantic seaboard, Great Lakes, and to a lesser degree, plains states toward the south and west. Nevertheless, the per-capita income figures show that despite losing ground to the south and west, New England and the mid-Atlantic states remain the most prosperous regions.

As interesting as these inter-regional changes are, relationships among people are a more direct indicator of social health and pathology. Table 2.3 presents an overview of the distribution of income among people over the last thirty years. The organization of income distribution

*"I'm afraid this is my last
visit, Mrs. Segarra. There's no money in social work."*

data in table 2.3 is called the size distribution of income, because it ranks income recipients by the size of their incomes. The figures are proportions of personal income (i.e., before-tax income).

A major omission in the data is income from capital gains, so the figures actually under-represent the proportions of income going to the top recipients who derive greater proportions and amounts from this source. Nevertheless, the table shows how increasing proportions of income have steadily accrued, especially to the top quintile (one-fifth or 20 percent) of income recipients since 1980. Well, not all that steadily; note the slight declines of the proportions of income received by the top 5 percent of

TABLE 2.2 Changes in Regional Personal Incomes	Percentage of Personal Income by Region		Per Capita Income by Region ($1,000)
	1969	2004	2004
New England	6.4	5.9	40.2
Mideast	23.6	18.4	37.8
Great Lakes	20.9	15.3	32.2
Plains	7.5	6.5	32.1
Southeast	17.3	22.5	29.8
Southwest	7.3	10.3	29.5
Rocky Mountain	2.2	3.2	31.5
Far West	15.2	17.8	34.5
United States	100.0	100.0	32.9

Source: Survey of Current Business (July 2005), p. D-60.

income recipients between 1970 and 1980 and between 2000 and 2002, with the top 20 percent behaving in a similar fashion in the latter period. This occurred because income from financial and real capital declines proportionally more during recessions than do wages and salaries.

The concentration of income does not, of course, mean that everyone else is receiving less in absolute amounts. The absolute numbers and percentages of families and individuals existing below the official poverty line began to decline in the mid-1990s. By the end of the decade, the percentages were lower than in 1980, but they turned up again in 2004. So while the increasing concentration of income does not mean declining material standards of living for everyone else, it is an extremely important economic and social process that calls for an explanation.

Before launching into the whys and wherefores, let's talk about how we might compare the size distribution of U.S. income of one year with

TABLE 2.3	Distribution of Personal Income among Families, 1970, 1980, 1990, 2000, and 2002					
	Percent Distribution of Personal Income					
Year	Lowest Fifth	Second Fifth	Middle Fifth	Fourth Fifth	Highest Fifth	Top 5 Percent
1970	5.4	12.2	17.6	23.8	40.9	15.6
1980	5.3	11.6	17.6	24.4	41.1	14.6
1990	4.6	10.8	16.6	23.8	44.3	17.4
2000	4.3	9.8	15.4	22.7	47.7	21.1
2002	4.2	9.7	15.5	23.0	47.6	20.8

Sources: *Statistical Abstract of the United States: 2000*, p. 471; *Statistical Abstract of the United States: 1999*, p. 479; *Statistical Abstract of the United States: 2004–2005*, p. 477.

that of another year or with another country in the same year. To start with the most obvious, how about taking the percentage of personal income (before-tax income) received by the top quintile (20 percent) of income recipients and divide it by the percentage of income received by the lowest quintile of income recipients? If you do this arithmetic from the numbers presented in table 2.3, you will find that this ratio changed from 7.6 to 11.3 between 1970 and 2002.

This is informative about directions and magnitudes, but it is pretty crude. So let's go another couple of steps up in complexity and look at the Lorenz curve—a visual device to display the size distribution of income. Figure 2.4 is a Lorenz curve derived from the 2002 data from table 2.3. The horizontal axis shows the percentage of income recipients, and the vertical axis shows the percentage of total personal income received by each proportion of recipients. So the first point, A, can be read directly off table 2.3: the poorest quintile of income recipients got 4.2 percent of the personal income. The second point, however, cannot be read directly off the table, because it is cumulative. The percentage of personal income received by the 40 percent of income recipients includes the percentage of income of the first quintile and the second quintile. So point B shows that the poorest 40 percent of income recipients received the 4.2 percent of the first quintile plus the 9.7 percent received by the second quintile, which equals 13.9 percent of personal income. This is what I meant as being cumulative. Point C shows that the 60 percent of the lowest income recipients got 4.2 plus 9.7 plus 15.5 percentages of personal income, which totals 29.4 percent of personal income. I hope that you could figure point D from table 2.3 by yourself and will not be surprised to find that at point E, 100 percent of income recipients received 100 percent of personal income.

This is the Lorenz curve, named after the U.S. economist who came up with this pictorial device in 1905 to represent distributions of income. If you got the idea, you understand that the diagonal (the line from 0 to E—the 45° line) is for the purpose of visual reference. It is what the

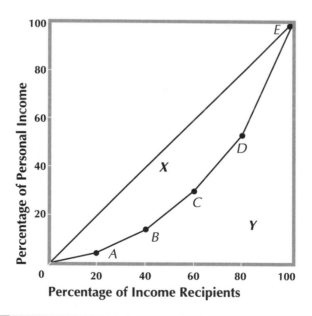

FIGURE 2.4 Lorenz Curve for the United States, 1998

Lorenz curve would be if income were distributed with perfect equality. That is, each 20 percent of income recipients received 20 percent of personal income through the entire array. The diagonal is not so much a goal or aspiration as it is a geometric baseline from which deviations from perfect equality can be compared. The other extreme (or reference point) is the axes themselves; if one family were to receive all of the income, then the Lorenz curve would simply run along the horizontal axis and then go up the vertical axis, showing that no one got anything until we hit 100 percent of income recipients. The conclusion from this is that the more an actual Lorenz curve is bowed out from the diagonal, the more unevenly is income distributed. If you are highly motivated, you can use graph paper to plot a Lorenz curve for 1970 and 2002 from table 2.3 and see that the 1970 curve lies within (closer to the diagonal than) the 2002 curve.

If you use deciles (10 percents) rather than quintiles (20 percents), the curve becomes a smoother curve, and if you use individual percentages, then the curve becomes even smoother. But no matter how smooth the curve becomes, it still is rather awkward for describing the distribution of income in verbal or quantitative terms. This is where the Gini coefficient comes in.

The **Gini coefficient** is derived from the Lorenz curve, and it is the ratio of the area between the Lorenz curve and the diagonal to the entire triangular area under the diagonal. That is, it is the area that indicates inequality as a percentage of the total area, and in figure 2.4, it is the ratio of area X to area $X + Y$. That is, it is X divided by $X + Y$. Perfect equality (the diagonal), therefore, would have a Gini coefficient of 0, and perfect inequality would have a Gini coefficient of 1. Get it? The larger the Gini coefficient, between 0 and 1, the more unevenly income is distributed.

Gini coefficients are quoted in newspapers, and they are very useful. Nevertheless, they are summary statistics, and like averages, their use entails the loss of information. Figure 2.5 illustrates the possibility of two economies with exactly the same Gini coefficients, but they could still be very different places. In one of them, Society A is an economy that is quite egalitarian except for an underclass that receives a very small percentage of total income. Conversely, in Society B, the same Gini coefficient $\left(\frac{X}{X+Y}\right)$ is consistent with most of the income being equally distributed among most of the population but the remainder of the income going to a high-income elite. Despite the same Gini coefficients, they would be very different societies in which to live.

Now that we have a grip on the measurement of income distribution, we can return to analyses and interpretations. The MRP of labor immediately points to the fact that some workers have greater amounts of human capital than others do. And it is clear that both age and education affect people's earnings. Average family incomes do indeed rise with age and experience but only up to 45 to 54 years of age. After that, average income falls rather abruptly for workers aged 55 and older. So a portion of the previously described income inequality has demographic origins; some individuals in the first (lowest income) quintile in 1970 will, for example,

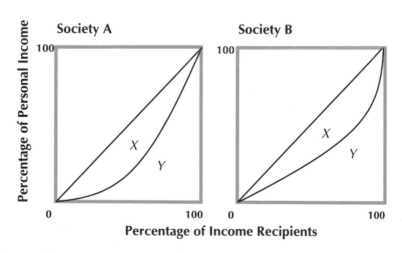

FIGURE 2.5 Two Lorenz Curves, One Gini Coefficient

AVERAGES

In our discussion of income, I always use "average" to refer to the median. The median is one of three types of averages: the mean, the median, and the least used, the mode. The median income of families is the middle income, the income at which half of the families lie below and half above. Unlike the mean income of families (the sum of all family incomes divided by the number of families), the median is not distorted by a few very high incomes pulling it upward.

have graduated from law school and moved up by several income categories by 1998. On the other hand, some in the middle or upper quintiles in 1970 will have retired from the workforce and moved down.

Unlike the life cycle in earnings, educational attainment has a more uniform effect on income. Income rises steadily for families and individuals as their educational attainment rises from less than a ninth-grade education to high school graduation, some college, bachelor's degree, master's degree, and professional degree. The only exception to the consistent relationship between education and family income, and one peculiarly poignant for an academic, is that those with the highest educational attainment—the doctorate—have a lower average income than those with professional degrees. Oh well.

Table 2.4 shows that "race" is another important facet of differential incomes. And gender turns out to be yet another determinant of difference in incomes. From the table, you can see that the gap between white and black families' incomes has been virtually unchanged since 1970, and the gap between Hispanic and white families' incomes has increased since 1980. Working women, however, now average about 80 percent of men's earnings, compared to 62 percent in 1980. Declining or stagnating wages for men helped narrow the gap.

TABLE 2.4 Median Incomes of Families by Race and Hispanic Origin in Constant (2002) Dollars

Year	All Families	White	Black	Asian, Pacific Islander	Hispanic*
1970	42,980	44,588	27,351	n.a.	n.a.
1980	43,456	45,277	26,198	n.a.	30,419
1990	47,167	49,251	28,582	56,364	31,261
2000	52,977	55,376	35,166	65,388	35,966
2002	51,680	54,633	33,525	60,984	34,185

Sources: *Statistical Abstract of the United States: 2000*, p. 471; *Statistical Abstract of the United States: 2004–2005*, p. 446.

*Persons of Hispanic origin can be of any race.

n.a. means not available.

The consistent and enduring differences of income by gender and race are not easily reconciled with MRP analysis. After all, the market creed is supposed to be "You give me a good day's work, and I do not care about your race, gender, religion, sexual orientation, national origin, or whatever." Moreover, this is not voluntary; it is not a matter of an individual employer's preferences. If competitive market forces make wages and salaries correspond to MRPs, any employer with a strong "taste for discrimination" would incur higher labor costs than the competitors. The employer would therefore be driven out of the market or at best limited to a narrow niche (e.g., "This product is guaranteed not to have been touched by an Antarctican").

One way to have labor markets equate everyone's wages to their MRPs and still disadvantage certain groups is to work through human capital. If you can effectively curtail some groups' access to education, training, and credit, you have a less competitive field and your own access to income-enhancing activities will pay off more.

Economists have been extremely inventive in using supply side characteristics like human capital to explain away pay differentials, and while those characteristics do go a ways toward explaining them, they go only part of the way. Behavior on the demand side (i.e., discrimination on the part of employers) cannot be so easily dismissed. After all is said and done, the claim that competitive markets will be a potent force in reducing discrimination on the employer/demand side has yet to live up to the standard that it sets for itself.

This discussion of disparities is important, but it does not adequately explain recent *changes* in the distribution of income. The usual explanations include both demand and supply elements, especially technological changes in the workplace and increased international competition, both of which have significantly affected domestic labor markets. The technical proficiencies needed for more and more jobs favor more educated workers, while at the same time, the greater access to foreign workers (through both trade and immigration) has increased the supply of unskilled labor. This pattern of labor demand therefore skews the distribution of income toward high wage and salary earners.

TWO GARBAGE COLLECTION MODELS

Steven Slavin (*Economics*, fifth edition [1990], p. 670) gives an intriguing presentation of such a process. He considers Memphis and New York City to have represented two different ways to get people to collect garbage. The Memphis model was to limit African American and Latino men's employment opportunities so severely that they had to work as garbage collectors at low wages. (Remember, Martin Luther King, Jr. was in Memphis to support a garbage collectors' strike when he was assassinated in 1968.) The New York City model is to pay garbage collectors relatively high wages and to have white men do it.

There is no question that both of these processes—technological changes and more integrated international labor markets—have been and continue to be at work in increasing the unevenness of income distribution, but there is more. Recognizing that wages and salaries are not the only sources of income is the next step, and the many income distribution studies that ignore this are oddly framed. This takes us to the **functional distribution of income**, where income data are organized by wages and salaries, interest, profits, and rent—by functional source rather than by size of income. Table 2.5 is suggestive; it shows that average real wages (i.e., corrected for changes in the cost of living) increased only slightly between 1960 and 2002, and in real (purchasing power) terms, they did not surpass the 1970 level until after 2000 despite strong increases in labor productivity.

I am sure that the first question that occurred to you is "how can these figures be reconciled with table 2.4, which, except in 2002, shows median family incomes rising considerably faster?" It's easy; more people in families are working more. Since 1970, the proportion of the civilian, noninstitutionalized population of 16 years and older who are in the labor force rose from 60.4 percent to 66 percent in 2004. There actually has been some decline in men's labor force participation, but it has been more than made up for by increased participation by women in paid employment. Women's participation rates steadily increased from 36.5 percent in 1960 to 42.6 percent in 1970 and to 60.3 in 2004. Another piece of the puzzle is that many workers hold multiple jobs and work long hours. These two changes help explain the seeming anomaly of rising median family incomes occurring along with median wages that were stagnant or even declining.

Back to the main event. Although table 2.5 presents a record of weak growth in earnings from wages, it displays a healthy growth of income from property (i.e., ownership of land and capital). This is especially evident in financial and real (corporate) capital and less so in real estate and the proprietorship of unincorporated enterprises. And it is important to

TABLE 2.5	Average Hourly Earnings and Indexes of Personal Income Sources, Productivity, and Gross Domestic Product (all at constant prices)					
	1960	**1970**	**1980**	**1990**	**2000**	**2004**
Average Hourly Earnings in the Private [Business] Sector (1982 dollars)	6.79	8.03	7.78	7.52	7.91	8.24
Index of Average Hourly Earnings in the Private [Business] Sector	100.0	118.3	114.6	110.8	116.5	127.7
Index of Personal Income from Dividends	100.0	138.5	171.9	279.9	502.2	549.9
Index of Personal Income from Interest	100.0	213.1	401.8	683.2	673.9	733.2
Index of Personal Income from Rent	100.0	95.6	69.5	68.7	157.2	170.6
Index of Personal Income from Unincorporated Enterprises	100.0	117.5	123.1	166.6	239.2	260.5
Index of Labor Productivity (Business Sector)	100.0	131.7	155.5	182.6	223.0	260.0
Index of Real GDP (total production of goods and services)	100.0	150.6	206.7	283.5	395.4	436.5

Sources: Economic Report of the President, 2000, pp. 306, 308, 336–39, 360, 373, 409; Economic Report of the President, 2001, pp. 276, 308–9, 330, 332, 343.

Note: The hourly earnings are for production and nonsupervisory workers, or around 82 percent of total nonagricultural employment. When dividends, interest, and rent are received by a firm, they are recorded as receipts of a corporation or of an unincorporated enterprise and become personal income as dividends from corporations and income from unincorporated enterprises. The dividend, rent, and interest incomes listed here, therefore, are only those accruing directly to individuals.

know that the personal income figures do not include income from capital gains, thus underreporting the income of the rich, who derive greater proportions and amounts of income from capital gains.

An emphasis on the importance of income from financial and real capital also helps explain a feature of table 2.3 that I did not mention but

"SEND US YOUR BRIGHTEST, BEST-TRAINED, . . ."

Not all immigrants are low-wage labor, unskilled, or just desperate. There are provisions in the U.S. immigration code (H-1B visas) that allow employers to bring in foreign workers with specialized skills that are needed but supposedly not available in the U.S. labor force. Nursing is an example of an eligible occupation, but employers in the electronics industry were especially successful in lobbying Congress to allow the immigration of technically proficient workers, who came mostly from Taiwan, China, India, and the former Soviet republics under a semi-indentured status. In fiscal 2000, there was a limit of 195,000 H-1B workers, and 166,000 workers actually arrived with H-1B permits. Although the limit of 195,000 lasted through fiscal 2003, the numbers of workers using them declined sharply due to recession and unemployment. In fiscal 2004, the limit dropped to 65,000 H-1B workers, and even fewer came. Especially during the boom years of the 1990s, however, this augmented supply of skilled labor no doubt dampened wage rises in the occupations involved. Moreover, in addition to concern about a "brain drain" from the countries of origin, many of the immigrant engineers and scientists received free educations in their native lands. This suggests that poor countries' taxpayers are in effect subsidizing them, their employers, and purchasers of computers and other electronic goodies.

Consistent with the optimism of the information technology sector in the 1990s, the laws enabling the immigration of these technical workers said nothing about what was to happen to these workers if they were laid off from their jobs. Those who were hit by the layoffs of 2001 and after, therefore, found themselves in an unpleasant legal limbo.

am confident that you noticed. The highest fifth of income recipients increased their proportion of personal income from 41.1 percent in 1980 to 47.7 percent in 2002, an increase of 6.6 percentage points. In the same time period, the top 5 percent of income recipients increased their share of total income from 14.6 percent to 20.8 percent, or 6.2 percentage points. This means that those in the top 5 percent of recipients received more than 95 percent of the entire increased proportions of income accruing to the top 20 percent of income recipients between 1980 and 2004.[11] And when you look at the rest of the table, you find that the top 5 percent and top 20 percent of income recipients are the only segments to have increased their proportions of total income since 1980. Up in the stratosphere of incomes, I am talking about big bucks, and CEOs are the most visible example of getting big bucks. Nevertheless, most of what is being hauled in by the very rich comes from property ownership—profits, interest, and income from land (including natural resources). And these are the fastest growing sources of income.

Wealth is much more concentrated than income, and by wealth here, I am not talking about fancy houses, cars, and boats but about the ownership of productive resources. For example, Edward Wolff's careful study (*Top Heavy* [1995], p. 11) found that between 1983 and 1990, the top 1 percent increased their proportion of total financial wealth from 43 to 48 percent. The top 20 percent (including that 1 percent) increased their proportion of total financial wealth from 91 to 94 percent. These figures indicate that the top 20 percent's increase was more than completely accounted for by gains by the richest 1 percent segment of the 20 percent. So much for people's capitalism and the vaunted dispersion of stock ownership among many small holders.

Now that we have some sense of the favorable position of financial and real capital, we should rethink the effects of technological change and greater international competition. In doing so, we will have to go beyond the conventional focus on wage and salary differentials. Both the technological and international changes have shifted the balance of bargaining power away from labor; the restructuring of work sites (sometimes called downsizing) together with the ability to use foreign labor both at home and abroad has created what in effect is a surplus labor market. This has enabled employers to create work situations in which more and more jobs are temporary, part time, and generally insecure, and they have few benefits and uncertain ladders of career advancement.

In the contemporary labor market, then, men's work has come to look more like women's work.[12]

With this background, it is easier to discern a couple of important recent processes. The first is that in the buoyant U.S. economy of the 1990s with very low rates of unemployment, there has been little upward pressure on wages. Chairman Alan Greenspan of the Federal Reserve Bank repeatedly (and ponderously) evoked the frightening specter of wages and salaries rising and causing some inflation if economic growth did not slow down. Table 2.5 along with table 2.3 show how successfully the "new economy" avoided the disaster of increasing wages for working families.

Closely related to this has been the decline of labor unions. Declining government protections for union organizing, internal governance problems, and employers' plausible threat of moving jobs, whether to less unionized domestic sites or abroad, have contributed to a much weakened U.S. labor movement. Union membership included around a full third of the nonagricultural U.S. labor force in the 1950s, and that proportion shrank to barely 15 percent in the 1990s.

It is no coincidence, moreover, that public employees constitute around half of current union membership, or that strikes by nurses, janitors, teachers, police, telephone workers, and United Parcel Service workers are the most effective. All of these service occupations are insulated from international competition by the fact that their work has to be performed on the spot, as it were. U.S. catalog companies can sell clothes made in Myanmar (Burma), use telephone operators in Jamaica, and farm out data entry to clerks in India. Nevertheless, their packages have to be delivered in the here and now, and that service cannot be imported. In a similar manner, hospitals can bring in Filipino nurses, and janitorial and security service companies can hire immigrants, but actual production—patient care, cleaning buildings, policing, classroom teaching, air transport, and telephone installation and repair—is not amenable to foreign production. The combination of increased service production

UNIONS AND LABOR MOVEMENTS

Calls to establish international labor standards (e.g., wages, work conditions, freedom to form labor unions) and prohibit the importation of goods produced under terrible work conditions have become audible positions in the public debate. But such efforts have often been accused of expressing an unseemly jingoism and the narrow interests of domestic labor at the expense of consumers interested in low prices. There is substance to this criticism, but the issue is more complicated than this. Let's ignore for the moment the conflict of interests between workers and consumers, which is probably a false dichotomy anyway. First of all, the creation of employment opportunities in poor countries is not unimportant. Moreover, many argue that policies that favor the workers in industrialized nations over workers in poor countries pits one set of workers against another and weakens the possibilities of creating an international labor movement that is necessary to balance the power of international capital. The counter-argument is that if the creation of employment in poor countries depends on worker poverty and degradation, it will not help the formation of an international labor movement, which necessarily will have to come from a vibrant labor movement in the industrialized nations. This is an important debate, and the historical record gives scant comfort to either side.

(see table I.2), international competition, and new attitudes by union leaders probably will produce a stronger union movement among such occupations.

Notes

1. The names of corporations in the United States often are followed by Inc. (for incorporated), those in Great Britain by Ltd. (limited liability), and those in Latin America by S.A. (Sociedad Anónima—Anonymous Society).

2. There are also Dow Jones indexes for utilities and for railroads listed on the NYSE, but they are seldom cited anymore. Moreover, the word "industrial" cannot be taken too literally, because a range of firms in service and other sectors is now included in the so-called Industrials index.

3. There are other NYSE indexes. For instance, the Standard & Poor's 500 index weights price changes for 500 stocks by each stock's share of total equity.

4. In actuality, the profit-maximizing level of production is a bit higher, but for our purposes, let's assume that it stays at 3,500 boots a week.

5. The Sherman Antitrust Act had also been used against labor unions, but the Clayton Act excluded them from anti-trust prosecution. In 1922, the U.S. Congress also exempted professional baseball from anti-trust action.

6. Extending the lesson in Greek-derived words, *monopsony* and *oligopsony* are market situations characterized (respectively) by a single buyer or a few buyers.

7. The 1990 percentages were higher in chemicals (32 percent), rubber and plastics (19 percent), stone, clay, and glass (25 percent), primary metals (19 percent), and electronic and electrical equipment (16 percent). For passenger cars, they were 13 percent, and for industrial machinery and equipment, 12 percent. These and the other data in the paragraph are from *Survey of Current Business* [(1958) 38(9), (1976) 56(8), and (1994) 74(1)] and from *U.S. Commodity Exports and Imports as Related to Output, 1960 & 1959* (Washington, D.C.: U.S. Department of Commerce, Government Printing Office, 1962) and *U.S. Commodity Exports and Imports as Related to Output, 1976 & 1975*. (Washington, D.C.: U.S. Department of Commerce, Government Printing Office, 1980).

8. This is not to say that the bureaucrats and policies of government regulation are immune to the influence of concentrated private economic power.

9. The high prices of many shops in poor urban neighborhoods are another matter. Before accusing store proprietors of exploitation, however, you need to check out the proprietors' standards of living and work as well as the reluctance of large, chain markets to pursue supposedly higher profits in poor neighborhoods. With a few exceptions, selling to the poor is not where big money is made.

10. Paul Samuelson in "Wages and Interest: A Modern Dissection of Marxian Economic Models," *American Economic Review* 47 (1957), p. 894.

11. This does not mean that the same individuals were in the top 5 percent in the two years. Some died and some moved up.

12. In the 1970s and early 1980s, there was quite a bit of excitement about new kinds of work organizations that would enhance workers' commitment to the job. These ranged from worker self-management plans to various kinds of teamwork to milder "Quality of Work Life" (QWL) efforts. By the 1990s, however, after the balance of bargaining power tipped in favor of employers, these experiments are much less prominent. The threat of job loss now seems to be enough to discipline workers.

Macroeconomics

The Economy as a Whole: Definitions and Analyses

A s we have seen, microeconomics is concerned with economic activity at the level of individual markets and generally concludes that competitive markets are efficient and work best when not encumbered by government intervention. In rather sharp contrast, macroeconomics is the branch of economics that deals with the relationships of large aggregates—all consumption expenditures added up, all exports added up, and so on—in order to analyze the performance of the national economy as a whole. The entire frame of analysis is oriented toward understanding how a central government (in the United States, the federal government) can deliberately manage total effective demand for goods and services through its budget (fiscal policy) and by altering financial conditions (monetary policy).

Why Macroeconomics?

The roots of macroeconomics and the idea that governments need to manage aggregate demand are not difficult to locate. Despite the usual portrayal of the 1920s as a decade of frivolity and good times, it was actually a time of economic instability and difficulty. Some state governments ineffectually attempted to regulate markets, and the federal government in the 1920s did little except to raise tariffs and experiment with a small agricultural price support program.

The U.S. stock market crash of 1929 and the onset of the Great Depression drastically altered all of this. The volatility of the international economy, the fragility of domestic financial systems, and the inability to match levels of aggregate demand with output capacity all converged to create the most serious worldwide capitalist crisis ever. Between 1929 and 1934, U.S. production declined by 30 percent and official unemployment rates rose to 25 percent of the workforce. The presidential election of Franklin Delano Roosevelt in 1932 signaled a new era—the New Deal—of active, interventionist government policies.

The short-lived National Industrial Recovery Act (NIRA) of 1933 was an early, ambitious attempt at national industrial planning, and it brought the force of federal law to attempts to stabilize markets. Even though businessmen dominated the councils empowered to make decisions about prices, wages, and output quotas, the NIRA's failure to bring order into markets soon turned the business community's initial support into opposition. In any case, the U.S. Supreme Court ruled it unconstitutional in 1935.

Two other general policies enjoyed greater successes. The Wagner-Connery Act (1935) established the National Labor Relations Board and legalized protections for union organizing and collective bargaining. The Social Security Act (1935) mandated a national pension system and some limited social insurance, even though it neglected large numbers of poor, minority, and women workers by excluding agriculture and domestic service. Both initiatives were resisted by business interests, and a large part of the entire New Deal endeavor has to be understood as an effort to put the business system back on its feet even if it had to overcome opposition by the business community to do so.

Augmenting the three pieces of legislation mentioned above, the New Deal included a myriad of more focused initiatives, ranging from financial market regulation, agricultural price supports, the Civilian Conservation Corps, Works Projects Administration, and other regulatory, public works, and relief policies. Nevertheless, the New Deal policies never adequately stimulated aggregate demand, and recovery was slow and uneven. When Hitler's army invaded the Polish corridor in late 1939, the U.S. unemployment rate was still around 15 percent.

World War II, more than any other factor, rescued U.S. capitalism from the Depression. As soon as large federal expenditures for war matériel raised profit prospects and unions agreed to a no-strike pledge, business opposition to federal regulation and control all but evaporated. During the war, the federal government successfully operated a regulatory regime that went far beyond the NIRA in its comprehensiveness, tight controls, and top-down lines of authority. By-products of the war effort included full employment, new occupational opportunities for women, modest improvements in the distribution of income, and new civil rights possibilities for African Americans.

Although most of the direct economic controls were dismantled soon after the war, they and the New Deal had established the foundations for substantial federal economic regulation and intervention (the "mixed economy"). These developments reflected political and economic elites' general loss of confidence in free markets and their conviction that if left alone, the vicissitudes of unregulated markets could jeopardize the very existence of a capitalist economy. At the same time, the New Deal and World War II controls seemed to show that active government policies of regulation and demand management could stabilize capitalist economies. These two lessons from experience encouraged a newfound faith in the efficacy of discretionary stabilization policies by public authorities.

The work of the Englishman John Maynard Keynes, in his *The General Theory of Employment, Interest, and Money* (1936), plausibly justified and systematically mapped interventionist strategies that did not upset the basic principles of a capitalist social order. The book established the theoretical bases of modern macroeconomic analysis, often referred to as "Keynesian economics."[1] The Keynesian approach emphasizes the need for sustaining levels of total (or "aggregate") demand adequate for the full employment of productive capacity. The policy tools of demand management are used to promote economic growth, reduce inflation and unemployment, and generally maintain a smoothly functioning economy with satisfactory levels of material prosperity. Advocates of such policies argue that the macroeconomic stability and buoyancy from prudent public policy are necessary for markets to work efficiently by satisfying some of the conditions, such as full employment and stable prices, that are assumed in microeconomics.

Two legislative acts immediately after the war are important to know about. The Employment Act of 1946 formally obligated the federal government to ensure "full employment" and illustrated these new sensibilities. This was followed closely by the Taft-Hartley Act of 1947, which constrained the freedoms that the Wagner-Connery Act had accorded organized labor, strengthened conservative union leaders' control over rank-and-file members, and mandated purging unions of left-wing influences. In addition to the Cold War, the Taft-Hartley Act was a direct response to the wave of post–World War II strikes often instigated by the rank-and-file membership against the wishes of union leaders. Moreover, employers feared that the Employment Act would weaken the threat of unemployment and strengthen labor's bargaining position.

It is important to understand, then, that the experiences of the Great Depression of the 1930s and World War II led political and economic leaders to have powerful doubts about the stability of free markets. Corresponding to these doubts were their convictions about the need for active economic guidance by central political authorities, thus leading to the rise of modern macroeconomic policy.

How Gross Is the Gross Domestic Product?

It is obligatory to begin with some formal definitions, simply so that we have a decent idea of what we're talking about. We'll start with the National Income and Product Accounts' most aggregate of the economic aggregates: **gross domestic product** (GDP), which is the total value of all goods and services produced in the nation in a year.[2] In the middle of the first decade of the twenty-first century, the GDP of the United States was over $12,000,000,000,000—that's right, over twelve *trillion* dollars (twelve zeros), or 12 million millions.

One of the key concepts underlying the National Income and Product Accounts and all of macroeconomics is that a buyer's expenditures represent some seller's receipts. Wages are costs to firms but receipts (income) for workers. Food that workers buy at the supermarket is a cost of living for them but receipts for the supermarket. An exception to this circular interdependence at the national level is that while the purchase of an imported good is a cost to the buyer, it is a receipt for a foreign seller and lies outside the domestic circular flow. The sale of an export is the mirror image: the receipt from the sale enters the national circular flow from the outside.

Table 3.1A presents the flow relationships within the nation and lists the GDP's components. Table 3.1B lists an alternative organization of the same data but by a different system of main headings ("aggregates"). These frequently used aggregates are important, but for now, let's concentrate on table 3.1A.

The left column of the table shows the expenditures for all final goods and services produced in that year. That is, the list includes the sale value of all goods and services except for those used for further production (e.g., steel, plastic, and glass for automobiles). The right column

TABLE 3.1 The Gross Domestic Product

A. Components of the Gross Domestic Product, 2004 (Individual Entries as Percentages of GDP)

Expenditures for Final Goods and Services

Consumption			70.1
Durable goods		8.5	
Nondurable goods		20.3	
Services		41.4	
Investment			16.4
Plant and equipment		10.4	
Residential housing		5.7	
Change in inventories		0.4	
Government Purchases			18.6
Federal		6.9	
Defense	4.7		
Nondefense	2.2		
State and local		11.7	
Exports		10.0	
−Imports		−15.2	
Totals			100.0
Gross Domestic Product (billions of dollars)			$11,735

Incomes

Wages and Salaries (including benefits)			55.2
Profits			17.5
Unincorporated Enterprises		7.5	
Corporations		10.0	
Profits taxes	3.6		
Dividends	3.3		
Retained earnings	3.2		
Interest			7.4
Rent			1.7
Indirect Business Taxes			6.6
Depreciation			11.6
Totals			100.0
Gross Domestic Income (billions of dollars)			$11,735

Source: Survey of Current Business (July 2005), pp. D-4, D-14, D-18.

(Continued)

TABLE 3.1 Continued

B. The Family of National Income Aggregates, 2004 (billions of dollars)

Gross Domestic Product	11,735.0
Plus income received from U.S. investments abroad	
Minus income to foreigners from their investments in the United States	
Equals: Gross National Product	11,778.97
Minus depreciation	
Equals: Net National Product	10,371.6
Minus indirect business taxes	
Plus subsidies to business	
Minus statistical discrepancy	
Equals: National Income	10,339.6
(total payments to productive resources for contributions to current production)	
Minus corporate profits taxes and retained profits	
(leaving dividend payments to individuals)	
Plus government transfer payments to individuals	
(payments not for current productive activity [e.g., pensions])	
Plus business transfer payments to individuals	
Equals: Personal Income	9,689.6
(total income received by individuals)	
Minus personal income taxes	
Equals: Disposable Income	8,646.9
(after-tax income of individuals)	

Source: Survey of Current Business (July 2005), pp. D-14, D-18.

shows how the receipts from the production and sale of those goods and services were distributed among recipients. The left side may be thought of as being the sales of all final goods and services, and the right side as the costs of producing and selling those goods and services. Even though there is no direct correspondence between individual entries, the sum of the two sides is equal—sales equal receipts; production equals income. This equality does not reflect the balance of an equilibrium condition; it simply expresses accounting definitions.

Table 3.1A suggests two ways to calculate the GDP. Look at the left side of the table, which represents one way to calculate the GDP—count up the total sales of only *final* goods and services. Since the only goods counted here are those that end up with the final users, we avoid the problem of double counting by not counting all the intermediate goods utilized in further production. For example, the value of the wheat sold to the miller, the value of the flour sold to the baker, the value of bread sold to the supermarket chain, and the value of the bread sold to consumers/shoppers cannot be added up into a meaningful total. One way to avoid double counting is to count only the value of the final product—the bread—which includes the value of the intermediate products used in its production. Table A.1 in the appendix to this book shows the magnitude of intermediate sales, which in several economic sectors was more than final sales. This demonstrates the need to prevent them from being included in the calculation of final product.

This is a fairly clear principle, right? Well, let's gum it up a bit by noting that investment goods constitute a major exception. When a firm buys a metal lathe from another firm, it is considered to be a final purchase, because even though the lathe is used for future production, its contribution to future production will occur over a period of years. For accounting convenience, such investment goods are classed as final purchases. The left side of table 3.1A represents the final-purchase/end-use strategy of calculating the GDP.

An alternative method to calculate the GDP is to add up the value of the wheat (assuming no intermediate products), the value of the flour minus that of the wheat, the value of the bread minus that of the flour, and the value of the bread sold by the supermarket minus the value of the bread from the baker. That is, each stage of production adds a certain amount of value to the final value, and this value-added approach is what we find in the right column of table 3.1A. After all, the value added at each stage of production is the value of its sales minus the value of the intermediate goods and services used up at that stage of production. Therefore, value added is what was received in wages and salaries, interest, rent, taxes, depreciation (wear and tear on plant and equipment), and profit (positive or negative—it's a residual) at each stage of production. The two approaches to the calculation of the GDP ought to add up to the same totals, but given the complexity of the calculations, perfect balance always requires adding some sort of statistical adjustment to one side of the account.

Now for some observations about what does not go into the GDP or any of the other aggregates. First of all, there is the resale of any good produced in a previous period (a used car, a thirty-year-old house). Although the commissions earned by the used car salesperson and the realtor are current services and thus counted toward this year's GDP, the sale prices of the car and house are not. Goods produced last year and kept in inventories and sold this year are counted at their current value, but that value is offset somewhat by the reduction in inventories, a component of the investment category.

Second, goods and services that do not pass through a market, even though currently produced, are generally not counted. One exception is an estimate of the value of food produced and consumed on farms (it used to be much larger), but food grown in your urban backyard and eaten by you at home is not. If your friend drops some books off at the library for you as a favor, that is not counted in GDP, but if you pay him $5.00 for the service, then it should be counted.

This takes us to one of the more contentious areas: the value of housework and child rearing is not counted in the GDP unless it is done under commercial auspices, by house cleaning, food, and child care service providers. When I began teaching economics oh so many years ago, many textbooks used the following example to illustrate this: if a man marries his (paid) housekeeper, he reduces the GDP. This once-common example seems to have become extinct.

Third, the value of leisure is not included in the GDP. If economic growth is possible by everyone working 60–80 hours a week, there is no way in the National Income and Product Accounts to acknowledge the costs from the loss of downtime. It simply is not measured as economic value in the National Income and Product Accounts.

Then there are genuine market activities that are not counted in the GDP because they are deliberately hidden. Evading taxes is definitely an incentive to under-report income and the value of production even if the economic activity is perfectly legal. Self-employed people are in the best position to evade taxes in this manner, whether they are self-employed professionals, house painters, bodyguards, or whatever. Tips are another income source that often is not reported.

Finally, there are illegal economic activities, where the incentive to keep under cover goes beyond chiseling on taxes. Maybe the product is not naughty but the manner of its production is frowned upon (e.g., employing illegal immigrants to make clothes or using unsafe chemicals to bleach paper). Completely illegal activities—the production and trade in amphetamines and other controlled substances, gambling, prostitution, contract killing, and other thoroughly criminalized economic production—are yet another subset of economic activity that is not noticed in the GDP.

Usually lumped together in the category of the **underground economy** (not the realm of the Hobbits), these market activities respond to the forces of demand and supply, even though the risks, costs, and returns of their illegality significantly condition their demand and supply curves. The very nature of the underground economy makes estimates of its size very tricky, and estimates range from 5 to 25 percent of GDP. Although the actual magnitude of these economic activities is uncertain, there is a suspicion that they are growing. One indication is the increasing amount of cash, especially $100 bills, in circulation compared to what people are holding in checking accounts.

Returning to the aboveground economy, government services that are not sold on the market (e.g., public education, fire and police protection, tax collection, standing army, most roads) are valued at the cost of public employees' wages and salaries. What governments buy from private firms (e.g., macadam, rockets, fire hoses, paper and pencils, surveillance equipment) are not considered to be intermediate products but rather final products purchased by the government.

Finally, some costs of production are generally not counted or else are severely undervalued in the GDP. Pollution and other sorts of resource degradation from production are the most obvious examples.

Once we have some idea of what GDP is, the next step is to figure out how to compare it over a period of time in order to discern growth or recession.Once we have some idea of what GDP is, the next step is to figure out how to compare it over a period of time in order to discern growth or recession. This can present a problem, because prices change in different amounts and directions over time. The GDP is the price of each final good and service multiplied by the quantity of the corresponding goods and services. Therefore, when comparing the GDP of 2004 with, say, the GDP of 2000, there is no easy way to know how much of the difference between the two figures is due to price changes and how much to "real" (quantity) changes. For this reason, it is necessary to use GDP at **constant prices** to compare GDPs over time. The idea is quite simple: use the prices of one period, say that of 2000, to calculate the GDP of 2004; then you can compare the two GDPs having avoided the distortions of price changes and isolated the changes in quantities. (Doing the actual calculations, of course, is far from simple.)

You can see this in table 3.2. The first row is GDP in current prices, and the second row is the GDP of each year using 2000 prices. The year-to-year changes of the GDP in the second row are changes only in quantities produced and sold, not of price changes because the same (2000)

TABLE 3.2 GDP in Current and Constant Dollars and Index Numbers						
	1999	2000	2001	2002	2003	2004
GDP in trillions of current dollars	9.25	9.32	10.12	10.44	11.0	11.74
GDP in trillions of 2000 dollars	9.47	9.82	7.89	10.07	10.38	10.84
Index of real GDP	96.4	100.0	80.3	102.5	105.7	116.6
GDP implicit price deflator	97.9	100.0	102.4	104.1	106.0	108.2

Sources: *Survey of Current Business* (April 2001), pp. D-3 and D-38; *Survey of Current Business* (July 2005), p. C-1; *Economic Report of the President, 2005*, table B-1.

prices have been used to calculate each GDP. Thus the GDPs in the second row are known as real GDP. If you want to construct an index number of real GDP in order to be able to read proportional changes more easily, you divide each year's real GDP by 2000 GDP and multiply by 100. For 2000, clearly the result is 100, but for 2001, it is 80.3, which shows that real GDP of the recession year 2001 was almost 20 percent less than real GDP for 2000. By 2002, however, the economy had recovered to 2.5 percent above the level of 2000. And so on, as presented in the third row of table 3.2.

GDP in constant prices illustrates the principle that one has to use the same prices ("hold prices constant") in order to measure changes in quantities. The converse is true for measuring changes in prices: quantities have to be held constant. An example of this is that now we have the 2004 GDP in 2000 prices, we can divide it into 2004 GDP in 2004 (current) prices (and multiply by 100) in order to measure how much prices had changed between 2000 and 2004. The quantities are constant—the goods and services produced in 2004—and the index so constructed is called the **GDP implicit price deflator**, which is shown in the fourth row of table 3.2. The Consumer Price Index (CPI) is the most familiar of the price indexes, and we will meet it in the next chapter when talking about inflation.

The general idea of standardizing prices for quantity indexes and standardizing quantities for price indexes is all well and good, but there is a problem. My example was to compare the 2000 GDP with the 2004 GDP calculated in 2000 prices in order to measure the changes in real

GDP between 2000 and 2004. Fine. But if instead, we were to calculate the 2000 GDP in 2004 prices and compare it with the 2004 GDP in 2004 prices, it would be just as acceptable a procedure. So what's the problem? The problem is that we would come up with a different figure for the change in real GDP over the period, and the GDP deflator would be different. This is because prices act as relative weights in a quantity index.

It's time for an example. Let us pretend that the price of a new Chevrolet Impala (very precisely specified by model and accessories) in 2000 was twenty times the price of an equally precisely specified Macintosh computer. This means that each Impala that was produced and sold in 2000 counted as twenty times more important (more heavily weighted) in the quantity index than each Macintosh. In 2004, however, the Impala's price was twenty-five times that of the Macintosh. Therefore, when you compare the two GDPs at constant 2000 prices, Macintosh production will be counted as more important (more heavily weighted) relative to Impala production than when you use 2004 prices as the constant. Exactly the opposite is true for price indexes, in which quantities serve as relative weights for price changes, and the results can vary significantly depending on the year selected. There is no obvious solution to this problem, other than to be clear about it and to name it: the **Index Number Problem**.

Just to nail this idea down, here is a quick exercise. In the liberating tradition of economic abstraction that allows one to make up whole worlds, you are the Minister of Economics of Stagnacia, a small country in which bread and ale are the only two goods produced and consumed. During your two-year term in office, ale production and prices have risen but the output of bread has fallen, although the price of bread has not changed. Now that you are running for reelection, you want to show the maximum increase (or minimum decrease) in total production and the minimum apparent inflation that have occurred while the economy has been under your guidance. Since outright lying and falsification are not feasible, which year's prices would you use to publish "real GDP," and which year's output would you use to calculate the published price index? (Think it over, and if you do not get prices in the second year for the quantity index and the quantities in the first year for the price index, think it over again.)

One way to tackle the index number problem is to calculate the implicit price deflator for both years and then take the *geometric* mean of the two. Usually when we speak of the mean as one of the averages, we are referring to the arithmetic mean. In this case, you would get the arithmetic mean by adding the two indexes and dividing the sum by two. To obtain a geometric mean, however, you multiply the two and take the square root of the answer. Obviously, this has to be more sophisticated, and the results are called chain-linked price indexes, which have begun to be used more often by the government. One criticism of the procedure is that the final number is a mush of the two procedures that tells you less than what you could figure out from looking at either one of the two individual indexes.

These problems and ambiguities suggest neither that it is useless to do the calculations nor that the results should be dismissed. What is suggested, however, is that one needs to be straightforward in calculating such indexes and to be careful in interpreting others' use of them.

Effective Demand

The focus of macroeconomics is on the left side of the table 3.1A, on the actual market expenditures or effective demand for all goods and services. The public policy emphasis on managing the levels of demand expresses the Keynesian conviction that aggregate demand is the most important determinant of employment, growth, and inflation. The lack of any consideration of supply conditions reflects the theory's origins in the Great Depression, when so much idle productive capacity (factories and people) meant that supply could be expected to respond easily to increases in demand.

The expenditures (which equal receipts) for final goods and services are divided up primarily by the type of buyer: households (consumption [C]); businesses (investment [I]); government (local, state, and federal

[G]); foreigners (exports [X]), subtracting the value of imports of foreign-produced goods and services in all categories [M]. I will go through each of these later, but it is important now to note that the categories are *not* defined by type of product. An automobile and even a shirt can belong in all of the categories.[3] We can express these relationships in shorthand: GDP = $C + I + G + X - M$.

Aggregate expenditures are divided in this manner because it is believed that they are behavioral categories that operate in relatively regular and predictable ways. That is, household decisions about consumption purchases are influenced by factors relatively uniform for all households; business investment purchases are predicated on factors different from those influencing household consumption levels but common for most businesses; and so on. I discuss exports and imports more thoroughly in chapter 5, and here I concentrate on the domestic components of expenditure: consumption, investment, and government. In chapter 4, I put them together to talk about changes in the level of economic activity and government policies that affect those levels.

Households and Consumption

Household consumption is the largest of the expenditure components, constituting 70 percent of all final purchases of goods and services (GDP) in 2004 and higher in 2005. Households are not only the white suburban families of four as depicted in the early TV shows (e.g., *Leave It to Beaver*). Households include all units that make up some sort of consumer decision unit, whether it is a single person, a three-generation family, a gay family, six recent college graduates sharing a one-bedroom apartment to beat exorbitant San Francisco rents, or whatever. By definition, households use their income to buy consumer goods and services or to save; with one exception, they do not invest. That exception is the purchase of a new residence, a situation in which the stream of future benefits is so long that it is included in the investment category.

Economists exclude such activities as buying stocks and bonds from the investment category. Most purchases of stocks and bonds are simply transfers of already-existing financial assets that affect GDP only through the brokers' fees. Even if a household bought newly issued stocks or bonds, an individual household's purchase of the asset is counted as savings. Only when the business issuing the stock or bond uses the money to buy plant and equipment or add to inventory does it become investment. The distinction between buying a stock and expanding plant and equipment is often expressed as the difference between financial investment and real investment. In a similar manner, financial capital includes stocks, bonds, and other financial assets, while real capital denotes plant, machinery, and other produced means of production that represent the economy's productive capacity.

Three types of consumer expenditures are listed in table 3.1A. Durable consumer goods are those expected to last three years or more and are usually big ticket items: automobiles, dishwashers, TV sets, furniture, and so on. Nondurable consumer goods include clothes, food, cigarettes, and whatever. Finally, services are intangibles, produced and consumed simultaneously, such as automobile repair, insurance, a concert, or lawn care.[4]

Determinants of Consumption Expenditure   As in the case of demand curves in chapter 1, it is clear that many factors influence the level of households' consumption decisions and expenditures. When all is said and done, however, the aggregation process, by which millions of separate consumption decisions are all added together, cancels out the influence of a fair number of individual idiosyncrasies, whether stemming from nature or nurture. This enables the generalization that household income is the major determinant of consumption expenditures. The income I am talking about is **disposable income**, which is listed in table 3.1B. As the name implies, it is the after-tax income from whatever source that accrues to households. This excludes all business taxes, depreciation allowances, and corporate retained earnings, and it includes private and public **transfer payments** (income such as pensions [private and public], insurance reimbursements, and welfare support) that are not compensation for currently rendered productive activity. As after-tax income, it is the income that households are free to "dispose."[5]

Disposable income is a reliable predictor of household consumption expenditures. There are two principal ways by which disposable income and therefore household consumption increases (or declines, but since the processes are symmetrical, I accentuate the positive). The first is general economic growth, which lifts all account entries. If the proportion of GDP that trickles down to disposable income does not change radically, a rise in GDP will generate increased disposable income that in turn will induce greater consumption expenditures.

The second way for disposable income to grow is through a change in the proportion of GDP received as disposable income. The most obvious source of such a change would be by a reduction in personal income taxes. This would allow households to keep more of their personal income and lead to an increase in disposable income and thus consumption expenditures even if there were no increase in GDP. In addition, if corporations were to shovel every available dollar of profit into dividends, disposable income would also increase as a proportion of gross domestic product.

The distribution of income, apart from its overall level, also used to be considered an influence on the levels of aggregate household consumption expenditures and savings. In the old days (whenever they were), it was believed that the rich saved more than the poor did, so if there were shifts in income to the most well-to-do, aggregate household savings would rise and consumption expenditures would decline. The idea that the rich save more and thus enable investment and general economic growth has been used as a justification for highly uneven distributions of income. The inefficiency of this mechanism, by which the rich in some sense function as stewards of economic resources for the good of the commonweal, has been revealed by recent history. Even though there has been a substantial increase in the concentration of income over the past two decades, the U.S. savings rate has declined to a fifty-year low. The rich spend almost all of their money, too, and what we have witnessed is an explosion of demand for expensive automobiles, restaurants, jewelry, and housing.

Interest rates are another secondary influence on household consumption expenditures. Interest rates are most important for consumer durables that are most often bought "on time" (i.e., with borrowed money and interest charges). Automobiles are a good example, but house purchases are particularly sensitive to interest rate changes. As I noted earlier, buying a new house is technically in the investment category, but households do it. Residential construction and purchase are particularly responsive to interest rate changes, because contractors borrow heavily to build houses, and mortgage interest costs are high proportions of total (and monthly) costs for buyers as well. Changes in interest rates, therefore, affect both the supply and demand sides of the market for new housing, and record low interest rates have substantially contributed to the recent boom in housing.

Another dimension of interest rate changes in respect to consumption expenditures is through credit cards. The usurious rates of interest charged on the unpaid balances of credit cards is truly breathtaking, but they do go up and down with general movements in interest rates. Interest rates' influence on the levels of unpaid credit card balances and of consumption expenditures in general, however, is not as clear as in the purchase of houses.

The Business Sector and Investment

As listed in table 3.1A, corporate profits are divided among dividends (paid out to stockholders), corporate taxes, and retained earnings (corporate savings). The depreciation allowance functions as a pool of liquid assets similar to that of retained earnings. The fact that corporate profits are taxed at the corporation level and then dividends are taxed as personal income when received by individuals is a source of chronic whining about double taxation.

Regarding the components of investment expenditures, again we find the magic number three. Purchase of new plant and equipment is the most straightforward form of investment expenditure. It is more volatile than consumption expenditures, and the reason for this can be illustrated by a simple example. Let's say that a company uses ten machines with ten-year life spans, and each year one machine falls apart, is swept up and thrown away, and then replaced as long as the demand for the company's product is stable. But one year, there is a 10 percent reduction in sales, so the company does not replace the worn-out machine that year. Therefore, a 10 percent reduction in the demand for the firm's output becomes magnified to a 100 percent decline in its new investment for plant and equipment. This process works for both declines and increases and contributes to volatile capital goods markets.

Inventories are the second component of investment, and they are a bit trickier. Some inventory investment is deliberate. The normal flow of production requires a reserve of components and materials and a number of finished products. Retailers maintain stocks of goods to keep shelves full. A distiller who sells six-year-old whiskey needs a six-year revolving supply. In addition, a firm may stockpile raw materials to hedge against anticipated price increases or keep back finished products in order to manipulate the market or outlast a labor strike. On the other hand, changes in inventory investment can also be involuntary and undesirable. If the company is not able to sell all it produces, it unwillingly builds up inventories of finished products, which probably means that it cuts back production in the near future. The inventory component of investment, then, is in a sense a residual category in that it helps ensure that the two sides of the account balance; everything produced is either sold or added to inventory; everything sold is either produced or taken out of inventory. But don't let this residual balancing of accounts mislead you. Changes in inventories are one of the most important signaling mechanisms in the economy, at both the microeconomic and macroeconomic levels.

Finally, residential construction and sales represent the third category of investment expenditure, and as I described earlier, it is the only way in which household expenditure is counted as investment.

Determinants of Investment Expenditures   At one level, the motive or cause of investment is very easy: expected profits. Behind the cost-benefit calculation of expected profits, however, are a large number of uncertainties about the markets for products, credit, intermediate products, labor, shifts in the competitive environment, technological changes, new government policies, and myriad other factors. The volatility of the business components of investment is a clear sign of the difficulty of identifying determinants with any precision.

Interest rates are one of the most important factors.[6] Even though they bear only on the cost side of the cost-benefit ratio, the heavy expenses and use of borrowed funds (or opportunity costs of already-acquired funds) of investment projects make interest rate considerations very important. For the plant and equipment component, any decline of interest rates (cost of borrowing money) increases the potential profitability of a greater range of investment projects and enhances businesspeople's willingness to take a shot at them, thus increasing expenditures on plant and equipment.

The plant and equipment component of investment is the only category of expenditures of final goods and services that is a factor of production. Recalling the discussion of marginal revenue product (MRP) in the previous chapter, the demand for investment goods is governed by the investment goods' (expected) MRP for real capital. So it is not hard to imagine a well-behaved, downward-sloping demand curve for investment goods in respect to interest rates, as in figure 3.1.

This is neat and clean, but the difficulty of determining the MRP of real capital does not stop with uncertainties about future earnings. The problem is that the returns from investments occur over extended periods of time, sometimes many years, and it is necessary to convert the value

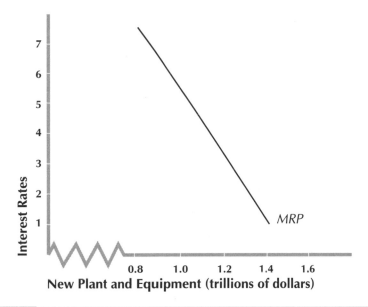

FIGURE 3.1 Demand Curve for New Plant and Equipment

of those future returns into present money, so to speak. This conversion is necessary, because future money, dollar for dollar, is worth less than present money. This is not in order to correct for expected inflation (easy and separate) nor is it a matter of how hard it is to defer gratification, although that may be a part of it ("I want that new car *right now!!*"). The conversion is required because any comparison between the value of future money and present money needs to take into account that one can earn future money with present money. Would you rather have $1,000 right now or one year from now? Any rational, calculating, economic type would jump at obtaining the $1,000 right now, because even if it could not be spent for a year, it could be deposited in a bank and in a year would turn into $1,050 (at 5 percent interest). Therefore, in order to compare the value of that one-year-away $1,000 with the immediate $1,000, the value of the future money has to be converted into present money. The actual process requires discounting the value of the future money by the potential earnings it could earn in the time it takes to get from the present to that future. It turns out that $1,000 in one year is worth $952.39 of present money if discounted by 5 percent, which is to say, if you put $952.39 in a bank at 5 percent interest, you will get $1,000 in one year. In the parlance of economics, $952.39 is the **present discounted value** (PDV) of $1,000 in a year discounted by an interest rate of 5 percent.

The formula for calculating the PDV of money one year away is (F_1) ÷ (1 + i), where $F_1 i$ is the amount of future money one year away, and i is the rate of discount—for our purposes, the interest rate. If you want to calculate the PDV of a lump of money two years away, you have to discount it for the first year by dividing it by (1 + i) and then for the second year by dividing it again by (1 + i). So you end up dividing it by (1 + i)^2. The formula is unusually handy, because the exponent (power) of the divisor is simply the number of years away from which the future income will be realized. So if you want the PDV of $7,000 to be received five years in the future, and the relevant interest rate is 6 percent, then you simply divide the $7,000 by (1.06)^5. This takes a few punches on the calculator, but I suspect that you're up to it. (You did get $5,230.81, right?)

So how about an example to illustrate this fancy new thing? Madeline has been the proprietor of a small dog grooming parlor in Providence for years and has decided to move on to new challenges that do not include ill-mannered dogs and worse-mannered dog owners. So she puts her shop, which is at the end of a small strip mall, on the market. Caitlin, cruising for a good investment opportunity, checks around a bit and realizes that there is no convenience store (e.g., 7-Eleven, Dairy Mart) within six or seven miles of the location. But Caitlin also finds out that Stop & Shop, Inc. is going to build a Super Stop & Shop in the open space across the street and open it in five years. The possibilities are still intriguing, however, because until the supermarket opens, a convenience store in this neighborhood would be a real moneymaker.

Caitlin goes into high gear and figures that it would take a year to buy the grooming parlor, purge it of fleas and smell, and turn it into a convenience store. In the second and third years, however, the store would clear at least $18,000 of profits a year, even if Caitlin hired all workers and did not have to work in the store at all. Moreover, in the fourth year, the store would make about $24,000 of profits because of the increased business from the workers constructing the Stop & Shop across the street. The supermarket would open in the fifth year, and although the convenience store business would be dead in the water, Caitlin figures on being able to sell the location in the mall for about $60,000 to someone interested in opening a video arcade, beauty salon, doughnut shop, martial arts studio, or whatever.

Caitlin needs to borrow the money to buy and renovate the store, and Adam, her banker, will charge her an interest rate of 9 percent. Is it really worthwhile? Or more precisely, what is the upper limit that Caitlin could put into buying and fixing up the store and have the investment make good financial sense? Try it out and check your results with table 3.3. Doing the arithmetic is a bit tedious, but presumably you came up with figures somewhere around those in the last row. With a little slippage for rounding off, the total PDV (the sum of the last row's numbers) is $85,033. So if Caitlin could buy and renovate the place for anything less than that figure, the chances are that she would be on to a good thing.

Moving beyond plant and equipment to the inventory portion of investment, it is expensive to hold inventories, whether of finished products

TABLE 3.3	Example of Present Discounted Value Calculation					
	Year 1	Year 2	Year 3	Year 4	Year 5	Total
Net Income (dollars)	0	18,000	18,000	24,000	60,000	
Divided by:	(1.09)	$(1.09)^2$ $= 1.188$	$(1.09)^3$ $= 1.295$	$(1.09)^4$ $= 1.412$	$(1.09)^5$ $= 1.539$	
Present Discounted Values (dollars)	0	15,150	13,900	16,997	38,986	85,033

or of raw materials and intermediate products. Even if the company is using its own money, those funds could be used for other purposes. So whether it is an opportunity cost or a direct cost paid to a bank, the cost of having funds tied up in inventories is substantial and varies directly with the interest rate. Despite the fact that businesses sometimes unwillingly have to increase inventories, we expect greater caution about growing inventories as interest rates rise. Finally, as mentioned in the discussion about household consumer expenditures, residential construction and purchases are especially sensitive to interest rate changes.

All together, the relationship between the volume of investment expenditures and the interest rate (the price of money) looks something like the familiar downward-sloping demand curve of figure 3.1. But since it includes all the components of investment, it would be farther to the right and probably have a different shape.

On the expected profit side of the investment decision, general economic growth also influences investment expenditures for plant and equipment as well as for inventories and residential housing. If economic growth proceeds to the point that it begins to put pressure on existing production capacities, it encourages managers to invest in new plant and equipment beyond depreciation and replacement needs. Moreover, higher levels of output and sales require higher levels of inventories, thus increasing the voluntary levels of investment in new inventories, and higher incomes enable house purchases. The response of investment expenditures to economic growth, graphically represented as an outward shift in the demand curve for loanable funds, is called, in the jargon of economics, the **accelerator principle**.

The Public Sector

One of the first things to keep in mind is that in budget preparation, including government budgets, expenditures can be planned and controlled with more precision than revenues, whose projections are more of an educated guess. A good part of budgetary struggles, therefore, takes the form of disagreements over estimates of projected revenues. The second thing to keep in mind is that economic theory, by and large, considers public sector policies and levels of expenditure to be determined by politics, and thereby the province of another discipline in the academic division of labor. What "real" economists deal with are the *effects* of public policies and expenditures.[7]

There are three levels of government: local, state, and federal. As shown in table 3.1A, the federal government's purchases of goods and services were a bit less than 7 percent of GDP in 2004, while state and local governments' purchases totaled almost 12 percent of GDP. These directly GDP-generating purchases of goods and services, however, do not constitute the whole of government budgets.

In addition to purchases of goods and services from private sector businesses, government budgets include transfer payments, such as pensions, grants, government subsidies to businesses, various forms of income support (Medicaid, Medicare, food stamps), and other payments not for a currently rendered productive activity (unless social peace and political campaign contributions are regarded as the quid pro quo). Finally, there are the wages and salaries paid to current public employees, and this is regarded as the main portion of the governments' value added.

Microeconomic rationales for government market intervention are couched in terms of market failure, which I discussed in the previous chapter. As noted there, market failure is a matter of markets failing to deliver efficiency, competitiveness, and so on—failures in terms of microeconomic theory's own variables and emphases. Government policies in public health, defense, anti-trust legislation, environmental protections, and regulation of food, pharmaceutical, and financial operations fall into this category.

I also have included the potential of an unregulated market system to generate serious unemployment and serious rounds of inflation as another dimension of market failure. Unlike the other kinds of market failure, economic stabilization efforts generally do not usually directly regulate the relations between demand and supply of individual markets. Nevertheless, the economy's producing at levels close to capacity and with stable prices is necessary for the smooth operation of markets (and assumed in micro-economics). Recession, inflation, and the role of government stabilization policy are the principal subjects of macroeconomics and of this and the next chapter.

Another reason for positive government policy, also outside the purview of (and assumed by) microeconomic theory, is the kind of public good that promotes *social cohesion*. This includes government activities that enable the economy and society to work in an orderly manner. A police and judicial system to enforce contracts, guarantee the security of private property and persons, maintain public order (e.g., stopping at stop signs), and punish transgressors are minimal levels of these functions. Since the New Deal years of the Great Depression, this category has expanded to encompass Social Security provisions, unemployment and accident insurance, welfare and income supports, Medicare, worker safety, and anti-discrimination legislation.

Many of these governmental functions have always been contested by sectors of the society. Some of these activities have been formally diluted in the past two decades, and others have simply been less vigorously enforced. In addition, even for those functions on which there has been at least nominal agreement, more are being performed by private enter-prises (**privatized**) under contract from local, state, and federal govern-ments. Schools, prisons, hospitals, product testing, solid waste disposal, and the monitoring of eligibility for welfare payments are some exam-ples, and there is continuing political pressure to turn more of health, education, and social insurance over to the private sector. Even Social Security, probably the most venerable federal program, is being consid-ered for some privatization. According to President G. W. Bush, the Social Security system is in a state of imminent financial crisis and in dire need of being "reformed." He stumped the nation with that message, but neither Congress nor their constituents were excited about the extent of the crisis or its proposed solution, and President Bush finally just gave up on it. Nonetheless, the issue is important, and it's worthwhile being clear about its dimensions.

So let's begin with how the Social Security system is financed. Current Social Security tax revenues—6.2 percent on wages and salaries from the employee and 6.2 percent from the employer—are used to make current benefit payments. Social Security trustees estimate that by 2018, these revenues will no longer be sufficient to cover benefit payments. This means that the Social Security system will have to draw on its accumulated surpluses ("the trust fund"), which will last until 2042, and after that, Social Security taxes will be able to cover only about 75 percent of obligations.

One reason for the projected shortfall is that the high U.S. birth rates of the baby boom years (1946–1964) were followed by a significant fall in birth rates. This pattern will reduce the ratio of people of working age to those under 20 years old and over 65 from the current 1.5 to 1.2 by 2050. That is, there simply will be fewer people paying into the system relative to the numbers receiving payments from the system. Another reason is that people in the United States are living longer; a 65-year-old person can now expect to live almost five years longer (to 83) than a 65-year-old person in 1940. This means that Social Security recipients will be recipients for more years. Moreover, women's greatly increased participation in the paid workforce means that they will be higher proportions of recipients of Social Security benefits, and on average, women live longer than men.

Now to the crisis. First of all, if you want to focus on a real, impending financial crisis, look at Medicare rather than Social Security. Second, if one-third of President Bush's tax cuts for the rich were rescinded, they would generate enough revenue to bail out the Social Security system. Finally, President Bush's proposal to allow some proportion of Social Security taxes to be invested by the individual is not a solution to the eventual problem; it would *exacerbate* the problem. Some flexibility along the cautious and restricted lines for private savings accounts suggested by the Commission to Strengthen Social Security, appointed by the president, may not be a terrible idea. Nevertheless, to represent private accounts as an answer to Social Security's financial problem is blatantly misleading. How can you solve a shortfall of Social Security revenues by diverting some Social Security revenues to private accounts without changing the amounts Social Security needs to pay out? The White House has been very slow to acknowledge that creating private savings plans would require immense borrowing anywhere from hundreds of billions of dollars to trillions of dollars, depending on the particulars of the plans. And this borrowing would be in addition to whatever changes the demographic shifts are going to require, because the hard fact is that eliminating the projected deficit is going to require some combination of raising Social Security taxes and reducing Social Security benefits.

One of the most frequently mentioned increases of Social Security taxes is to raise the limit on taxable income without changing the limit on benefits. In 2005, only the first $90,000 of an individual's wages and salaries was subject to the Social Security tax, and the limit changes every year due to cost-of-living adjustments. This meant that 15 percent of wages and salaries were not taxed by Social Security in 2005, while only 10 percent of wages and salaries were not taxed in 1983 with the then limit of $35,700. If the limit were abolished and current benefit maximums retained (somewhere around $2,000 a month in 2006), it would affect 6 percent of Social Security taxpayers and eliminate the financial shortfall. And of course, there are all sorts of partial measures. If the limit were to be raised to $140,000 for both taxing and benefit calculations, the income missed by the tax would go back down to 10 percent, and it would alleviate 40 percent of the revenue-expenditure discrepancy.

The most frequently discussed reductions in benefits are to reduce the annual cost-of-living benefit increases and to raise the age at which one is eligible for full benefits. Congress changed the full retirement age in 1983, and by 2012, the gradual rise in the full retirement age will end at 67. Raising the retirement age once again seems to many to be an easy change, but those who advocate that change are out of touch with the fact that much work is boring, stressful, demeaning, physically punishing, and/or dangerous. Most people are eager to retire and grasp at the chance to retire early if feasible.

If people are so eager to retire, why have we seen a recent reversal of a century-long trend of lower labor market participation by people over 65 years of age? This is because there is a genuine crisis around private pensions and benefits. Corporations are finding it increasingly difficult to fund full pensions and health care in the globally competitive environment. As an extreme example, Lucent Technologies has 20,000 workers and 120,000 retirees, and General Motors may be worse off. One ploy, of which Bethlehem Steel in 2002 is a good example, is to declare bankruptcy, find a sympathetic judge who will say that shedding underfunded pension obligations is necessary for emerging from bankruptcy, and shift $3.7 billion in unfunded obligations to the federal Pension Guarantee Corporation (PGC) that cannot pay the full promised pensions. Congress created the PGC in 1974 to protect workers, but it has been transformed into a business strategy employed by United Airlines, Polaroid, US Airways, Federal Mogul, Cone Williams, WestPoint Stevens, and over 300 other companies.

Some economists have hoped that the proper domain for government regulation could be neatly and cleanly derived from theoretical foundations, such as public goods and externality principles. But there is no clean and simple boundary between the rights of private production and the larger public good. Such issues as smoking in public places, gun control, environmental preservation, product liability, contagious disease control, airline safety, and even speed limits arouse highly charged political debates around private freedoms versus public regulation that are periodically conducted anew.

Financing Public Expenditures—Taxation Although all three levels of government derive some revenue from fees for services (driver's and

TABLE 3.4 Federal, State, and Local Government Taxes and Other Receipts (billions of current dollars)

	1970	1980	1990	2000	2004
Federal Government					
Individual income taxes	90.4	244.1	466.9	1,007.7	794.6
Corporation profits taxes	32.8	64.6	93.5	244.0	218.1
Social insurance and retirement	44.4	157.8	380.0	695.6	806.0
Other tax and nontax receipts	25.2	50.6	91.5	118.4	153.1
Total Receipts	192.8	517.1	1,032.0	2,065.7	1,971.8
Percentage of current GDP	18.5	18.5	17.8	20.6	16.8
State and Local Governments					
Property taxes	34.1	68.5	155.6	248.5	321.6
Sales taxes	30.3	79.9	177.9	331.7	364.4
Individual income taxes	10.8	42.1	105.6	216.3	225.1
Corporate profits taxes	3.7	13.3	23.6	40.2	40.2
Grants from federal government	21.9	83.0	136.8	244.6	350.4
Other tax and nontax receipts	30.0	95.5	250.0	148.8	283.6
Total Receipts	130.8	382.3	849.5	1,230.1	1,585.3
Percentages of GDP	12.6	13.7	14.7	12.3	13.5

Sources: *Economic Report of the President, 2000*, pp. 306, 399, 405; *Survey of Current Business* (April 2001), p. D-9; *Survey of Current Business* (July 2005), D-22.

automobile licenses, and state and national parks, for example), the majority of government revenues comes from taxes and from borrowing (deficit financing). Table 3.4 outlines the magnitudes of various taxes in the United States.

By looking along the row of table 3.4 that shows federal government tax receipts as proportions of GDP, we get a peek at some recent economic history. The last year of the Eisenhower administration, 1960, was a year of mild recession, which helped John F. Kennedy to be elected to the presidency. The Vietnam War and some war taxes helped boost the 1970 pro-

YOU THINK THAT YOU PAY HIGH TAXES!

The World Bank, using definitions different from table 3.4, calculates that U.S. residents paid less than 20 percent of GNP (gross national product) in taxes in 1997. For a sense of perspective, it is worthwhile to look at those proportions for some nations with per capita incomes close to or greater than those in the United States. (I ignore high-income anomalies such as tax havens for the very rich [e.g., Luxembourg] and small societies floating on pools of oil.) Taxes as a proportion of GNP for Belgium, the Netherlands, France, and Italy were around 40 percent. Taxes were around one-third of GNP in Austria, Denmark, Norway, and the United Kingdom, and around 25 percent in Australia, Finland, and Germany. Income in all of these countries is more evenly distributed than in the United States.

portion, and the 1980 figures show the great rise in federal government revenues in dollar terms with no change in the percentage of GDP, reflecting the inflation of the 1970s. The sustained growth of the 1990s, however, generated significant increases in tax revenues that fueled a federal budget surplus. But then President Bush's large tax cuts for the rich, a slowing economy, and the occupation of Iraq quickly wiped out the surplus. The deficit will become even greater if promises are kept to rebuild the Gulf Coast after Hurricane Katrina, continue a drug prescription benefit through Medicare, and cut additional taxes. But promises are not always kept.

Now let's look at the nature of different kinds of taxes. A tax is defined as **progressive** if its average rate rises with the income of the taxpayer (i.e., marginal tax rates on additional income are higher than the average tax rate on all income). A progressive tax does not only mean that more prosperous taxpayers pay more of that tax than do their less prosperous contemporaries. They do, but in order for a tax to be progressive, more prosperous tax payers have to pay *higher proportions* of their incomes in that tax than do the less well-to-do. The federal income tax is somewhat progressive, although not as much as it had been before the 1986 and 2001 tax reforms.

A **regressive tax** is the opposite: the poor pay higher proportions of their incomes for a regressive tax than do those with higher incomes. Sales taxes on clothes and food at the grocery store are good examples. State lotteries, which are surrogate taxes, have also been found to have a regressive impact.

As I mentioned in chapter 2, figuring out who actually bears the burden of a particular tax—its incidence—is difficult. Often the nominal taxpayer who writes the check to the taxing authority can effectively shift the actual burden on to someone else. It is especially difficult to determine the incidence of property taxes, which account for almost 80 percent of local government tax revenues. How much of the tax is passed on to renters in higher rent? If property taxes rise, do the current property owners bear the entire burden of the increase because any future buyer will discount the value of the property by the amount of the higher tax? One argument used to defend a corporate profit tax is that it is difficult for the firm to shift this tax to consumers. That argument has obviously not carried the day, since corporate profit taxes have been steadily declining as a proportion of all taxes.

Another issue is whether taxes should be more oriented toward user fees, like the sewage and water bills in towns and cities. That is, why should poor people from the East Coast pay taxes to support a national park in Montana that they will never visit? Should those who send their children to private schools pay for public schools? Needless to say, the politics of taxation are highly fraught, and patterns of taxation are a first-order indication of who has how much political influence.

A final observation about taxation is the idea of **tax expenditure**, a somewhat oxymoronic-sounding term. A tax expenditure is a tax credit or deduction to encourage some particular spending or saving activity. Tax breaks that reward those involved with individual retirement accounts, health insurance, college savings accounts, income from municipal bonds, and interest payments on home mortgages are examples of tax expenditures. The *expenditure* part of the term expresses the fact that each one of these tax breaks costs the federal government in forgone tax revenues and

"Other folks have to pay taxes, too, Mr. Herndon,
so would you please spare us the dramatics!"

therefore are parallel to policies that require explicit public expenditures. For example, the home mortgage interest deduction costs $100 billion a year in reduced revenues, and that cost should be considered in the same light as the money that the government actually spends, say, on creating affordable housing, even though it comes from the other side of the ledger.

Nevertheless, legislators do not scrutinize tax expenditures with the same rigor as explicit expenditures, and they seldom challenge their effectiveness in stimulating the rewarded activities. Tax expenditures too easily appear to be costless and painless. This illusion of bargain-basement benefits is one reason that tax expenditures seem to have become the principal tool of social policy. Instead of expanding federal housing programs, expand tax credits for home ownership. Instead of universal health insurance, award people tax deductions for purchasing health insurance. Instead of helping pay for college education, permit tax-free savings accounts for college costs. And so on down the list.

In 2004, the U.S. Treasury reported 146 different tax expenditures, and all of these exemptions, exceptions, deductions, and so on render the tax code extremely complex. This benefits tax accountants and lawyers in addition to those directly targeted for benefits, and there are periodic calls to simplify the tax system. President Bush has opened the discussion again, and as in the past, three quite radical suggestions are in the air. All three of them involve replacing the current income tax with one of the following: a consumption tax (i.e., a sales tax); a value-added tax (a sales tax at each stage of production); or a flat income tax. The last could be made mildly progressive by exempting, say, the first $25,000 of family income and then everyone would pay the same proportion of all income in tax. It is interesting to read about the debate, but the last major over-haul of the U.S. income tax system was 1986, and it is clear that the Bush administration is not going to provide the leadership and engage in the negotiations and compromises that a serious effort would entail.

Financing Public Expenditures—Deficit Finance   The second principal source of revenue, especially for the federal government, is borrowing. The U.S. Treasury can borrow from the private sector or it can borrow from the Federal Reserve System (the Fed). Borrowing from the Fed effectively creates new money. Both kinds of borrowing accumulate and increase the national debt, but they have different implications, which I describe later in this chapter.

Much of the agitation about the federal government deficit subsided with the economic expansion of the 1990s that produced such tax rev-enues that the federal government budget went into surplus. But now that we have returned to large federal deficits, the debate has returned, too, although the sides are divided up rather oddly. In any case, opponents of budget deficits often sound the theme that the federal government should adhere to the financial discipline of households and business enterprises that have to limit expenditures to income or net receipts.

TABLE 3.5 Major Components of Debt in the United States at Year End, 1970–2000 (billions of dollars)					
Public Debt		**Private Debt**			
Federal	State & Local	Home Mortgages*	Consumer Debt	Non-Financial Corporations	Financial Sectors
1970	299.5	150.3	274.3	133.7	367.4	127.8
1980	735.0	744.4	904.6	355.4	911.6	578.1
1990	2,498.1	992.3	2,461.3	805.1	2,522.5	2,615.8
2000	3,385.2	1,279.3	5,021.9	1,568.8	4,740.8	8,430.8
2004	4,395.6	1,674.8	7,568.2	2,140.7	5,172.0	11,794.3

Source: Board of Governors of the Federal Reserve System, *Flow of Funds Accounts of the United States, June 9, 2005,* table D.3.

*These figures do not include commercial and agricultural property. The combined value of those mortgages was about one-third or one-quarter the value of home mortgages.

This analogy is fatally flawed. As table 3.5 shows, both household and nonfinancial corporate expenditures are not limited to current income; in fact, both carry more debt than the federal government. But the major problem with the formulation is that it does not distinguish between investment for capital expenditures and consumption (or current) expenditures. Although both households and businesses soon get into difficult straits if current expenditures are greater than current income for an extended period of time (and both often do), households and businesses both depend on borrowing (that is, spending more than their income). Households engage in deficit financing (borrowing) in order to invest in a future stream of important consumer services (for example, automobile transportation and housing). Businesses routinely have to borrow in order to expand or even maintain productive capacity (plant and equipment) to take advantage of long-term profit prospects. The corresponding types of public investment are constructing schools, roads, bridges, airports, and health clinics as well as ensuring clear air and clean water. All of these hold promise of promoting future economic growth, and therefore future tax revenues, as well as reducing the cost of some public services, such as health services and perhaps police and prisons.

A considerable amount of the murkiness that surrounds discussions about the federal government's expenditures and their significance would dissipate if there were greater respect for the distinction between current versus capital expenditures. There would, of course, be continuing disagreements over whether a particular item should be in the capital or current category, but at least the conversation would have a greater likelihood of being meaningful.

Economists' Criticisms of Public Expenditure   Economists have several ways to cast suspicion on the efficacy of the public sector's role in the economy. This reflects a general tenet of classical liberalism: the market is a realm of freedom and efficiency, and government is a realm of coercion and inefficiency. One of the most frequently heard criticisms is at the microeconomic level: the public sector is more or less sheltered from the "discipline of the market," decisions are not profit motivated, and employment in the public sector does not contain sufficient numbers of carrots and sticks to be efficient. This includes the organization of public agencies, the motivations of individual employees, and insulation from strict accountability.[8] The evidence for these claims is, to be charitable, mixed, but this has very little to do with the frequency and intensity of the assertions.

Another oft-heard criticism at the microeconomic level is that the public sector competes unfairly with private businesses in providing goods and services in certain markets. Unlike the public sector, private firms have to pay taxes and full market prices for their resources, and they bear the risk of personal investments.

On the other hand, it is politically acceptable for the federal government to spend large amounts of money on armaments. Such expenditures do not compete with private interests at either the national or local level but definitely benefit a number of domestic corporations, employees, and regional economies. As recently as the late 1980s, the military portion of the federal government's purchases of goods and services was three and half times the nonmilitary portion. The end of the Cold War led to lower expenditures for "defense," but between 2001 and 2005, federal military spending increased over 40 percent to finance the war on terrorism, the occupation of Iraq, the National Missile Defense Shield, and so on.

The increasing privatization of public services, including education, health, and incarceration, has been a response to these criticisms. In this section, however, I am going to discuss two less obvious but important criticisms of public sector economic activity: crowding out and public choice theory.

Crowding Out   Much of the controversy about federal revenues and expenditures revolves around how much the federal government's activities **crowd out** private economic activity, and here, I do not mean only the previously mentioned public production that competes with private enterprise. In order to look more closely at this phenomenon, let's posit a situation in which all economic resources are fully employed and, therefore, the economy is not able to expand output. By definition any increase in the public sector's command over goods and services has to crowd out private expenditure by an equal amount—a 100 percent crowding out. In order to understand the mechanisms by which this occurs, we need to look back at how the federal government is financed.

The most straightforward crowding out mechanism is for the government to raise taxes by an amount equal to the increased expenditure. This is simply a matter of taking purchasing power away from the private sector and using it in the public sector.

When raising taxes is not feasible or desirable, the federal government can engage in deficit financing. If the government borrows by selling its bonds to private purchasers, it competes with private borrowers for investable funds, and when the government bids those funds away from private borrowers, thus raising interest rates, this becomes the crowding out effect. On the other hand, if the deficit is financed by the sale of government bonds to the Fed, the Fed credits the amount of the bonds to the Treasury's account, and when the Treasury spends that money, it increases the total amount of money in the economy. In this situation, the crowding out effect comes through the public sector bidding goods and services away from prospective private buyers, thus raising prices in product markets.

It is important to remember that the clarity of the operation of these three dimensions of crowding out—taxation, financial markets, and product markets—is due entirely to the original assumption: that all economic resources were fully employed and the economy was incapable of expanding output. When there is a recession and substantial unemployment, augmented government expenditures probably increase production and income and crowding out is substantially lower. In addition, a good amount of the inflow of foreign funds has gone into U.S. government bonds and thus helped alleviate the crowding out of domestic private investment by public sector debt. This help, of course, may be the source of other problems.

Public Choice Theory   One of the more interesting criticisms of the public sector's economic activities comes from **public choice theory**. One of the key ideas here is that many government policies and expenditures benefit very specific interest groups, but that the costs of these group-specific policies and expenditures are diffused among the entire tax-paying population. Therefore, when particular special interest groups mobilize campaigns to achieve the desired policy or expenditure, there is very little resistance to them. The cost for an individual is almost negligible, and indifference reigns. It is argued, then, that the politics of concentrated benefits and widespread, low per-person costs systematically produce a series of public policies and expenditures not justified by general public benefits.

Building on this background, the next chapter continues the macro-economics discussion by focusing on the tools of fiscal and monetary policy used to stabilize the economy and stimulate economic growth.

Notes

1. Keynes's theoretical formulations also created the categories for the National Income and Product Accounts through which national levels of economic activity are measured.

2. Instead of measuring all (gross) final production, a better indication of the significance of that year's production would be to subtract (net) from that total the reduced productive capacity from the wear and tear on productive resources resulting from that year's production. Look at table 3.1B for GNP minus depreciation—the Net National Product (NNP). The difficulty of measuring real depreciation, however, and its sensitivity to changes in tax codes make it such an unreliable number that GDP is generally preferred.

3. The idea of a shirt as an investment good sounds a bit odd, but in a given year, it could be added to a producer's or retailer's inventory, which is a component of investment.

4. There is a certain counter-intuitive quality to the highly manufactured Big Mac being counted as a service. Restaurants technically combine both goods and service production but are generally counted as services.

5. Discretionary income is substantially less than disposable income; it is the income after subtracting necessary expenditures such as food, clothing, shelter, and transportation.

6. Occasionally I speak of "the interest rate," which stands for an array of interest rates that vary primarily by the length of time and amount of risk of the loans.

7. The principal caveat to this generalization is the theory of public choice, for which its major proponent, James Buchanan, received a Nobel Prize in economics. I describe aspects of this theory later in this chapter.

8. The "rational choice" branch of political science employs microeconomic assumptions of individual maximizing motivations to analyze public policy and its implementation. This rapidly growing field in political science is another example of the extent to which the economics paradigm is penetrating other social sciences.

Fiscal Policy, Monetary Policy, Recession, and Inflation

T his chapter describes the principal means by which the federal government deliberately affects the level of economic activity in order to reduce adverse fluctuations. As I have already mentioned, the federal government does this through managing the level of aggregate demand. **Fiscal policy** is the government's intentional use of its budget, including both the revenue and expenditure sides, to affect the levels of aggregate demand and therefore of general economic activity. The second principal tool of demand management is monetary policy, which I describe after fiscal policy.

Fiscal Policy: Taxing and Spending

It does not take years of intense study to figure out that without an unlikely 100 percent crowding out, if the federal government increased its total purchases of goods and services from the private sector without changing anything else, it would have a positive effect on the volume of goods and services produced and sold. The GDP would go up. The same amount of analytical insight yields the parallel observation: if the federal government were to reduce personal income taxes and not change anything else, the chances are that it would have a positive effect on the volume of consumer goods and services produced and purchased. Again the GDP would go up. This is indeed the essence of fiscal policy, but I can be a bit more precise and interesting than this.

Let's say that the federal government increases its purchases of privately produced goods and services by $400 million, and there is no offsetting crowding out. This immediately increases GDP by $400 million, and since we will pretend that disposable income equals three-quarters, or 75 percent, of GDP, disposable income rises by $300 million. But this is only the beginning; there is an echo effect through household consumption expenditures. Ignoring imports for the moment, we'll imagine for the sake of arithmetic convenience that households' consumer expenditures always gobble up 80 percent of any increase of disposable income, and thus 20 percent of added income goes into new savings. The proportion of additional income that goes to additional consumption is called the **marginal propensity to consume** (mpc).[1] Now we're ready to trace the echo effect through the system.

The $400 million increase in GDP trickles down to a $300 million increase in disposable income (75 percent of the change in GDP), and that $300 million rise in after-tax income induces $240 million more in household consumption expenditures (mpc = .80 × $300 million). But the echo has not died away yet. The $240 million of new consumption expenditures means $240 million more in GDP, and therefore it generates $180 million more in disposable income. That increase in turn triggers $144 million in new consumption expenditures (.80 × $180), which means that GDP increases by the $144 million, and thus a new round begins again. Successive rounds continue around and around in a steadily declining manner, and the final result is that GDP has been stimulated by a multiple of the government's original spending increase. The process is called (surprise, surprise) the **multiplier**.

In my numerical example, the multiplier would work out to be 2.5, which means the initial stimulus of $400 million generates a total increase in GDP of $1,000 million (or $1 billion). I portray this more concretely below, where G is government purchases of goods and services, DY is disposable income, and C is consumer expenditures.

Change G = Change GDP → Change DY(.75) → Change C(.80) =
  ($400M)   ($400M)   ($300M)   ($240M)

= Change GDP → Change DY(.75) → Change C(.80) = Change GDP →
    ($240M)   ($180M)   ($144M)   ($144M)

→ Change DY(.75) → Change C(.80) = Change GDP → and so on.
   ($108M)   ($86.4M)   ($86.4M)

So adding up all of the Change GDPs yields $400M + $240M + $144M + $86.4M + $51.8M + $31.1M + · · · = $1,000M (2.5 times the initial $400 million increase). This kind of exercise is useful for illustrating the process, but it is not worthwhile spending much time in calculating a precise multiplier. There are too many other factors involved. For example, some of the impact of the initial $400 million is offset by crowding out effects; some consumption expenditures go for imported goods that siphon increased expenditures out of the system; and the size of the mpc depends on the composition of the increased government expenditure in ways that are not specified in the model. In regard to the last point, whether the expenditure goes for a new space station or new schools affects whether well-to-do professionals or less prosperous construction workers receive the bulk of the new income. This in turn may influence the kinds of goods and services purchased and the employment effects of the next round of spending.

Without getting caught up in false precision, the general principle is important: induced consumption through the marginal propensity to consume means that an initial change creates an echo effect that goes though a series of diminishing rounds that cumulate into a total effect greater than the initial increase.

The multiplier gives extra leverage to government policies aimed at stimulating or cooling off the economy, but the multiplier is not limited to government expenditure. An increase in investment expenditures spurred, say, by a drop in interest rates, technological changes, mistaken expectations, or the need for expanded productive capacity would set off a similar round of diminishing changes working through the marginal propensity to consume. A sudden boost of exports would have identical effects. The basic idea behind the multiplier is that when increased production generates increased income without bringing to the market the corresponding values of consumer goods on which that income is spent, there is a multiplier effect.

Let's pretend that Stonewall, Mississippi (population 1,189), received a million-dollar bequest from a local boy who made it big in Chicago. The town council decides to use the money to erect a large statue of their favorite Civil War hero astride an even larger horse. The people working on the statue are paid, the suppliers of the stone and tools are paid, and they create a million dollars' worth of statue. All of this new production and income, however, did not create the equivalent value of consumer goods and services for those workers and suppliers to buy. Ergo, the statue produces a local multiplier effect parallel to that of a million-dollar increase in, for example, exports.

In all of this, of course, there is nothing to prevent exactly the same set of relationships generating cumulative negative changes of GDP in response to a decline in government, investment, or export expenditures.

Fiscal policy working through the tax side has a similar effect, but there is a significant difference. If the federal government returns $400 million in income taxes in a one-year, lump sum rebate, it kicks off a multiple chain reaction, but a smaller chain reaction.[2] The first increase in expenditure (and thus of GDP) is not $400 million; it is the consumption expenditures induced by the $400 million increase in disposable income: $320 million (mpc of .80 × $400 million). That $320 million (making for an identical change in GDP) then rebounds around the system in a similar way, increasing disposable income by $240 million (.75 of $320 million). This in turn stimulates an increase in household consumption expenditures by $192 million (.80 of $240 million), and on and on until the total increase of GDP adds up to $800 million. Granting a tax break, then, results in a smaller ultimate increase in GDP than increasing government expenditures on goods and services by the same amount, and that difference is due to the smaller initial change in expenditure that sets off the rounds of consumption expenditure.

If the government were to stimulate the economy by increasing transfer payments or hiring more people (increased government wages and salaries), we expect a resulting increase in GDP closer to the tax break rather than to government purchase of goods and services. This also paves the way to describe the balanced budget multiplier.

The **balanced budget multiplier** is a hypothetical policy in which both taxes and government expenditures on goods and services are increased by the same amount. By the reasoning above, the two do not cancel each other out. Using the same numerical example, the government increases expenditures by $400 million and raises taxes by the same amount. The higher taxes reduce households' consumption expenditures by $320 million, which is $80 million less than the $400 million increase in government purchases of goods and services.

On the other hand, if the increase in government expenditures (which is equal to the tax hike) had been used for transfer payments and/or wages and salaries, personal income would rise by $400 million. The gain in disposable income, however, would be reduced by the amount of extra income tax payments, and the net effect would probably be slightly negative. (Think this through; it's not all that obvious.)

The discussion of the multiplier and the government budget reveals the logic behind the occasional fiscal strategy of lowering taxes with the expectation of stimulating the economy to the point that total tax revenues would increase, even with lower tax rates. This worked better in the early 1960s than in the mid-1980s, when the **supply side economics** strategy, which was supposed to stimulate private enterprises by increasing pecuniary incentives, simply did not come through as hoped. As a consequence, President Ronald Reagan's administration holds the title for piling up more federal government debt than any other peacetime administration before or since.

PYRAMIDS AND CATHEDRALS?

John Maynard Keynes, writing in the depths of the Great Depression, was convinced that modern capitalism was chronically plagued by deficient levels of aggregate demand and needed continual boosts of a multiplier-type stimulus in order to be viable. In his inimitable style, he wrote:

> Ancient Egypt was doubly fortunate, and doubtless owed to this its fabled wealth, in that it possessed *two* activities, namely pyramid-building as well as the search for the precious metals, the fruits of which, since they could not serve the needs of man by being consumed, did not stale with abundance. The Middle Ages built cathedrals and sang dirges. Two pyramids, two masses for the dead, are twice as good as one; but not so two railways from London to York. Thus we are so sensible, have schooled ourselves to so close a semblance of prudent financiers, taking careful thought before we add to the "financial" burdens of posterity by building them houses to live in, that we have no such easy escape from the sufferings of unemployment. (John Maynard Keynes, *The General Theory of Employment, Interest and Money* [1936], p. 131)

It is clear that Keynes, for all his brilliance, did not foresee the policy of permanent war readiness that makes pyramids and cathedrals pale in comparison.

President G. W. Bush's tax cuts were not designed to fight recession. He proposed them well before the recession, which began in March 2001, but he did take the opportunity of the recession to convince enough people in Congress and the public of the need for tax cuts. The general justification was to stimulate economic growth by cutting income taxes on high earners, reducing tax rates on capital gains and dividend income, eliminating the estate tax temporarily, and allowing businesses to write off the cost of new capital purchases more quickly. The rhetoric justifying this shift of the tax burden from financial and real capital to wages and salaries suggests that the very rich need to be bribed heavily to use their resources productively. The inefficiency of tax cuts targeted in this manner as an economic stimulus is shown by an economic recovery so sluggish that it was not until 2004 that the *absolute* number of jobs returned to 2000 levels—never mind the quality of the jobs.

Money Is as Money Does

The adage that serves as this section's title aptly defines money; anything that performs the three functions of money—medium of exchange, standard unit of value, and store of value (or of deferred payment)—is money. A wide range of things have served these purposes and thus been money, things that included large stones in the South Pacific, mollusk shells among Native Americans, sticks of chewing gum in occupied Germany after World War II, pieces of printed paper, and notations in bank ledgers and electronic files, among others. Gold no doubt holds the historical record for being most closely identified with money, in good part because of its scarcity, malleability, ease of dividing it into small units, and a chemical inertness that prevents it from rusting and otherwise deteriorating over time. (The last three qualities make gold useful for filling cavities in teeth as well.)

Confidence is the key to something functioning successfully as money. You willingly accept some form of money in payment for a service or commodity only if you believe the value of that money will be maintained in the eyes of others at least until you wish to exchange it for a good or service. The psychological element has imparted a mysterious, even mythical and transcendental, quality to money, despite its rather mundane and socially determined character. The U.S. government no longer backs up its currency with gold or any other tangible commodity. Instead, its paper currency boldly declares: "This note is legal tender for all debts, public and private."[3] The source of the U.S. dollar's value, then, depends on the authority of the U.S. government and the confidence that the dollar will hold its value in the eyes of others.

Currency, however, is only one component of what functions as money in the United States. There is a whole array of financial instruments, including currency, various kinds of bank accounts, stocks, bonds, IOUs for gambling debts, life insurance certificates, and arcane forms of option contracts. Each of these has some possibility of performing the three monetary functions, albeit with widely varying degrees of satisfaction, but they possess very different degrees of **liquidity**—how easily, quickly, and cheaply one can convert a particular asset into another kind of asset. Cash (currency and coins) is the most liquid of assets, and with cash one can pretty much buy anything (i.e., convert it into another kind of asset, whether a shirt or another financial instrument) immediately and with no transaction costs. Over 80 percent of transactions in the United States are in cash, but these transactions constitute less than 1 percent of the value of total transactions.

Checking accounts (or **demand deposits**, including interest-bearing NOW accounts) are almost as liquid as cash, but they are not legal tender. People can, and often do, refuse payment by check—try an out-of-town check in New York City. Various kinds of interest-bearing savings accounts are less liquid than checking deposits, U.S. government bonds are even less liquid, and so on.[4] Where does one draw the line on what is money in the here and now?

At the risk of sounding like a grumpy old man again, it was easier to answer this question when I began teaching economics. Cash and checking deposits constituted money, and all interest-bearing assets that were less easily convertible were not strictly money. Well, this definition still holds, but now it is called M_1. And there is also an M_2 and an M_3. The problem is that in the past twenty years, pushed by demand and enabled by the deregulation of the financial industry and electronic communication technology, financial instruments have proliferated to the extent that many of them blur together in terms of the liquidity criterion.

Anyway, M_1 is cash and checking deposits, and as we left the year 2005, we did so with about $716 billion in currency and $641 billion in various kinds of demand deposits, adding up to around $1,356 billion in total.[5] M_2 includes M_1 plus a set of somewhat less liquid financial assets (e.g., savings accounts), and it equaled about $6,588 billion at that time. M_3 includes M_2 plus a range of financial assets that are even less liquid, and it was around $9,977 billion. Which definition is the most appropriate depends on the use to which it is put, and I use M_1, which fits my purposes the best because it includes the financial instruments that are most often involved in transactions.

Financial Markets, the Federal Reserve System, and Monetary Policy

The first thing to know about banks is that they accept deposits in one window and lend them out another window, and they make their profits by charging a higher price (interest rate) for the money they lend than the price (interest rate) they pay depositors. Lending depositors' money is possible because they work on a **fractional reserve system**, in which banks do not have to keep all their deposits on hand. If they had to keep all the deposits behind the counter, they would simply be warehouses and would charge depositors for keeping their money rather than paying depositors for the use of it.

Banks cannot lend out everything that they get in deposits, however, because they do have to be able to cover themselves in the event of experiencing **adverse clearing balances**—when withdrawals are greater than new deposits. The fraction of deposits that banks keep for the contingency

of net withdrawals is determined by bankers' prudence and, more impor-
tantly, by state and federal regulatory agencies.

This process of accepting deposits and making loans is called **financial intermediation**, which is conventionally described as gathering
together large numbers of small deposits in order to lend out large lumps.
Although the size patterns of bank deposits belie the notion that many
small deposits are the principal sources of funds, the function played by
financial intermediaries is clear—they act as brokers connecting lenders
(depositors) with borrowers, putting the money to work, as they say.
Financial intermediaries in the United States used to be quite specialized,
with each type of institution legally restricted to certain sources of funds
and to specific kinds of lending. Financial deregulation, however, beginning in the late 1970s, accelerated in the next decades, and continues to
blur the distinctions among financial institutions. As a result, commercial banks, investment banks, savings and loan associations, mutual savings banks, and even brokerage firms, insurance companies, and mutual
funds are increasingly able to cross over and compete in what had for-
merly been one another's particular domains.

In 1913, the U.S. government established the Federal Reserve System
(the Fed) to regulate banks in order to reduce the incidence of financial
panics, and later, in 1933 it established the Federal Deposit Insurance
Corporation, or FDIC, which guarantees deposits currently up to $100,000
through an insurance program. When the public lost confidence in a bank,
large proportions of the bank's depositors tried to withdraw their money
at the same time. Of course, the bank could not meet the demands of all
(or even most) of its depositors, whether the initial loss of confidence was
or was not justified. The bank had to close, at least temporarily, an action
that undermined depositors' confidence in other banks. The contagion
thus had the potential of escalating into a full financial panic that severely
disrupted financial markets and economic activity in general. Two of the
most serious pre–Federal Reserve panics occurred in 1873 and 1907, and
the bank panics and closings of the 1930s led to the FDIC.

The Fed is the central bank for the United States, although uneasiness about centralized political authority gives the U.S central bank some unique features: the Fed is organized into twelve regional banks; and it has substantial insulation from elected government officials. Its headquarters and major policy-making bodies, however, are located in Washington, D.C., and its regulation of financial institutions is subject to and dependent on federal legislation. Nevertheless, in formulating and implementing monetary policy, the Fed operates with considerable autonomy.

Monetary Policy

Although not a part of the original intention, it soon became clear that the Fed's acting as the financial agent for the U.S. Treasury had the potential of affecting financial markets in ways that significantly influenced levels of general economic activity. It did this by being able to expand or contract the amount of money in circulation and therefore to change interest rates. The deliberate use of this influence is called **monetary policy**. There are three major mechanisms by which the Fed affects the availability of financial liquidity—money, which for the sake of clarity here I consider as M_1.

Open Market Operations The most important mechanism is the Fed's purchase and sale of federal government bonds on the open market. The first step in describing this process is to understand the counter-intuitive relationship between a bond's price and its yield (interest payments). If you buy a $100 government bond, you are lending the government $100. If that bond promises to pay you $110 in one year (the original $100 plus $10 extra) then the yield of the bond is 10 percent $\left(\frac{10}{100}\right)$—the rate of interest that the government is paying you for lending it the money. If you were to pay only $98 for the same bond that pays $110 in one year, the net $12 you earn means a rate of return is 12.24 percent $\left(\frac{12}{98}\right)$. On the other hand, if you were to pay $102 for that bond, your rate of return would be 7.84 percent $\left(\frac{8}{102}\right)$. Get it? As the price of the bond falls, the absolute and

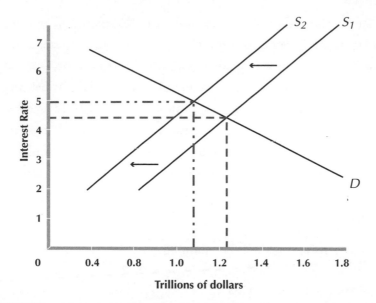

FIGURE 4.1 The Market for Loanable Funds and Fed Policy

relative differences between what you are paying for the bond and the fixed value of what you will get for it rises. The equal and opposite hold for rising bond prices.

With that under our belts, let's look at what happens when the Fed sells a large volume of bonds. It soaks up liquidity in the private economy by selling relatively illiquid bonds in exchange for private buyers' liquid checking deposits and cash (money). This net loss of liquid assets reduces the amount of loanable funds available to banks and other financial intermediaries. This is shown in figure 4.1 as a shift to the left of the supply curve of loanable funds from S_1 to S_2. The demand curve for loanable funds includes all demand for borrowed money, including for plant and equipment, inventories, home and auto purchases, international commerce, stock market speculation, and three-day funerals. Although the supply curve for loanable funds is determined principally by Fed monetary policy, it is usually drawn with some positive slope, because economists still like to believe that higher interest rates induce people to save more, and therefore make more money available for lending.

In our example in figure 4.1, however, the Fed's policy reduces the availability of loanable funds, which puts upward pressure on interest rates (the price for renting/borrowing loanable funds) as potential borrowers compete with one another for loans. The rise in interest rates chokes off some investment and consumption expenditures and may slow down exports. This restrains the general level of economic activity.

Why would people necessarily buy the bonds offered by the Fed? All the Fed has to do is to reduce slightly the price of the bond and thus raise the rate of return slightly above what is generally available. These are offers that professional money managers cannot refuse. Whether the money managers work for banks, mutual funds, pension funds, insurance companies, manufacturing corporations, rich individuals, or whatever, they are paid by their employers to take advantage of any such opportunities and to rush to get such a deal. Moreover, those money managers probably had to sell some financial assets in order to buy the government bonds, and to do so, slightly discounted their prices in order to sell them quickly to take advantage of the good deal. So the initial transaction begins the process of raising the yield and effective interest rates, and the process works itself throughout financial markets, raising interest rates and discouraging primarily investment and consumption expenditures.

On the other hand, when the Fed buys bonds, in an appropriately massive volume, it pays by check. Let's say that those selling the bonds to the Fed had done so only because they got an especially good deal (a slightly above-market price), but they really did want interest-bearing bonds rather than a liquid checking deposit that earns little or no interest. These people would turn around and replace the bonds sold to the Fed by buying some other bonds from private bondholders. This process of excess liquidity chasing through the system continues the process of bidding up the price of bonds and lowering interest rates, thus encouraging new borrowers to enter the market and stimulate investment and consumption expenditures.

When private parties buy and sell bonds between them, one private party (corporation, individual, church) gives up money from a checking account or from cash and another private party gains the same amount in a checking account or cash. But it is different with the Fed's purchases and sale of bonds, because the Fed's checking balances are not available to the public as loanable funds. When private parties buy bonds from or sell bonds to the Fed, the change in the amount of money (e.g., checking account balances) in the private sector declines or rises, respectively. Well, yes, there is a certain arbitrariness, even sleight of hand, to all of this, but the money available to be lent for private expenditures is, for all intents and purposes, the money circulating in the private sector.

An extremely important aspect of this process is that when the Fed injects more liquidity/money into the economy by buying bonds, it is *not* a direct increase in incomes. The Fed is not handing out money on street corners. The increase in the amount of money in the economy is due to money managers' having been induced to adjust their portfolios of financial holdings by exchanging relatively illiquid bonds for liquid cash and checking deposits. The creation of more money in the economy, therefore, is not done by directly increasing anybody's income (aside from some fat commissions); it is due to changes in the composition of previously held financial assets. Any increase in GDP and income from these transactions comes about through a drop in interest rates that stimulates more expenditure and production.

The Fed's open-market transactions are big, but they have an even greater effect on the money supply. The fractional reserve banking system means that banks create liquidity in the form of demand deposits in their day-by-day lending operations, because every time they make a loan, they create new deposits that the borrower can draw upon. This gives the Fed increased leverage over the money supply. Any given change in the amount of privately held checking deposits due to the Fed's selling or buying government bonds affects bank reserves and lending capacities and thus magnifies that initial change in the money supply.

One last note on language. The Fed usually announces its actions in terms of changing the **federal funds rate**, the interest rate that banks charge one another for very short-term loans (often just overnight) to tide the borrowing bank over a temporary shortfall of what it needs to meet its reserve requirements. The Fed and many others watch this particular interest rate very closely, because they consider it to be a significant indicator of financial market conditions in general, and the Fed uses the sensitive federal funds rate as its target. When the Fed announces, let's say, that money markets need to be tightened and it is raising the federal funds rate by a quarter of a percent, it means that it intends to sell enough bonds that the reduction in loanable funds is almost immediately registered as a quarter of a percentage point in the federal funds rate. The federal funds rate is merely a target variable, and its rise soon is felt in rises throughout the highly integrated financial markets. A wide range of different interest rates coexists at any one time, depending primarily on the length and risk of each type of loan.

AN ORACLE OF OUR TIMES

In the early 2000s, the U.S. economy rode the crest of a long expansion, achieving a combination of high employment and low inflation that was due to structural changes largely independent of the policy actions of the Fed. Nevertheless, the public pronouncements of the Fed's chairman, Alan Greenspan, coupled with small tweakings of the interest rate, came to be viewed as the primary instrument of government policy for sustaining the remarkable period of economic expansion. By contrast, if Mr. Greenspan had been at the Fed's helm in the early 1970s, coping with the aftermath of the Vietnam War, high government deficits, an oil embargo, high unemployment, and double-digit inflation, it is unlikely that either the Fed or its chairman would have been so celebrated. In any case, Mr. Greenspan's inconsistency about the dangers of federal deficits and this Fed's disappointing record in bringing the U.S. economy out of the doldrums of 2001–2002 dimmed some of the luster of Mr. Greenspan's reputation before he retired.

Reserve Requirements A second policy option for the Fed is to change the fraction of deposits that member banks have to hold as reserves. Although banks chartered by the Fed ("national banks") are only around a third of the total—most are chartered by states—they are the larger banks and hold most of total bank assets and significantly affect general financial activity. A rise of the reserve requirement immediately reduces the capacity of member banks to lend, thus tightening financial markets and raising interest rates. On the other hand, lowering the reserve requirement increases the supply of loanable funds and reduces interest rates.

Changing reserve requirements is an extremely blunt instrument used when immediate and large changes seem to be needed. For more precisely targeted changes, the Fed prefers open-market operations.

Discount Rates The **discount rate** is the interest rate that the Fed charges for lending money to its member banks, usually for augmenting their reserves to the desired levels. Most of such lending now takes place among banks in the federal funds market rather than between the Fed and the banks, and the discount rate has become primarily a matter of symbolic value. This does not mean that symbols are without significance, however. The Fed uses changes in the discount rate as explicit signals to the financial community of its concerns about the economy, concerns that might soon result in more than symbolic gestures. People ignore such declarations of the Fed's stance at their peril.

Business Cycles, Inflation, and Unemployment

At the end of every long economic upswing, one always hears claims that the business cycle has been abolished, but the fact remains that overall levels of economic activity do fluctuate over time. By the summer of 2001, the U.S. economy was definitely slowing, and the unusual expansion of the past eight years appeared to be over. The terrorist attack in early September added to problems already apparent.

In studying economic fluctuations, the interaction between the multiplier and accelerator makes it relatively easy to explain why, once begun, economic upswings continue going up, and once begun, downswings continue down. For example, when a vigorous multiplier effect is working its way through the economy with new rounds of consumption expenditure, demand for particular goods and services may begin to outrun firms' capacities to produce enough to keep up with the increased demand. Those producers are likely to invest in enlarging their productive capacities, encouraged by a generally optimistic business climate created by the expansion. This induced investment is called the accelerator, and one can think of it as renewing the multiplier. That is, any new investment induced by heightened demand kicks off a new multiplier impact, which in time induces more investment, and so on. The same mechanism can also work in reverse, and downward-spiraling levels of general economic activity, with attendant underutilized productive capacity and business pessimism, lead to the cancellation of investment projects and plunge the economy even deeper into the doldrums.

Inadequate levels of economic activity create unemployment, and the Employment Act of 1946 charged the federal government with the responsibility of maintaining rates of job growth sufficient for full employment. Although the Employment Act seems to have been unofficially repealed in the 1980s, low or negative rates of economic growth reduce income, innovation, profits, consumer satisfaction, as well as the likelihood of a public official's being reelected.

The U.S. Congress has not codified the goal of avoiding inflation, but the Fed is staffed with bankers and it functions as the frontline defense against inflation. Bankers and their colleagues in other financial institutions are extremely allergic to inflation. In inflationary times, banks have to pay higher interest rates for deposits while many of their previous loans were made at lower interest rates. More generally, inflation can disrupt financial markets by introducing uncertainty into the value of the units in which all financial instruments are calibrated.

Employers do not mind a bit of unemployment in order to keep workers disciplined, and those most interested in full employment do not mind a bit of inflation as part of the process. Nevertheless, it is obviously in the interests of elected government officials to steer the economy safely between the Scylla of inflation on one side and the Charybdis of unemployment on the other.[6] Public stabilization policy is interested in reducing the size of business fluctuations in a way that promotes steady economic growth. This also means reversing or reducing the momentum of an established upswing or downswing that threatens to have unfavorable effects.

Up, Up, Up, . . .

Inflation is defined as a general rise in prices, but you do have to keep in mind that prices never rise uniformly across the board. The principal explanation for inflation is excess demand—too much money (expenditures) chasing too few goods leading to prices being bid up. In the latter half of the nineteenth century, this was taken literally through the **quantity theory of money**. It was believed that a change in the amount of money circulating in the economy would have a fairly immediate and proportional effect on general price levels. Although there are economists who still pay lip service to the quantity theory of money, most economists today agree that changes in the money supply affect the economy primarily through changes in the interest rate.

Although I mention a couple of exceptions below, modern economics sees inflation to be primarily a demand-driven process, despite disagreements about the sources of the excess demand. So think of all those individual short run demand and supply curves for particular markets with demand curves shifting to the right and new equilibria established farther up the respective supply curves at higher prices and increased output. In competitive markets, short-term supply curves slope up and to the right because increased output increases the derived demand for labor and inputs, leading to their prices rising. Producers cannot continue to produce more goods and services without higher product prices to compensate for higher production costs.

In contrast, supply side explanations for inflation depend on the existence of noncompetitive markets. If a firm, a group of firms, or a labor organization gains sufficient market power in a certain market, it may exercise this market power by raising its prices in order to increase returns, be they profits or wages. The resulting higher prices are then registered as inflation. This strategy requires not only market power, whether in markets for intermediate products, labor, or final products; it also requires a generally buoyant economy. Without strong demand for the product or service, declining purchases of the higher-priced good or service would offset the benefits from the rise in price.

When OPEC used its market power to quadruple the price of petroleum in the early 1970s, it was so effective that the **supply side shock** threw most of the capitalist world into a recession. The jumbo price rise also stimulated conservation and the use of substitutes (coal, natural gas, nuclear, solar, and wind energy, bicycles, and feet). Although OPEC withstood these pressures from reduced demand for petroleum for a while, these strains eventually undermined (but did not destroy) the cohesion that underlies OPEC's market power.

Turning from causes to effects, inflation by its very definition reduces the real value (purchasing power) of a unit of currency (e.g., dollar); that is, any given number of dollars commands fewer goods and services. Any assets whose values are fixed in units of a currency experiencing inflation lose real value. This means people who are holding cash, deposits in banks, bonds, and other financial instruments denominated in specific dollar terms. The same is true of wages, salaries, pensions, unemployment compensations, and any other income flow either fixed or only slowly changing.

On the other hand, people whose assets are in equities (they *own* physical assets) are likely to be better off in inflationary times. Whether those equities are textile mills, office buildings, pieces of corporations (stocks), homes, antique cars, or paintings by Renoir, their values are not fixed in monetary terms and thus their values can appreciate to keep up with inflation. And again, people with more flexible incomes—profits, rents, commissions, and adjustable fees—come through inflation in better shape than those living on fixed or sticky incomes.

An important principle to keep in mind when thinking about winners and losers in inflationary times is that there is no net loss of purchasing power within a closed economy (i.e., without any foreign trade and investment). What are involved are *shifts* of purchasing power. For example, inflation often produces significant shifts of purchasing power from lenders to borrowers. This is the same idea described above—people with assets fixed in dollar terms (lenders holding IOUs) receive repayments of loans in dollars whose purchasing power has been eroded by inflation. On the other side, those whose liabilities (debts) are fixed in dollar terms tend to benefit from inflation. The federal government and those with home mortgages, both substantial debtors, clearly make out well in times of inflation when the real value of their debt is being reduced.

In the United States during the 1970s, the double-digit inflation led to considerable innovation by some in creating ways to protect themselves from inflation. One way was for lenders to adjust the interest due on the loan according to current interest rates, a frequent practice in mortgages that last twenty and thirty years. Let us say that a loan's interest rate is defined as always being three percentage points above that of the U.S. Treasury's thirty-day bonds ("bills"). As current interest rates respond quickly to current and anticipated inflation, **variable interest rates** better protect the lender from inflation.

A related device is that lenders occasionally **indexed** the amount (principal) of each loan—tying the dollar amount of the bond/loan to an indicator (index) of inflation, such as the Consumer Price Index (CPI). So if you borrow $100 for a year and the CPI increases 4 percent during that year, you have to pay back $104 plus interest. Some union contracts provided for indexing wages, and Social Security payments are adjusted for price changes. It is time, therefore, to look more closely at the CPI, the most important measure of inflation.

Since values are prices times quantities, we have to standardize *quantities* in order to measure changes in prices. But the CPI is not a general price index; it is an index intended to measure price changes that are the most important for families. So how does one find out which prices are most important, and how important? The Bureau of Labor Statistics of the Department of Labor takes surveys, and in this case, surveys of the expenditures of "average urban families." (No, I have never known one either.)

So the surveys tell us that the average urban family buys a particular pattern of goods and services and pays such and such prices for them— the typical "market basket." The CPI is based on price changes of around 200 items, but for the purposes of illustration, table 4.1 lists only eight large categories. The first and last columns are real, and I made up the other numbers for illustrative purpose. Now we know which prices are important and their relative importance (weights). We're in business.

Table 4.1 shows how the CPI is constructed: calculate the value of the identical market basket of goods and services (i.e., holding quantities constant) in each period's prices; establish a base point (not necessarily the same year as the weighting year) by dividing the value of every year's market basket by the value of the year that you want to be 100 (the base point), and multiply by 100. The CPI generated by the table ($44,240 / $38,393 x 100 = 115.5) is close to the actual mid-2005 CPI if 1999 is the base year (= 100).

Before leaving Table 4.1, let's talk about the behavior of some of the categories. The decline in apparel prices sounds like China, right? The rise of

TABLE 4.1 Calculation of the 2005 Consumer Price Index

	Annual Expenditures (Weights)	Total Annual Expenditures in 1999	Cost of Identical Market Basket in 2005 Prices	Changes in Prices of Each Category
Food and beverages	15%	$6,126	$6,941	13.3%
Apparel	4%	$1,532	$1,403	-8.4%
Housing	42%	$16,083	$18,592	15.6%
Transportation	17%	$6,510	$8,079	24.1%
Medical care	6%	$2,298	$2,843	23.7%
Recreation	5%	$1,915	$2,039	6.5%
Education and communication	6%	$2,298	$2,535	10.3%
Other goods and services	4%	$1,532	$1,808	18.9%
Total	100.0	$38,292	$44,240	CPI = 115.5

Sources: The first and last columns are from http://www.bls.gov/cpi/home.htm#data; the numbers in the middle columns are simply for illustration.

transportation prices was larger than in medical services, due to the price of fuel. Because food and fuel prices are very volatile, a separate CPI is calculated without them and is called Core CPI. Why don't we see the sharp rises in house prices more strongly reflected in the numbers? Because houses' sale prices are not included in the index. Rentals and rental equivalences are used instead, and rents have not risen as much as houses' sale prices.

The CPI no doubt exaggerates the amount of inflation, because it considers virtually all price increases as inflation, whereas some price increases represent quality improvements in the product. Automobiles and shoes are examples of current products that are definitely superior to the corresponding 1970 products. In the case of electronic products, price reductions have accompanied improved quality, so if you acknowledge quality improvements, prices should be shown to have fallen even farther. The second principal problem with the CPI is the difficulty of introducing new products,

LOTS OF INFLATION?

In discussing people's tendency to exaggerate the amount of inflation, an eminent monetary economist used to say to his class, "We all know that there has been a substantial amount of inflation in the last fifty years. But if you were given $5,000, would you rather spend it in the 1950 Sears and Roebuck catalogue or in the 2000 Sears and Roebuck catalogue?" (Presumably he ruled out reselling the 1950 merchandise in retro stores.) The question does force one to think more seriously about the extent and nature of inflation in the post–World War II decades. In doing so, the first step is to acknowledge the differences among categories of goods. If you need hand tools, basic tables and chairs, underwear, socks, sweaters, and warm coats, and you are not especially worried about fashion, you would leap at the opportunity to spend the money in the older catalog. On the other hand, if you are deep into stereos, TVs, computers, mag wheels, running shoes, and whatever, you would probably opt for the newer catalog. How does the level of income affect such a choice, and what does that say about the character of inflation over the past fifty years?

such as cell phones. Some recent estimates claim that the CPI overstates inflation by as much as a full percentage point or even a point and a half each year, and when payments are indexed to the CPI, this becomes a significant issue over time.

The **Producer Price Index** (PPI) is the second most frequently used price index. Like the CPI, the PPI is based on a market basket made up of goods and services bought by firms, in other words, they are intermediate, not final products. The PPI's earlier name was the Wholesale Price Index, which is a bit clearer about this. The PPI is watched closely, because if it begins to rise, can the CPI be far behind? Table 4.2 shows some of the recent inflation history in the United States.

Down, Down, Down, . . .

The rate of unemployment is one of the most visible and important indications of productive capacity utilization and also of social health. The calculation of the rate is quite straightforward: divide the number of unemployed people by the size of the civilian labor force. But of course, it is not quite that straightforward. Beginning with the denominator of the ratio, who is in the civilian labor force? Everyone who is sixteen years old or older and employed or actively seeking work in the past four weeks. Since we explicitly are talking about the *civilian* labor force, it

TABLE 4.2	Percentage Changes of the Consumer Price Index in Five-Year Increments							
	1965–1970	1970–1975	1975–1980	1980–1985	1985–1990	1990–1995	1995–2000	2000–2005
% Change of Index	23.2	38.7	53.2	30.6	21.5	16.6	13.0	13.0

Sources: The Federal Reserve Bank of Minneapolis
(http://minneapolisfed.org/Research/data/us/calc/hist1913.cfm) and the U.S. Department of Labor, Bureau of Labor Statistics (http://data.bls.gov/cgi-bin/surveymost).

excludes the one and a half million people in the military and all institutionalized persons. Among the institutionalized, the number of prisoners in the United States doubled between 1987 and 1997 and in 2004 numbered 2,267,787—40 percent larger than the armed forces (active and reserves). Although women were only 7 percent of the prisoners, their number is growing at more than twice the rate of men.

One final note on the definition of the labor force: those over sixteen years of age neither employed nor actively seeking work in the past four weeks are not considered to be in the civilian workforce. This includes students and retirees who are not working because they are presumably doing something they prefer doing. But it also includes perhaps 300,000 to 400,000 people who had sought jobs but became discouraged and stopped trying to find something decent.

Now let's look at the numerator of the unemployment ratio: the number of unemployed people. The seventeen million people who hold part-time jobs are defined as being employed, even if they wanted to work full time. The skilled machinist who lost his job to computerized methods of reconfiguring production machinery and is working as a clerk in a liquor store is employed.

Now that we have some idea about the measurement of unemployment, we can explore the different types. The usual distinctions among kinds of unemployment are seasonal unemployment, frictional unemployment, structural unemployment, and cyclical unemployment. **Seasonal unemployment,** as the name might have suggested to you, bears most heavily on those working in agriculture and tourism. In addition, there are a range of other specific jobs and places that go through predictable seasonal employment cycles.

Frictional unemployment is made up of people temporarily in transition into the workforce and into and out of particular jobs. The following examples all fall into the frictional category. Michael decides that harsh winters are not for him any more, quits his job, moves to Arizona, and looks for work. Eva tells her supervisor what she thinks of his style of personnel management. Mary and Frank's book and record shop goes under because a Borders bookstore opened down the street. Torsten graduates from college and begins job hunting. Frictional unemployment generally is thought to be a rather benign sort of thing, illustrating both the adjustments necessary to accommodate changes in the economy and the freedom of workers to move from job to job. Nevertheless, better access to information makes the job search more efficient and satisfactory, and there is some hope that on-line services are beginning to perform that function.

Structural unemployment is less nice. This is the type of unemployment that is due to a mismatch between the skills of the workforce and the requirements of the jobs. Structural unemployment is when the technical proficiency required for jobs rises beyond the skills and training of the available workforce. Recruiting, say, foreign nurses and engineers relieves this shortage of trained workers—or at least a shortage at the wages employers are willing to pay. Some structural unemployment is hidden from statisticians by the structurally unemployed having to find new but inferior jobs, as in the case of the former machinist now working in the liquor store.

This process used to be called technological unemployment, but **displaced workers** seems recently to have become the euphemism of choice. Economists argue about the magnitude and implications of this form of unemployment, but there appears to be some agreement that in the past twenty or thirty years, it has affected older workers (over forty) more severely than previously. It is not clear whether this reduced protection from seniority is due to cost-saving efforts, difficulty of training older workers, or what, but it is clear that compared to younger workers, those over forty have more difficulty finding new employment and have to take larger cuts in pay when they do find new work.

Economists usually prescribe retraining and relocation to combat structural unemployment. These are certainly worthwhile endeavors, but they do not guarantee the creation of appropriate jobs.

Deskilling is closely related to displacement of this kind. **Deskilling** occurs when technological changes enable what had previously been workers' skills to be incorporated into machinery whose operation requires a less skilled worker. A mundane but clear example is the use of bar codes in supermarkets. By this device, stores do not have to pay people for their abilities to know the prices of items, the difference between iceberg lettuce and parsley, or how to make change. Deskilling does not mean that the workers are less skilled; it simply means that the jobs do not require the skills and therefore employers do not pay for them. In selected neighborhoods, some grocery stores have taken the next step: customers can check themselves out by using bar code scanners and payment machines. One employee can cover as many as four checkout stations, and the effect of bar code technology has gone beyond deskilling and become technological unemployment.

The last category is **cyclical unemployment**. As the level of economic activity enters the negative phase of a business cycle, cyclical unemployment rises. In the past twenty years, the peaks of unemployment (corresponding to the troughs of the business cycle) have resulted in unemployment rates close to 10 percent in the early 1980s and almost 8 percent in the early 1990s. Although these rates include frictional, structural, and cyclical unemployment, only the last accounts for rapid changes in the overall rates. Cyclical unemployment is the type of unemployment that fiscal and monetary policies are designed to offset by stimulating aggregate demand, and table 4.3 shows how unevenly unemployment

TABLE 4.3	Civilian Unemployment Rates in July 2005		
Total Civilian Labor Force Unemployment Rate			5.0
Adult males	4.3	Blacks	9.5
Adult females	4.7	Hispanics/Latinos	5.5
16- to 19-year-olds	16.1	Asians	5.2
Whites	4.3		

Source: Bureau of Labor Statistics (http://www.bls.gov/news.release/empsit.nr0.htm).

affects different groups of workers, an unevenness that has proven to be extremely durable.

By adding up frictional, structural, and seasonal unemployment rates (i.e., excluding cyclical unemployment) we get what some economists view as the **natural rate of unemployment**. (When anybody calls something in the social world "natural," you should immediately be on your guard.) In any case, the natural rate of unemployment is supposedly the minimum rate possible without setting off inflationary pressures. We discuss the trade-off between inflation and unemployment later in this chapter, but now it is worth noting that just a few years ago, economists who subscribed to the idea of a natural rate of unemployment believed that it was around 5.5 percent of the civilian workforce. This meant that "full employment" was 5.5 percent unemployment, because the remaining unemployment could not be reduced by demand management counter-cyclical policies without causing substantial inflation. Since the rate of unemployment in the late 1990s and early 2000s stayed well below that natural rate, and for all intents and purposes, there was no inflation, this entire construction has lost some of its appeal. The response that the natural rate has changed is not all that satisfactory, because if the natural rate is unstable and unpredictable, then it is useless as a benchmark for policy.

There is another economics construct that gets into the news occasionally. This is the **misery index**, which is the sum of the rate of inflation and the rate of unemployment. So inflation at 6 percent and unemployment at 7 percent add up to a misery index of 13. The notion that a 1 percent rise in the inflation rate is somehow equivalent, in social policy objectives, to a 1 percent rise in the unemployment rate is deeply suspect. I discussed the undesirable effects of inflation in the previous section, and by contrast consider the impact of a 1 percent increase in the unemployment rate. This means an additional one and a third million people have lost job opportunities. The true social costs of unemployment go beyond the losses in income and include greater incidences of family stress, domestic violence, alcoholism, mortgage foreclosures, and crime.

Additional Aspects of Stabilization Policy

Before describing monetary policy and fiscal policy, which are used deliberately, there are some built-in economic mechanisms thought to reduce the size of business fluctuations. The so-called **automatic stabilizers** work to insulate disposable income, and therefore consumption expenditures, from the full effects of the swings in GDP. One of these stabilizers is the federal personal income tax system. The extent to which that tax is progressive means that tax liabilities rise and fall *more* than the rise and fall of before-tax income, thus affecting after-tax disposable income somewhat less. This suggests that consumption expenditures do not fluctuate as much as the ups and downs of GDP and therefore help stabilize the entire economy.

Public policies of unemployment insurance and income-support programs (food stamps, welfare payments) and corporations maintaining dividend levels despite changes in profits are two additional automatic stabilizers that shield disposable income and consumption expenditures from the full brunt of changes in GDP. The public policy side of these is probably weakening as a result of welfare reform and smaller proportions of the unemployed being eligible for unemployment benefits.

Automatic stabilizers are not potent anti-cyclical defenses, and often government authorities feel the need, as it were, to manufacture the turning points of cycles.[7] In the case of an inflationary expansion, the Fed's monetary policy, especially open-market policy, is the principal way to cool down an overheated economy. By selling government bonds in the financial market, the Fed reduces the amount of loanable funds available and raises the price of borrowing (interest rates). After some point, this tightening of financial markets dampens both investment and consumption expenditures and at least reduces the rate of growth of aggregate demand.

On the other hand, monetary policy is less likely to be effective in stimulating the economy than in reining it in. Fed policy that increases the amount of loanable funds and reduces interest rates is merely permissive:

It allows people to borrow at lower costs. But if conditions are such that firms have idle plant capacity and see few prospects for new investments yielding high returns, and if consumers are worried about whether their employment is secure, lower interest rates are not a powerful inducement to increase spending. There are a number of aphorisms that usually appear in textbooks to illustrate the asymmetry of monetary policy. Two of the most commonly seen are "You can lead a horse to water, but you can't make him drink" and "You can bring a balloon down by pulling on its string, but you can't make it rise by pushing on the string."

The Fed's restrictive policies, however, really do raise the cost of doing business and buying new consumer goods, and it does so in a very definite, tangible manner. This asymmetry does not weigh too heavily on the Fed, because it has historically been much more concerned about the dangers of inflation than the effects of recession and unemployment. The Fed's members tend to be drawn from the banking community and are not elected.

Government fiscal policy has therefore been the main tool for responding to serious recessions, but there are political problems. Politicians from both parties have competed with each other in condemning "big government" (federal expenditures) and budgetary deficits. This leaves tax cuts sounding as though they are the only legitimate anti-recession fiscal policy. The listless recovery from the 2001–2002 recession, however, was not an impressive record for that tactic.

There are at least three factors outside of politics and policies working against a more vigorous economic rebound. Let's begin with record high oil prices. As noted in chapter 1, the price hikes in 2005–2006 are not due to supply-side manipulations by OPEC, the cartel of oil exporters. All oil producers benefit from the high prices, but apart from domestic political difficulties for some (for example, in Nigeria and Iraq) they are pretty much producing at or near capacity. Nevertheless, demand has risen so strongly, driven especially by the United States, China, and India, that prices are rising. The vulnerability of the United States is obvious. For example, if the U.S. government continues to bully the Iranian government about their nuclear program (for electrical power? for bombs?), the Iranians could withdraw their oil from the international market, and then there would a real price spike. This move would not be costless to Iran, of course, but we have managed to put ourselves in the position of having to hope that they would not do it.

The rise in the price of petroleum has an odd double whammy on the U.S. economy. It contributes to inflation, which is usually associated with hearty economic growth. At the same time, a sharp rise in petroleum prices usually has negative effects on economic growth. The quadrupling of petroleum prices in 1973 forced most industrialized nations into recession, and the 1979 price hike by OPEC dampened economic growth and contributed to the election of President Ronald Reagan in 1980. But our experience recently is that the U.S. economy is continuing to plod along, driven by continuing consumer shopping, taking the rise in petroleum prices in stride. In thinking about this, remember that petroleum is also the chief source of a number of chemicals that are fundamental to making fertilizer, plastics, tires, and paints, among other products.

As chapter 1 described, the rise in one commodity's price usually causes consumers to substitute other commodities for the one becoming more expensive. Since petroleum is almost uniquely the energy source for transportation, this is not easy. Our living patterns, where so many of us work quite far from home without adequate public transportation, forces most of us to use automobiles to get to work, kids to school, groceries to the kitchen, and so on.

Some diesel engines can be converted to burn vegetable cooking oil, but ethanol, made from corn in the United States, is the gasoline substitute with the most political clout. The major problem is that the process to make a gallon of ethanol requires about forty percent of the energy contained in a gallon of ethanol without counting the energy consumed in the cultivation of corn. There are, however, some pilot programs underway with the potential of reducing the amount of energy absorbed in producing ethanol.

There are critical voices that argue that the federal subsidy for ethanol is wasteful and that increasing fuel standards on cars and trucks would be a more effective way to reduce gasoline consumption. The Bush administration reluctantly has done so, and they have included light trucks and SUVs. One way to achieve even higher average mileage performance is through the use of so-called hybrid vehicles that combine gasoline and battery power and thus offer a way to make a gallon of gasoline go much farther. It is a perfect expression of our culture, however, that some vehicles (for example, the Honda Accord and the Lexus 600hL) utilize hybrid technology to give vehicles more power at the expense of little or no miles-per-gallon advantage over conventionally powered vehicles.

Turning to the other major avenue of energy use, the U.S. Department of Energy predicts that the demand for electricity will rise 50 percent by 2025. Natural gas fuels around 20 percent of the generation of electricity in the United States, but like oil, natural gas prices have gone through the roof. Nuclear power plants, which also account for 20 percent of electricity production, are making a comeback in response to the market as well as to the federal government's program of incentives. Nine power companies have indicated their intention to build nineteen nuclear plants, and all but one are sited in small depressed southern towns. This is the first new wave of nuclear generators in the pipeline since the 1980s, when the partial meltdown in a reactor at Three Mile Island, Pennsylvania, and the explosion of a reactor at Chernobyl, Ukraine, cooled earlier enthusiasm. NIMBY (Not In My Back Yard) will continue to be a factor in the placement of new power plants and refineries.

The federal energy bill makes some generous provisions to coal producers and coal-fired electricity production, which accounts for about half the national electricity generated. Although the price of coal has also risen in the last few years, it is still cheaper than petroleum and natural gas. And unlike petroleum and natural gas, U.S. coal reserves could supply much of the U.S. power needs for more than 200 years. In addition, industrial researchers believe that they will soon be able to extract from coal the chemicals currently derived from petroleum and to liquefy coal in such a manner that it will work as diesel fuel. So what's the problem with a coal-powered future?

Despite heavy advertising to change the image of coal, it is still dangerous to mine and dirty to burn. Coal mining is often fatal for miners, and even after mines have been abandoned, the mines constitute fatal hazards to dozens of hikers, hunters, children, and others who accidentally fall into old mine shafts each year. Open pit mining and "mountaintop removal" are not as dangerous for workers, but they destroy the landscape and surrounding ecology. Mountaintop removal has leveled almost 380,000 acres in Appalachia and destroyed 700 miles of streams.

Older coal-fired generators are important contributors to the 24,000 premature deaths that the American Lung Association attributes to pollution by power plants. The carbon dioxide and sulphur dioxide emissions have been significantly reduced in new power plants, but the Bush administration has rolled back regulations on the older utilities. It seems unlikely that those utilities are going to make costly changes voluntarily.

Even President Bush is beginning to talk more about alternative energy sources like wind, sun, and hydrogen that are renewable and less harmful to people and environments. One of the problems with the entire endeavor has been that when petroleum prices rise quickly, more attention is paid to alternative sources of energy. Then when petroleum prices go down, resources for research and experimentation dry up. One economist has suggested that there should be a federal tax on petroleum that would adjust in ways that would guarantee high petroleum prices in order to draw into the alternative energy sector more long-term investments that would sustain the necessary efforts. If energy pessimists are right and petroleum supplies are going to continue to be very tight, demand and supply might be enough to keep very high energy prices. But if they are not, it would be hard to imagine a politician willing to say out loud that the government ought to prop up gas prices at high levels for the indefinite future.

The second negative economic force outside of politics is Katrina. Although the response to the hurricane by all three levels of government was disgraceful, irresponsible, and tragic, it would be meaningless to blame the not-quite-natural disaster and its damage to deliberate government policy. Katrina killed fewer people than the September 11, 2001 terrorist attack in the United States, but focusing narrowly on the economic effects of the two incidents, the employment effect of rebuilding the Pentagon and high-rise structures in the very south of Manhattan is bound to be significantly less than reconstructing large portions of New Orleans—one of the premier cities of the United States. Estimates for the costs of such Gulf Coast reconstruction are murky, due in part to the political complexity of specifying how much rebuilding would constitute reconstruction. For example, how many of the tens of thousands of houses destroyed by the hurricane and flooding will be replaced? And replaced by what? Or in another vein, would reconstruction include restoring the delta's valuable shrimp beds that took such a hard hit?

Two U.S. senators have casually mentioned cost figures: $150 billion (Harry Reid, Minority Leader); and $200 billion (Gregg Judd, Chairman of the Senate Budget Committee). But these are offhand comments and pertain only to hopes about the federal government's share of reconstruction funding, and in light of the $100 billion a year for wars in Afghanistan and Iraq and a massive federal deficit, it will be surprising if federal funding for Katrina's destruction approaches those levels. Even if such budget-busting allocations were to happen, the federal role is primarily to repair infrastructure (levees, roads, port facilities, bridges, schools, post offices, and maybe water, power, and security services). The $150 to $200 billion aspirations, therefore, do not include the reconstruction costs that have been and will continue to be borne by state and local governments, insurance companies, corporations (for example, repairing damaged oil rigs and refineries), and families. Altogether, then, after the initial shocks of Katrina and of the dispersion of people immediately affected are worked through the system, Katrina may be a shot in the arm for national employment and for a wide range of industries.

Finally there is the war in Iraq. This was a deliberate policy, but despite suspicions about oil conspiracies, it is difficult to discern what its purpose was. Even so, it is probably safe to say that stimulating the U.S. economy was not the principal intention behind the decision to invade Iraq, although the extra expenditures associated with the war and occupation no doubt have acted as a net macroeconomic boost to employment and production.

So was it worthwhile to invade and occupy Iraq? There have been a number of studies by economists who try to weigh the benefits of the invasion and occupation against its costs and compare that ratio with the benefits and costs of the prior policy—containing Saddam Hussein and conducting inspections.[8] It is revealing that in a discipline with pretensions of being a value-free science, complex and extensive calculations by conservative economists demonstrate that the policy of going to war was superior to the alternative policy of containment, and equally complex and extensive calculations by liberal economists show exactly the opposite.

Estimating the dollar costs and benefits of going to war has a somewhat mystical aura about it, and a much more concrete and less frequently studied question concerns who bears the costs of the invasion and occupation. The current cost of the war and occupation is being borne almost entirely by the U.S. troops in Iraq and the Iraqi people, since there has been no war tax to share the burden among U.S. noncombatants. One would normally expect the massive borrowing to finance the war would at least raise interest rates, which would function as a sort of tax. But as I have mentioned, Asian purchases of our Treasury bonds have kept interest rates low despite the Fed's efforts and thus reduced the cost to the U.S. government of financing the war. There is the argument that we are all helping pay for the war through higher prices for goods and services (including gasoline) being bid up by the military, but it is difficult to take that burden too seriously. If war expenditures were to be financed in part by cutting Medicaid and food stamps, which has been proposed in Congress, there will be another easily identified group—the nation's poorest—sharing the burden with the troops and Iraqis.

Returning now to issues of economic policy, fiscal stimulus is not the only reason elected officials are fond of repeated tax cuts. These gifts can be targeted to help friends, family, campaign contributors, future employers, certain constituents, and so on. Moreover, large tax cuts not only restrain the growth of government, they pressure government to downsize. Conservatives call this strategy "Starve the Beast," and it pleases those who wish to have few restrictions on their activities, have an underdeveloped sense of community, and are able and willing to stay in the private sector for such services as health, education, security of persons and property, transportation, and recreation.

On the other hand, federal expenditures for the war on terror and the occupation of Iraq are politically safe, even if they entail massive budgetary deficits. Such expenditures do not compete with domestic economic interests, and voting for them gets confused with a loyalty test. Rebuilding the U.S. Gulf coast, however, is another matter; some lawmakers are reluctant to increase the deficit in order to rebuild the areas damaged by hurricanes. The irony in all of this is that the Bush administration's fiscal policy has inadvertently been the policy prescribed by standard Keynesian macroeconomics to reinvigorate a sagging economy.

Both monetary and fiscal policies have serious lags in their effects. Although monetary policy can be implemented almost immediately when Fed decision makers decide that aggregate demand has to be controlled, it can take considerable time before the change in the credit markets registers significantly on behavior. Fiscal policy, however, has a much more immediate impact once implemented, but its serious lag is between recognizing the need for the policy and the time it takes to wind through the executive and legislative branches before it can be put into effect.

These patterns of lags have led some economists to claim that discretionary government stabilization policies have, on balance, been *destabilizing*. They argue that by the time the effects of monetary policy are felt and/or fiscal policy is implemented, the economy often had already turned around and that the policy thereby ended up exacerbating the direction of an already-existing upswing or downswing.

Doubts about the Inflation–Unemployment Trade-Off

Policymakers do have to worry about lags in effectiveness, but the principal doubts about the efficacy of discretionary government stabilization policies come from different directions. The first batch of doubts stems from the U.S. economy behaving in ways not expected by the conventional notion that inflation is the consequence of too much aggregate demand, and that recession is the mirror image—the result of too little aggregate demand. This notion has governed our entire discussion so far. The second set of doubts is based on the suspicion that the greater integration of international product and financial markets has changed national economic circumstances in ways that substantially dilute the effectiveness of demand management policies in influencing domestic levels of economic activity.

The standard reading of the demand-based causation for inflation and recession implies that public policy must guide aggregate economic performance along the very narrow path between the dangers of inflation on one side and recession on the other ("razor's edge"; or Scylla and Charybdis), and that there were definite trade-offs between the two. That is, the cost of full employment was the toleration of some inflation, and the cost of no or slight inflation was tolerating some underutilization of productive capacity, most notably registered as unemployment. This conception was graphically expressed in the **Philips Curve**. Figure 4.2 is a Philips Curve based on observations from the 1960s, and it indicates the expected negative relationship between inflation and unemployment.

The problem is that the U.S. economy has generated two kinds of anomalies that undermine the idea of an orderly universe in which the relationships between inflation and unemployment are regular, stable, and

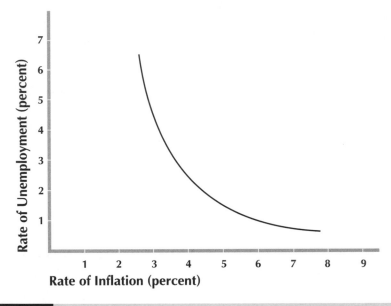

FIGURE 4.2 The Philips Curve

inverse. The first aberration was that the U.S. economy went through a couple of periods of simultaneous inflation and recession called **stagflation**.

Stagflation had been a regular feature of the economic landscape in several Latin American nations (especially Brazil, Argentina, and Chile) throughout the post–World War II decades, but it was not evident in the United States until the late 1950s. Its first appearance lasted only a short time, however, and in the 1960s, the economy acted in ways that at least in retrospect appeared reasonable in terms of the conventional ideas of excess or insufficient demand. Stagflation came back with a vengeance, however, in the 1970s, and it was more sustained. A decade of a more "normal" inflation-recession relationship again followed in the 1980s, when public policy deliberately created a severe recession and high rates of unemployment and succeeded in breaking inflation.

A new anomaly appeared in the 1990s. Instead of the aberrant appearance of inflation and unemployment together in stagflation, we saw the aberrant *absence* of both inflation and unemployment. During most of the 1990s and the early 2000s, the U.S. economy grew vigorously with very low rates of unemployment and inflation.

Implications of Greater International Economic Integration

We discuss the international economy at greater length in chapters 5 and 6, but here I list some of the factors thought to have weakened national demand-management modes of stabilization policy in the past two or three decades. As imports become a larger proportion of U.S. purchases,

ANOMALIES

The ways in which the U.S. economy operated in the 1970s and 1990s are not completely mysterious. The supply side shock of OPEC raising petroleum prices by a factor of four hit the United States (and other economies) hard in the early 1970s and produced some unusual responses. And for the U.S. economy's ability to experience full employment growth with low inflation during the 1990s, three factors significantly weakened U.S. workers' bargaining power vis-à-vis employers and allowed substantial economic growth and very low rates of unemployment with little upward wage pressure.

- The increasingly integrated international economy of the 1990s put U.S. workers into direct competition with workers throughout the world;

- The restructuring of the U.S. economy, in good part a response to international competition, increased the uncertainty of workers' jobs at a time that weak support for income maintenance policies (e.g., welfare, unemployment compensation) increased workers' dependence on steady employment; and

- The federal government, over the past two or three decades, has systematically eroded legal protections for workers to organize, bargain collectively, and strike.

more and more of any increase in domestic demand leaks off to foreign producers instead of stimulating local production and employment. As exports become higher proportions of domestic firms' production, local production and employment respond increasingly to demand in foreign economies and less to domestic U.S. demand. As barriers against the instantaneous movement of financial capital decline and the volume of footloose capital seeking the highest short-term rates of return rises, the Fed has less control over U.S. financial markets, and global financial markets increasingly gain influence over the volume and the terms (interest rates) of loanable funds available to U.S. borrowers. For example, the Fed has raised short-term interest rates almost every month between late 2004 and mid-2006, but to the Fed's surprise, the long-term rates did not respond until April 2006. Why is that? In part because the Chinese and Japanese governments invested so much money in long-term U.S. government bonds that they were keeping the bonds' prices up (and thus the yields/interest rates low), and in integrated financial markets, it holds all long-term rates down, including those for mortgages. Until the East Asians' purchase of U.S. Treasury bonds began to slow down in early 2006, their buying spree held down long-term interest rates in the United States despite the Fed's attempts to raise them. And all this time you thought that U.S. monetary policy was made in Washington, D.C.

There are plausible explanations for stagflation of the 1970s and low unemployment and inflation in the 1990s, but these explanations do not fit comfortably into either Keynesian or other standard views of how the economy works. In addition, while international economic integration is a political choice rather than an inevitable force of nature, the very process of integration produces strong political support among those in a position to take advantage of it. The 1960s were the high-water mark for optimism about controlling the economy through Keynesian-inspired policies, which were portrayed as being administered by neutral technocrats insulated from the irrational or narrowly self-serving resistance of the benighted. By the 1980s and 1990s, however, changes in the relationship between inflation and recession, together with increasing global economic interdependence, have strengthened general skepticism about the place of government macroeconomic stabilization policy in our society.

Beyond the specific policy issues, these transformations raise the possibility that the underlying logic of the economy has changed significantly. There is the definite possibility that the economy is operating along principles different from those taught to economists when they were in graduate school and, with little or no change, are still being passed on to current undergraduates.

Notes

1. So while the mpc in respect to disposable income is .80, in respect to GDP, the mpc is .60 (.75 × .80).

2. The complications around an arithmetic example of changing tax *rates* rather than amounts is a bit daunting, because altering tax rates also changes the ratio of disposable income to GDP and therefore one of the key parameters of the multiplier.

3. Checks, credit cards, and wheelbarrows full of pennies are not legal tender and do not have to be accepted in payment "for all debts, public and private."

4. Credit cards are not money; they are a means of deferred payment, essentially a short-term loan from the card company to the cardholder with the services of a collection agency to the retailer thrown in, but not free. It takes money to pay a credit card bill, and if it is not paid on time, unpaid balances become longer-term and much more expensive loans.

5. The composition of such holdings is a matter of individual preference. The highly unusual increase in currency holdings from November to December of 1999 suggests that Y2K fears may have led people to worry about bank deposits.

6. In Greek myth (and Homer's *Odyssey*), Scylla was a sea monster, and she lived in a cave opposite the whirlpool Charybdis above the Strait of Messina (between Sicily and Italy). Ulysses, and metaphorically those after him, tried to steer a narrow path between these two evils—Scylla and Charybdis.

After the initial discussion, I critically evaluate the assumption that inflation and unemployment are due to opposite causes (too much demand and too little demand, respectively) and represent a trade-off.

7. This suggests the possibility of manipulating levels of economic activity for political purposes. There is literature about the "political business cycle" that argues, for instance, that incumbents have deliberately used federal fiscal policy to pump up the economy during election years. Such calumny!

8. Alan B. Krueger, "The Cost of Invading Iraq: Imponderables Meet Uncertainties," *New York Times* (March 30, 2006), is a clear and informative survey of several such studies.

International Economics
and National Economies

International Economics and Comparative Advantage

I have described some of the effects of heightened international economic integration throughout the book, but here I focus specifically on the international realm. There is a continuing debate about whether recent increased foreign trade and investment signify distinctive new patterns or whether they are simply more of the same. As you will see from this chapter and the next, I tend toward the belief that the quantitative changes have been sufficiently large to have qualitatively transformed relations among nations and thus internal national dynamics.

The two chapters in this last section have quite different emphases. This chapter describes how economists analyze the principal types of international economic activity; it is about international economics.

Chapter 6 draws on the theories of this chapter as well as of previous chapters in order to outline the principal events, processes, and eventual transformations in the international economy. With the changes of the past thirty years, it is becoming more difficult and less useful to draw hard and fast lines between "international" and "domestic" economies, and this is reflected in chapter 6.

The Idea of Comparative Advantage

The argument for international specialization and trade among nations is parallel to the argument that specialization among individuals within a nation leads to mutually beneficial exchange. The specific case for international trade is called the theory of **comparative advantage** (or comparative costs), and David Ricardo appears to have come up with its first precise formulation in his *Principles of Political Economy and Taxation* (1817). Ricardo's theorizing had a very practical application; the theory of comparative advantage was one of the major arguments in British manufacturers' successful effort to abolish British tariffs on imported grain (the "Corn Laws") in 1846.

The basics of the modern theory of comparative advantage have not changed much since Ricardo's time, and like Ricardo, modern textbooks frequently introduce the idea of comparative advantage in the language of the labor theory of value. This is cumbersome and confusing, and it is easier just to state the essential point: the gains from trade are based on the ratios of product prices *within* the nation, and if these differ *among* nations, it benefits all to trade.

We presume that a fairly efficient market system will generate relative prices that reflect real opportunity costs, which in turn reflect relative availabilities of productive factors/resources.[1] Let's look at a numerical example, adhering to the time-honored tradition of creating an example from an imaginary world of two countries (here, the United States and Japan), two commodities (here, Digital Versatile Disc [DVD players] and grain), and no transportation costs. I begin with the exchange relationships between the commodities within each country.

United States: 1 DVD player = 3 bushels of grain (i.e., the price of a DVD player is three times the price of a bushel of grain)

Japan: 1 DVD player = 2 bushels of grain (i.e., the price of a DVD player is twice the price of a bushel of grain)

In this example, the DVD player-grain exchange ratio within each country is different, and therefore, there is the basis for mutually advantageous trade. If the ratios were the same, there would be no benefits from trade. In the example, DVD players in the United States are more expensive (in terms of grain) than they are in Japan, while grain is relatively cheaper (in terms of DVD players) than in Japan. The actual extent and terms of the exchange that would result from opening trade between the two countries depend on the demand and supply conditions for both commodities in both countries and therefore is indeterminate from the information here.

Nevertheless, what we do know from these ratios is that U.S. consumers would be willing to buy a DVD player from Japan for anything less than three bushels of grain and willing to buy a bushel of grain from Japan for anything less than one-third of a DVD player. On the other hand, Japanese consumers would be willing to buy a DVD player for anything less than two bushels of grain and buy a bushel of grain for anything less than one-half of a DVD player.

These limits preclude the United States exporting DVD players in exchange for Japanese grain at mutually agreeable exchange ratios (figure it out), but (surprise! surprise!) U.S. exports of grain in exchange for Japanese DVD players look very promising as a basis for trade. Any terms of trade between a DVD player = 3 bushels of grain and a DVD player = 2 bushels of grain would benefit the consumers in both countries. (The same relationships can be expressed in terms of a bushel of grain and are simply the reciprocals: 1 bushel of grain for anything between $\frac{1}{3}$ DVD player and $\frac{1}{2}$ DVD players would look good to both sides.)

Exchange Rates and Adjustment Mechanisms

The U.S.-Japan example illustrates the core of the comparative advantage argument: international specialization and trade benefit each national participant. Consumers in the United States and Japan, however, do not live in barter economies; they live in monetized economies where the value of goods and services is denominated in monetary units rather than in terms of other goods and services. The potential advantages from trade have to be reflected in money prices of the commodities in order for markets to respond appropriately. Every time you buy a foreign-produced good or service, think of it as two distinct transactions: you buy the necessary amount of that foreign nation's currency with your dollars, then you buy that foreign-produced good or service in the foreign nation's currency. In other words, the domestic money prices (and therefore price ratios) within the United States have to be translated into the Japanese currency (yen, or ¥), and vice versa: so many yen per dollar is, at the same time, so many dollars per yen. The price of a currency in units of other currencies is called its **exchange rate**.

Extending the previous example to show how exchange rates affect market signals and reveal comparative advantage, let us say that the prices in the United States and Japan in their respective currencies are the following:

United States: DVD players sell for $150 and bushels of grain for $50.

Japan: DVD players sell for ¥14,000 and bushels of grain for ¥7,000.

Note that these prices represent the previous ratios: DVD players are worth three bushels of grain in the United States; and a DVD player is worth two bushels of grain in Japan. Again, we would expect decently functioning markets to generate prices reflecting relative costs of production.

In order for international trade to work, the dollar-yen exchange rate needs to be such that U.S. grain is cheaper in yen than is Japanese grain and that Japanese DVD players are cheaper in dollars than are U.S. DVD players. So how do exchange rates get set at levels that highlight nations' respective comparative advantages and thus facilitate trade? For the purposes of illustration, we look at a situation in which the exchange rate turns out to be such that both U.S. DVD players and U.S. grain are more expensive in dollars and in yen than are Japanese DVD players and Japanese grain.

Let's say that for completely mysterious reasons, the initial exchange rate is $1 = ¥200 (or reciprocally, each yen = $0.005 (or 1/2 of a U.S. cent). This exchange rate means that Japanese DVD players and grain are

EXCHANGE RATES AND STANDARDS OF LIVING

Although exchange rates are indeed the prices by which currencies are converted into others, it is very tricky to use them to compare income figures. That is, if we know the per-capita income of Mexico for 1999 (in pesos) and the per capita income in the United States for 1999 (in dollars), current exchange rates are not a reliable way to convert them into a common currency in order to compare them. Exchange rates are determined primarily by the markets of international transactions and do not necessarily reflect the actual prices of goods and services produced and consumed locally. Think about how tenuous the relationship is between the exchange rate for the Saudi Arabian currency (the riyal) and the prices of the goods and services most important for most Saudi citizens. There is a school of thought in economics that argues that in the long run, exchange rates do tend toward a level that expresses relative costs of living in different nations (the purchasing power parity doctrine), but it is not clear how helpful it is even if true. The World Bank creates separate indices for converting and comparing national income figures.

TABLE 5.1   Summary of the Illustrative Arithmetic (Comparative Advantage)

A. Initial Situation:

Domestic Prices

U.S. DVD players	$150	Japanese DVD players	¥14,000
U.S. Grain	$50	Japanese Grain	¥7,000

B. When the exchange rate is $1.00 = ¥200:

Foreign Prices

U.S. DVD players	¥30,000	Japanese DVD players	$70
U.S. Grain	¥10,000	Japanese Grain	$35

C. The Gold Standard: The exchange rate is still $1.00 = ¥200, but the United States has experienced a 20 percent deflation and Japan has experienced a 30 percent inflation.

Domestic Prices

U.S. DVD players	$120	Japanese DVD players	¥18,200
U.S. Grain	$40	Japanese Grain	¥9,100

Foreign Prices

U.S. DVD players	¥24,000	Japanese DVD players	$91
U.S. Grain	¥8,000	Japanese Grain	$45.50

D. Flexible Exchange Rates: The exchange rate has changed to $1.00 = ¥100, but domestic prices have not changed.

Domestic Prices

U.S. DVD players	$150	Japanese DVD players	¥14,000
U.S. Grain	$50	Japanese Grain	¥7,000

Foreign Prices

U.S. DVD players	¥15,000	Japanese DVD players	$140
U.S. Grain	¥5,000	Japanese Grain	$70

cheaper in U.S. dollars than are U.S. products, and that U.S. DVD players and grain are more expensive in yen than are Japanese goods (you do the arithmetic and check it out with table 5.1). U.S. consumers then buy both DVD players and grain from Japan, and Japanese consumers buy nothing from the United States. This obviously cannot go on for any length of time, because in the example, the only source of Japanese yen for U.S. consumers is through the sale of U.S. products to the Japanese; and if they do not sell, they cannot continue to buy.

This would represent a massive deficit in the U.S. **balance of trade**—the balance between the value of a nation's exports and its imports. Since the Japanese have no incentive to buy from U.S. producers, there are not enough yen around for U.S. consumers to be able to keep buying from the Japanese. Whatever there might have initially been in the way of trade would quickly dry up.

This leads to an important observation: one nation simply cannot continue to undersell another in all products without compensating financial flows in the opposite direction. In the case of China, Japan, and to a lesser degree, South Korea, those compensating flows are their massive purchase of U.S. federal government bonds. I discuss this later in this and the next chapter, but here it is worth noting that without massive counter-flows, there is no danger from cheap foreign labor producing a flood of imports into the United States that destroys our economy. Apart from the fact that labor is cheap (or expensive) only relative to its productivity, the above example demonstrates why this is not a likely outcome. The extent and composition of a nation's involvement in and gains from international trade are not governed by the absolute costs of a nation's goods and services. The key relationships are the nation's relative prices of goods and services compared to other nations' relative prices: the ratios of prices *within* a nation compared to the ratios of prices *within* other nations. The clarity of this conclusion is less compelling when we add some complications to this simple model, but this is a worthwhile starting point. In any case, the cheap labor threat is not all that apt in this

A CAUTION ABOUT UNITS OF ANALYSIS

Comparative advantage models are usually couched in terms of nations—
the "United States" exported this, "Japan" imported that, both "Japan" and
the "United States" benefited from the international division of labor and
trade. Although using nations as units of analysis is appropriate for first-
order understandings, it can be misleading if pushed too far. For example,
let's look at the trade between Guatemala and the United States, where the
prices of Guatemala's exports (principally coffee) fluctuate relative to the
prices of its imports (mostly manufactured goods and foodstuffs). An
increase in Guatemala's **terms of trade** (the ratio of export prices over
import prices) indicates that each unit of Guatemala's exports pays for
more imports; and a decrease indicates that each unit of Guatemalan
exports pays for fewer imports. Does that mean, then, that a substantial
decrease in Guatemalan terms of trade can be described in the anthropo-
morphic terms of a small, poor nation being exploited by a large, wealthy
nation? No. It simply means that the value of coffee produced by
Guatemalan workers is being divided between Guatemalan coffee planters
and U.S. coffee purchasers in ways less favorable to the coffee planters. It is
imperative not to mistake (in this case) the material benefits of coffee
planters with those of Guatemalan society as a whole.

particular example, since Japanese workers are on average paid more
than U.S. workers, and most of U.S. international economic relationships
are with other prosperous, high-wage nations.

Returning to the numerical example, remember that the potential
benefits from trade between Japan and the United States cannot be
realized at the existing prices and exchange rate. So what is the mechanism to adjust the prices and exchange rates in ways appropriate for trade
to proceed? The gold standard and flexible exchange rates are the two
principal types of adjustment mechanisms that work in that direction.

Gold Standard

The **gold standard** was the adjustment mechanism that more or less prevailed during most of the nineteenth century and into the early decades of the twentieth. The rules of the gold standard required that gold be the ultimate medium of international exchange and that a nation's money supply be directly linked to the volume of gold that it possessed. Therefore, a nation that imported more goods and services than it exported experienced net outflows of gold that contracted the domestic money supply and reduced the price level of the deficit nation (recall the discussion of the quantity theory of money in chapter 4). The resulting deflation made the nation's exports more competitive in international markets because their prices, in both domestic and foreign currencies, had declined, and the deflation made imports less competitive in local markets, because domestic goods' prices had declined while the prices of imports had not. This double whammy—increasing exports and decreasing imports—thus eased the previous import-export imbalance. The mirror image was that a nation that exported more than it imported received net inflows of gold that expanded its domestic money supply, and the consequent inflation made imports less expensive in its domestic market and its exports more expensive in foreign markets. Both of these effects moved the surplus nation's exports and imports closer to a balance.

The gold standard adjustment mechanism that brought exports and imports into some rough equivalence worked through changes in the price levels of both deficit and surplus nations without any change in exchange rates. So let's try this with our example of U.S.-Japanese imbalance.

If both nations adhere to the rules of the gold standard, the United States is shipping gold to Japan to cover the balance-of-trade deficit, and one would expect inflation in Japan and deflation in the United States. So let's say that the United States-to-Japan flow of gold led to a 20 percent deflation in the United States and a 30 percent inflation in the smaller

Japanese economy. These alterations in price levels (but not in relative prices) would produce the following prices:

United States: DVD players sell for $120 and bushels of grain for $40.

Japan: DVD players sell for ¥18,200 and bushels of grain for ¥9,100.

Converting these prices at the unchanged $1.00 = ¥200 exchange rate, U.S. DVD players would sell for ¥24,000 in Japan and U.S. grain for ¥8,000 in Japan. Meanwhile, Japanese DVD players would sell in the United States for $91.00 and Japanese grain for $45.50. Now we can do business; this is within the range of price levels that work. Japanese producers sell DVD players to U.S. consumers, U.S. farmers sell grain to Japanese consumers, and mutually beneficial trade based on comparative advantage is possible.

It is not coincidental, of course, that the arithmetic example seemed to work the first time. The actual operation of the gold standard was considerably less certain, but even when it did work with textbook tidiness, neither inflation nor deflation makes a government popular with citizens. Moreover, governments did not like to abdicate the determination of their domestic money supplies to the vicissitudes of international trade and investment or to the serendipity of major gold strikes (causing worldwide inflation) and shortages (exerting deflationary drags).

Flexible Exchange Rates

The principal theoretical alternative to the gold standard is a very different, even polar method of adjustment. The **flexible exchange rate** system operates through the international demand for and supply of national currencies that have no direct connections with gold. In international currency markets, the supply of the currency of a nation that was importing more than it was exporting would exceed the demand for it, causing that currency's price in respect to other currencies (i.e., its exchange rate) to be driven down by market forces. This devaluation would reduce the price of the deficit nation's exports in foreign markets, encouraging more exports and raise the price of imports in domestic markets, discouraging imports. Both of these processes would propel the nation closer to balance. The equal and opposite would happen for nations that exported more than they imported. The scarcity of those surplus nations' currencies in international markets would cause a rise (appreciation, or revaluation) of its exchange rate, which in turn would raise the price of its exports in foreign markets, discouraging exports, and reduce the price of imports in domestic markets, encouraging imports.

So like the gold standard, the flexible exchange rate adjustment mechanism works symmetrically in both deficit and surplus nations, but unlike the gold standard, it relied on changes in exchange rates rather than in national price levels. Now let's return to our example of U.S.-Japanese trade imbalance, starting with an exchange rate of $1.00 = ¥200 and the initial domestic prices:

United States: DVD players sell for $150 and bushels of grain for $50.

Japan: DVD players sell for ¥14,000 and bushels of grain for ¥7,000.

In the flexible exchange rate scenario, the U.S. balance-of-trade deficit does not lead to inter-nation flows of gold; rather, the supply of U.S. dollars is significantly in excess of the amount that anyone wants at that price. As a consequence, the price of the U.S. dollar in respect to other currencies (here, the Japanese yen) declines until its demand and supply are roughly equivalent.

Let's say that the value of the U.S. dollar continues to fall until it reaches a level of $1.00 = ¥100—that is, it falls to half its former value in yen. At this point, the price of Japanese DVD players in U.S. dollars is still less than the price of U.S. DVD players, but the price of Japanese grain in U.S. dollars is considerably more. U.S. DVD player producers still have no market in Japan, but U.S. grain farmers do. At an exchange rate of $1.00 = ¥100, then, we can do business. With no changes in the dollar prices of U.S. goods or the yen prices of Japanese goods, international trade between Japan and the United States can go forward on the basis of comparative advantage. Use table 5.1 to check your calculations.

THE ANCHOR

The understanding that flexible exchange rates were potentially destabilizing was significant in Chile in the early 1980s. The "Chicago Boys"—Chileans who studied at the free market–oriented economics department of the University of Chicago and worked as economic advisers to the Pinochet dictatorship (1973–1990)—were reluctant to adopt flexible exchange rates, because they believed that a fixed exchange rate would work as an anchor to stabilize the Chilean economy. The problem with a fixed rate, of course, is that it never is really set in concrete; it remains fixed only as long as the nation's Central Bank can defend it. It does this by buying its own currency on world markets, drawing down its (sometimes borrowed) foreign exchange reserves of "hard" currencies (generally accepted national currencies—dollars, yen, deutsche marks, and so on). As soon as a fixed-rate currency gets into trouble and devaluation looks likely, speculators begin selling off that currency (even if they have to borrow it) and eventually force the devaluation—an excellent example of a self-fulfilling prophecy. This is what happened to Chile when the debt crisis hit in 1982; the Chilean Central Bank soon ran out of reserves and the Chilean economy took the worst beating in the hemisphere. The International Monetary Fund and the U.S. Agency of International Development, however, helped to bail out the Pinochet regime with a generosity not extended to other Latin American nations.

Despite the free market character of flexible exchange rates, not all free market economists are enthusiastic about them because of the fear of destabilization. Flexible exchange rates work better to protect a nation's economy from the effects of changes emanating from the international economy and less well in responding to changes from domestic economic activity. If Economy A is expanding faster than its trading partners and experiencing inflation, the rising consumer expenditures in the growing economy will lead to its imports increasing faster than its exports. In a flexible exchange regime, the market pressure on the country's exchange rate would be to devalue its currency. This devaluation would raise the price of imports (in domestic currency), thus discouraging them and stimulating domestic substitutes, and it would lower the price of exports (in foreign currencies), thus encouraging them. This means that a flexible exchange rate would move in a direction that would cause more inflation in an overheated economy. The way in which the appreciation of a flexible exchange rate would exacerbate an economy's downward slide is parallel. (Work out this contention!)

International Investment and the Balance of Payments

In order to be clear, I have described the two adjustment mechanisms as ideal types. In practice, however, nations did occasionally change their exchange rates even during the heyday of the gold standard; and in current exchange rate systems, which more closely approximate the flexible exchange rate model, governments often interfere in currency markets in order to influence exchange rates. But the most important simplification is that the entire conversation so far in this chapter has been conducted under the assumption that the purchase and sale of goods and services—imports and exports—are the only kinds of international economic transactions. As soon as I enlarge the scope of our analysis to include international investment, there is a substantial increase in complexity and some of the heretofore tidy conclusions are put at risk.

The first step is to recognize that the demand for a nation's currency is not exclusively for buying that nation's exports. It also can be used to invest in that country. This can take myriad forms: purchase of another nation's financial assets, such as bank deposits, bonds, derivatives, options, and so on. Or foreigners might build a cement plant, buy an auto repair shop, or acquire some farmland in another country. When foreigners purchase financial assets, it is called **foreign portfolio investment**; and when they acquire "real" assets (the cement plant, shop, land), it is called **foreign direct investment**.[2]

I occasionally run into the contention that the U.S. balance-of-trade deficit is the reason for so much foreign investment entering the United States. I guess that it is the idea that all those U.S. dollars slopping around outside the United States have to be used in some manner. Whatever, the proposition mistakes cause for effect. The U.S. currency is one, if not *the* principal, currency generally accepted as an international medium of exchange, so many foreigners wish to maintain balances of U.S. dollars for their liquidity. In addition, the U.S. economy continued to prosper through most of the 1990s, with record rates of return in the stock market, and many foreigners have desired to get a piece of the action by buying U.S. stocks. Finally, the United States is considered to be an attractive site for investment because, even after the events of 11 September 2001, it is still a (relatively) safe haven.

While liquidity, security, and good returns are never irrelevant, they are not the only motives. East Asia's massive purchases of U.S. federal government debt helped to sustain their large balance-of-trade surpluses with the United States by keeping the price of the U.S. dollar higher in their currencies than it would be without their purchases of federal bonds. East Asians began reducing their purchase of U.S. government bonds in March and April 2006, and long-term interest rates in the United States began to rise.

If I wanted to be cute, I would say that the United States appears to have a comparative advantage in producing and exporting debt that is

highly desirable by foreigners. After all, foreigners' ownership of U.S. publicly held federal debt rose from less than 20 percent in 1989 to about 40 percent in 2000, and they held around 20 percent of U.S. corporate bonds. But I resist the temptation, because it violates the distinction between comparative advantage–trade balances and international financial flows, a distinction that is so firmly rooted in the canon of international economic theory that I hesitate even trying to be funny about it.

So what does this mean for the relationship between U.S. trade deficits and foreign investment in the United States? When foreigners invest heavily in the United States, they can force the U.S. trade balance into deficit. Foreigners' desire to acquire financial and real assets in the United States creates a demand for U.S. dollars that drives up the value of the U.S. dollar in foreign exchange markets. That is, its exchange rate appreciates, and this discourages U.S. exports by raising their prices in foreign currencies and encourages U.S. imports by making them cheaper in U.S. dollars. That is, the desirability of U.S. assets to foreign investors tips the U.S. trade balance (deeper) into red ink. The conclusion, then, is that foreign investment is not passive in respect to trade balances; it can decisively affect trade balances. This is not a matter of the tail wagging the dog. Rather, foreign investment in its own right is a powerful force that cannot be obscured by focusing narrowly on the balance of trade.

Now that we have gotten our feet wet in the realm of international investment, we ought to look briefly at the **balance of payments**, which is the most comprehensive measure of international transactions and includes two principal accounts. The first part is the **current account**, of which exports and imports (the balance of trade) are components. As table 5.2 shows, the current account also contains unilateral transfers (for example, U.S. government grants to foreign militaries and private U.S. residents' remittances to the folks in the old country) as well as repatriated earnings from foreign investment (profits from foreign-owned enterprises operating in the United States sent out of the country and profits from U.S.-owned foreign enterprises brought into the country). The second part is the

TABLE 5.2	United States Current Account, 2004 (billions of U.S. dollars)				
					Balance
Receipts from Rest of World		1,750.0	Payments to Rest of World		2,455.3	−705.3
Exports of Goods and Services		1,275.2	Imports of Goods and Services		1,992.0	−716.8
Goods	894.6		Goods	1,490.8		−596.2
Services	380.6		Services	290.8		89.8
Income Receipts from U.S. Investments Abroad		471.7	Income Payments from Foreign Investments in the U.S.		454.1	17.6
			Transfer Payments (net)		86.1	−86.1
			Private (net)		48.4	−48.4
			Government (net)		37.7	−37.7

Source: Survey of Current Business (July 2005), p. D-33.

capital account, which records the financial transactions involved in both foreign portfolio investment and foreign direct investment.

In order to calculate a nation's balance of payments, all you have to do is look at the changes in its Central Bank's reserves of foreign currency plus the short-term financial flows that simply compensate for imbalances in other accounts. But this raises a serious problem: How does one distinguish between compensatory short-term portfolio investment and, for example, foreigners' deposits in New York banks to avoid taxes in the foreigners' home country? This has always been a problem, and as the

size of short-term foreign portfolio investments has increased exponentially over the past two or three decades (for instance, speculative "hot money" and money laundering), it has become even more difficult. As a result, the current account along with the direction of exchange rate changes are the best measures of a nation's financial standing in the international economy.

International financial movements introduce two more complications that need to be mentioned here. The first is that foreign investment may to some extent reduce the destabilizing nature of flexible exchange rates. As described earlier, if Country A is growing rapidly and experiencing inflation, it is likely that its imports are outrunning exports and will force changes in Country A's exchange rate in the wrong direction (depreciation), wrong because it exacerbates the already inflationary tendencies in Country A. But if foreign investors are attracted to the opportunities in a vigorous economy and to what are probably rising interest rates, inflows of foreign investment may offset some of the effects that the balance-of-trade imbalance has on depressing the exchange rate.

The effect of foreign investment on the cheap labor argument, however, is probably more important. In our two-country, two-product example, I showed that cheap labor is not an important determinant of comparative advantage. But what if we open the example to allow Japanese DVD player producers to relocate some labor-intensive stages of DVD player production (e.g., assembly and packaging) to South Korea, where labor was cheaper (relative to productivity)? It might be argued that the effect of the foreign investment in Korea as well as Korean exports of assembled and packaged DVD players would force an appreciation of the Korean currency (the won) that would neutralize labor cost differences. But once we include foreign investment in the picture, the picture loses its clarity. Korean direct investments in Indonesia and Vietnam (even cheaper labor) and portfolio investments in the U.S. stock market could offset these forces. I return to this issue at the end of

the next chapter, but the point here is to illustrate that once international financial flows are incorporated into our thinking, things get more complicated and what had appeared clear and solid becomes murky and contingent. Conclusions predicated on simpler models often have to be qualified.

Government Policy and the International Economy: Tariffs, Quotas, and Exchange Rates

The comparative advantage argument about the mutual benefits of free international trade has the corollary that government intervention in international market relationships is generally not a good idea.[3] Nevertheless, governments have continually intervened in international economic transactions in order to shield their economies from international competition, an effort called **protectionism**. The extreme point is a completely self-sufficient, hermetically sealed economy with no foreign trade and investment—a condition of **autarky**.

Government protectionist policies usually include tariffs and quotas on imported goods. A **tariff** is simply a tax on selected imported goods, while a **quota** imposes a quantitative limit on the import of particular products. If a tariff on a particular product is so high that it effectively precludes imports of that product, then it acts like an import prohibition, or a zero-level quota. As noted in my previous discussion of taxes, there is a definite trade-off between using a tariff for revenue purposes and using it to discourage imports of a particular good or service. As an illustration of this process's importance, up until World War I, tariffs routinely accounted for 40–50 percent of the U.S. federal government's revenue.

In any case, the effects of tariffs and quotas are similar in that they both raise the domestic price of the imported good, thus subsidizing domestic producers of import substitutes at the expense of domestic consumers who pay extra for the product.[4] Foreign producers are also disadvantaged, but usually they do not vote in the country in question.

Economists tend to be derisive about most of the reasons advanced to protect the domestic economy from international competition. The logic of comparative advantage that I described above seems to be all that is needed to dispose of claims that protection is necessary to increase or maintain domestic employment and to protect ourselves from cheap foreign labor and/or unfair competition. I revisit the apparent firmness of these conclusions later, but even within the limits of a strict comparative advantage model, there are a couple of arguments for government intervention that economists do not dismiss quite as readily, although most remain pretty skeptical.

The first is the belief that certain kinds of productive capacity should be preserved within the nation for reasons of national security. This is straightforward (as a conception even if not in practice), but the second—the infant industry argument (described below)—is more complex. First of all, comparative advantage theory is static. That is, the comparative advantage argument assumes that a nation's productive capacity is fixed. The analysis, therefore, is conducted entirely in terms of how an existing set of productive resources might be allocated more efficiently to achieve a one-time gain. In order to overcome this limitation, the theory has been supplemented by some ideas about dynamic relationships between international trade and economic growth. Increased competition galvanizes local producers, forces them to innovate, and makes foreign technologies more accessible. This last is possible through being more open for foreign investment as well as by trading products with "low growth potential" (e.g., bananas) for products with "high growth potential" (e.g., robotic-controlled assembly lines). In addition, greater specialization from international trade may enable local producers to capture increasing economies of scale.

These add-ons improve the theory, but they do not adequately address the question about how a nation might establish an entirely new line of production that initially entails high costs and thus needs protection from foreign competition. And if carefully chosen, the new line of

"Your Majesty, my voyage will not only forge a new route to the spices of the East but also create over three thousand new jobs."

production could become internationally competitive and a new source of comparative advantage. That is, the **infant industry argument** suggests how a national government might change production and trade patterns so that over time a nation might shift the entire structure of its comparative advantage from, say, sugar into machine tools, and generate higher rates of labor productivity growth over time. This was the argument of Alexander Hamilton in late eighteenth-century United States, Friedrich List in early nineteenth-century Germany, and African, Asian, and Latin American governments in the three decades after World War II, when protection was part of a general industrialization policy known as **import-substitution industrialization**.

As you might guess by now, economists are chronically doubtful about the claims of both national security and infant industry arguments, suspecting that they are either entirely fictitious or, at best, highly inflated by those who stand to benefit directly. But for better or worse, economists seldom run governments, and protective measures happen, whether due to

real economic conditions or to the mechanism described in the previous chapter as public choice theory: concentrated benefits (to a limited number of producers) and widely dispersed costs (higher prices for all domestic consumers of the protected product) create a political situation in which some protective measures can yield very high political returns for politicians irrespective of the logic of economic theory.

So let us say that in a nation that wishes to duck out of globalization (or at least mitigate its effects), the government ignores economists' recommendations and decides to institute some protectionist measures. Even so, the economists should not just go away and pout, because they still have something to offer. For instance, tariffs are probably better than quotas. Quotas, like tariffs, raise domestic prices for particular articles and thus increase the returns of those producing those articles domestically at the expense of purchasers. But in the case of quotas, there is another set of beneficiaries: those who receive a government license to import some portion of that quota. Government officials' ability to choose who receives the import licenses often leads to corruption of one kind or another, and even if licenses are distributed by an honest auction, the perception of favoritism is unavoidable. Tariffs do not include the politically fraught need to allocate import licenses, and in addition, tariffs yield more public revenues than do quotas. Finally, tariffs are superior to quotas because they still require price competition among foreign sellers of a tariffed item. When a product is subject to a quota, there is little incentive for foreign sellers to try to reduce their selling prices, because administrative decisions by government authorities determine the volume and suppliers of those products.

The problem with letting the economists back into the conversation, however, is that they do not let go of the general point that while tariffs may be superior to (or less inferior than) quotas, interference with the free market is probably a mistake. Moreover, if you are going to interfere with the market to stimulate some sort of domestic production, whether justified by claims about national security, an infant industry, or campaign contributions, economists generally argue that the best mechanism would be a direct government subsidy to the firm or firms in question. Then the size of the subsidy and who is getting it are perfectly obvious, and the general tax system rather than the purchasers of targeted products would finance the subsidy. This greater transparency makes it easy to compare the policy's costs with the value of the policy's goals. The disadvantage, of course, is that subsidies require government expenditures and therefore are politically more difficult.

Free Trade Determining Public Policy

In the final part of this chapter, let's turn the analysis around. Instead of looking at the effect of government policies on international trade and investment, what might be the effect of international trade and investment on some areas of government domestic policy? There is a strong suspicion that free international trade is an obstacle to a government's pursuing a range of domestic social policies. That is, under conditions of significant international competition, how can a nation sustain a welfare safety net, universal health insurance, provisions for worker safety, and environmental safeguards? Such policies do raise the costs of doing business for domestic firms, either through direct cost increases (e.g., scrubbers on smokestacks and safety equipment) or by increased taxes for health, pension, and welfare benefits. In such circumstances, negatively affected firms forcefully advance the argument that the extra costs imposed by these policies allow firms in countries without the same extent of social policies to undersell them in the international and maybe even domestic marketplace.

The logic of comparative advantage does have something to say about this issue. If the costs from social policies are imposed *comprehensively*, across the board, they increase all domestic firms' costs fairly evenly. A uniform increase of production costs does not change a nation's pattern of comparative advantage. The domestic costs of production are not what make the differences in comparative advantage; what makes the difference are the relative prices within a nation rather than "absolute" prices between or among nations. Nevertheless, the policy program still does entail some cost in regard to international trade, because the comprehensive social policies may mean some decline in its terms of trade—the ratio of export prices to import prices. That is, looking back at the earlier numerical example, it may mean that if the United States were to implement a wide range of social policies, the resulting depreciation of its exchange rate would require it to export more grain to pay for the DVD players that it imports.

If the cost of social policies bears more heavily on some domestic producers than on others, then the configuration of comparative costs may indeed be affected and international competitiveness impaired in certain branches of production. In general, however, there is nothing in the comparative cost argument that contains the necessity of a nation's participating in a "race to the bottom" in which governments successively unload social and environmental protections and put downward pressure on wages in order to compete in international markets.

Once out of the comforting confines of a narrowly construed comparative advantage, there are other considerations. What are the implications of capital mobility (not just trade in products), the ability of individual firms (not "countries") to pursue profit maximizing strategies across borders, and in the process, move labor-intensive production *stages* (not entire product lines) to nations without social policies? This may very well establish the competitive mechanisms capable of setting off a race to the bottom even though the logic of comparative advantage, limited to international trade in goods and services, does not.

Notes

1. Chapter 2 describes the conditions for market failure that might prevent prices from reflecting these so-called real relationships.

2. Neither foreign portfolio nor direct investment is necessarily "investment" as defined in chapter 3. The acquisition of financial instruments certainly is not, and even in regard to foreign direct investment, it is called investment even

when the transaction is simply a transfer of an already-existing real asset (e.g., a ten-year-old office building). This inconsistency in national income and product account definitions may simply be to assure everyone that government accountants are not pathologically obsessive in their drive for consistency.

3. Economists' consensus about the benefits of unrestricted free trade and investment has an odd limit: despite fearless advocacy of reducing barriers to the international movement of products and finance, they are strangely silent about the increased efficiency to be achieved by unrestricted labor migration. Economists apparently respect prevailing political sensibilities in their silence on the international movement of people.

4. Multiple exchange rates, frequently employed by Latin American nations in the three decades after World War II, are another device with similar results. This comprehensive form of controlling international trade and exchange required a government monopoly on holdings of foreign currencies, which they sold to domestic buyers at various prices (exchange rates), depending on whether the buyer's use was considered to be of high or low priority.

6

The International Economy: The Rise and Fall of Bretton Woods

The industrial, financial, and naval power of Britain was essential for the working of the gold standard, but by the late nineteenth and early twentieth centuries, other countries, especially Germany and the United States, increasingly challenged Britain's dominance. World War I severely crippled Britain, and political opposition in the U.S. Congress prevented the United States from assuming the responsibilities, risks, and benefits that would have accompanied its becoming the new international financial center.[1] When the leading industrial nations tried to resurrect the gold standard in the 1920s, despite unpropitious conditions, the result was unstable and unsuccessful.

The Great Depression of the 1930s swept aside all attempts to reestablish the international economy along previous lines. The crash of the U.S. stock market in late 1929 and subsequent worldwide capitalist depression caused a precipitous contraction of the international economy. Imports of the largest seventy-five trading nations entered a downward spiral so steep that by the first quarter of 1933, the value of their total imports was little more than one-third of what it had been in early 1929. National declines in income and consumption account for much of the extended contraction of international economic activity, but "beggar thy neighbor" policies pursued by individual nations exacerbated the downward spiral. Governments utilized tariffs and quotas, export subsidies, capital controls (restrictions on international financial movements), and competitive devaluations in mutually defeating efforts to stimulate domestic economic recovery at the expense of trading partners.

Although New Deal policies mitigated some of the worst effects of the Depression in the United States, it was World War II that made the greatest contribution to pulling the capitalist world out of the Depression. At the same time, the war also destroyed a large portion of the productive and transport infrastructure in all of the major industrialized nations except the United States. The United States was not the site of battles, and the U.S. economy expanded its productive capabilities under tight wartime governmental controls and regulations that we might call War Capitalism. The resulting economic dominance, especially in manufacturing, together with a new political will to assert that dominance, added up to the U.S. ability to call the shots in the immediate post–World War II world.

As an Allied victory in World War II became imminent, the Allies began to make concrete plans to reconstruct an international financial framework robust enough to support a vigorous postwar expansion of international trade and investment. The experiences of the 1920s and 1930s demonstrated the futility of exhuming the nineteenth-century gold standard, and in any case, the mechanism by which the gold standard maintained some sort of equivalence between exports and imports among trading nations had become riskier. The 1930s demonstrated that in advanced industrial nations, deflation was not just a neutral reduction in price levels; it also meant a contraction of output, a rise in unemployment, and the creation of political difficulties. Inflation also had significant economic and political costs. Flexible exchange rate systems did not have these problems, but they sounded too much like the competitive devaluations and exchange rate volatility that had destabilized the international economy during the 1930s.

The design of the postwar international financial system reflected political and economic elites' general loss of confidence in free market adjustment mechanisms and signaled a new willingness to rely on discretionary policies by public authorities. That is, and as noted in chapter 3, the experiences of the New Deal and War Capitalism seemed to demonstrate that active government policies of regulation and demand management could stabilize capitalist economies and that such deliberate intervention was necessary.

The Dollar Exchange Standard, 1944–1971

Officials in the U.S. Treasury Department were the principal architects of the new international framework, which was ratified by the 1944 international conference convened at **Bretton Woods**, New Hampshire. The U.S. dollar became the new **key currency** (essentially an international legal tender); it was made convertible to gold at $35 an ounce, and exchange rates were to be fixed and defended by their governments. In this, the new framework was less than a bold move; it essentially substituted the United States and the dollar for a greatly weakened Great Britain and the British pound. The principal Bretton Woods innovations were to break the direct link between gold and national currencies and create two new international financial institutions—the International Monetary Fund (IMF) and the International Bank for Reconstruction and Development (subsequently known as the World Bank). These two new institutions were charged with monitoring and helping to stabilize the international trade and payments system.

A major problem with the new managed system, however, was that the signatory governments were unwilling to cede significant power to supranational agencies, and they narrowly circumscribed the operational scope of the IMF's and World Bank's regulatory authority. In addition, these anxieties about national sovereignty led to the quick demise of the International Trade Organization (ITO), which Bretton Woods had established to reduce trade barriers. The ITO was replaced in 1947 by the General Agreement on Tariffs and Trade (GATT), a forum to negotiate multilateral reductions in tariffs, quotas, and other restrictions on international trade in manufactured goods.

The Bretton Woods framework paid lip service to the function of the free market and genuinely tried to protect national sovereignty and the role of government policies. Nevertheless, it still authorized the IMF and the World Bank to take steps to rectify problems stemming from imbalances in member nations' balances of international payments. The goal of the new institutional framework was stability. The delegates at Bretton Woods feared that unrestrained devaluations of exchange rates and restrictions on international commerce would tempt competitive retaliations by other nations, and that such anarchy could lead to an international economic contraction reminiscent of the 1930s. Therefore, measures that directly attacked an individual nation's payments deficits, such as exchange rate devaluations, were to be used only as a last resort and then through orderly, managed, and approved procedures.

In this, however, the definition of the problem had changed. Both the gold standard and flexible exchange rate systems force adjustments on both deficit and surplus nations as constituent parts of destabilizing payments imbalances. Although it is obvious that there cannot be balance-of-payments deficits without equal balance-of-payments surpluses in the world, the Bretton Woods system singled out deficits as the problem. Unlike the gold standard or the flexible exchange rates, therefore, it placed the burden of adjustment entirely on deficit nations.

The responsibility of both the IMF and the World Bank, therefore, was to work with nations experiencing balance-of-payments deficits, and although the functions of the IMF and World Bank became blurred in the 1980s and 1990s, there was initially a definite division of labor between them. The IMF's primary responsibility was to deal with balance-of-payments problems considered to be of a short-term, cyclical nature. It did this by allowing a deficit nation to withdraw in hard currency (for example, U.S. dollars) the equivalent of its IMF "quota" (a country's assessment paid into the IMF, almost a deposit). And a nation could even borrow beyond its quota in order to defend its exchange rate and weather a payments deficit without taking actions considered inimical to the international economic structure. Borrowing beyond one's quota, however, often required the borrowing government to agree to certain conditions—the IMF's "**conditionality**."

Similar to the medicine of the gold standard, the IMF's standard prescriptions to reduce a balance-of-trade deficit have consistently been deflationary domestic policies. The specific target has been reductions in government expenditures, seen as the most effective means to reduce domestic incomes, wages, and inflation in deficit nations. This was thought to lower the offending nations' domestic demand for imports and the prices of their exports, making them more competitive in international markets. In addition, the IMF strongly pressured nations to abolish government regulations and controls over domestic and international exchanges, seen by the IMF as impeding the operation of efficient free markets.

There are, however, problems with the IMF one-size-fits-all policy formula. IMF prescriptions were (and are) aimed narrowly at imports and exports (the balance of trade) and tended to ignore international flows of investment (the capital account), which could offset whatever positive changes might occur in the balance of trade. Forcing a deficit nation into a recession discourages new international investment, and abolishing restrictions on capital movements enables foreigners to divest funds and local residents to engage in **capital flight** (sending liquid assets abroad to avoid local risks), all of which pull funds out of the weak economy and push the capital account into deficit. The effects of deflation and deregulation could exacerbate balance-of-payments deficits even if the balance of trade turned positive.

The World Bank, in contrast to the IMF, made long-term loans to countries where chronic balance-of-payments deficits were seen to be due to the very structure of the deficit nation's economy. The purpose of these loans was not to tide the nation over a temporary shortfall of international receipts. The World Bank was to help nations change the domestic composition of their production, create new patterns of comparative advantage, become more competitive internationally, and thus bring their international payments into balance.

Since the Soviet Union ultimately chose to join neither the IMF nor the World Bank, the United States and its allies have had little trouble dominating both institutions, where voting power is proportional to the quota each nation paid into the institutions. The decisive influence by the United States in the IMF and World Bank, then, was different from its position in the United Nations, where the Soviet Union had veto power in the Security Council. As a consequence, the U.S. government has preferred to work through the IMF and World Bank, ensuring the Bretton Woods institutions' place as the premier international economic institutions.

But in the decade after World War II, the U.S.-sponsored Marshall Plan eclipsed the World Bank and the IMF in financing the reconstruction of Western Europe. The Marshall Plan was a genuine foreign aid program, and through it, the United States pumped over $13 billion into the European economies between 1948 and 1952, along with associated programs for Japan. This reconstruction program was augmented by such institution-building efforts as the North Atlantic Treaty Organization (NATO) and what became the European Economic Community (EEC, and eventually the European Union [EU]). All together, this first large-scale venture in foreign aid was extremely successful in rebuilding the war-ravaged economies and in inoculating these regions against anti-capitalist movements in general and Soviet influence in particular.

Despite these successes, rapid and disquieting changes in the wider world in the late 1940s and early 1950s fueled U.S. policymakers' fears about a world out of control. These years witnessed the convulsions of independence and partition of India and Pakistan (1947); the Berlin blockade (1948); the creation of Israel in Palestine (1948); the Communist revolution in China (1949); the Soviet's detonation of an atom bomb (1949); bitter anti-colonial struggles in Greece, Malaya (now Malaysia), Indonesia, Vietnam, and Algeria; the Korean War (1950–1953); and growing resistance to colonial rule throughout the rest of Africa, Asia, and the Caribbean. Both the United States and the Soviet Union began to pay more attention to Africa, Asia, and Latin America, and especially with the triumph of the Chinese revolution, the Cold War broadened to a truly global scale.

The Cold War and armaments expenditures enabled the U.S. federal government to engage, willy-nilly, is what was essentially a Keynesian agenda of large-scale expenditures that stimulated production and employment in the United States. Cold War weapons programs were politically palatable forms of U.S. government expenditures, because they did not compete with any significant interest groups, and anti-communism bred a fear of "internal subversion" that effectively prevented government programs from going too far in redistributing income or restricting the prerogatives of business. Moreover, foreign military expenditures ensured the flow of key-currency U.S. dollars into the world economy beyond the expiration of the Marshall Plan.

Complementing the explicitly military aspects of the Cold War, the U.S. government launched programs to encourage economic development in Africa, Asia, and Latin America. President Harry Truman's Point Four doctrine, enunciated in 1949, formally announced the intention of the U.S. government to promote poor nations' economic growth and to alleviate worldwide poverty and misery—conditions that were "breeding grounds for communism." Foreign aid, sponsored research, and expert advice underwrote an elaborate and extensively interlocked development establishment of U.S. government agencies, universities, and foundations, international institutions, and some foreign agencies. The principal intellectual paradigms that informed North American thought about economic development framed the issues in terms of "poor nations" and "rich nations" rather than of poor peoples and rich peoples, thus avoiding uncomfortable questions about class disparities at home and abroad.

A NOTE ON ELUSIVE TERMS

"Third World" was a term adopted at the 1954 Bandung conference of unaligned Asian and African nations. Many of these nations had recently become independent of European colonial empires or were struggling to do so, and they rejected the tutelage of either the industrialized capitalist First World or the communist Second World. The Third World category always included an extremely heterogeneous bunch of places, but the differences among the Third World nations increased rapidly by the 1970s and 1980s. The oil-rich nations of the Middle East and the "Newly Industrialized Countries" (NICs, such as South Korea, Taiwan, Brazil, Mexico) experienced substantial material progress and others (e.g., sub-Saharan Africa) became even poorer. Moreover, the dissolution of the Soviet Union in the early 1990s has meant that an identifiable Second World has been replaced by so-called Economies in Transition (to market capitalism). These problems with the Third World designation have led some observers to favor the use of "South" versus "North," a designation with its own difficulties (e.g., Australia, New Zealand, South Africa?). I recognize the problems of any shorthand term, but convenience demands something, and I have chosen the bland Less Developed Countries (LDCs). I use a variety of terms for the industrialized, prosperous nations, terms such as metropolitan countries, rich countries, and whatever.

The World Bank and its spin-off associated agencies—the International Finance Corporation (1956) and the International Development Association (1960)—increasingly became incorporated into the development project. During the 1950s and 1960s, its functions were most notable in funding large-scale transportation, irrigation, and hydroelectric projects, similar to those being realized at the same time in the western United States by the U.S. Army Corps of Engineers and the U.S. Bureau of Reclamation. The World Bank's approach did evolve, however, and by the 1970s, it was beginning to fund health, education, and other projects that targeted the needs of the poorest. The evolution of World Bank thinking is not surprising when one considers the scale and complexity of the goals, but it has made the World Bank vulnerable to charges of intellectual faddism. This is in contrast to the IMF, which has consistently stuck to its version of free market analysis and maintained a posture generally seen to be anti-development in its consequence.

During these decades, shifts in the directions of U.S. foreign direct investment in the Less Developed Countries (LDCs) introduced a new actor—the **transnational corporation (TNC)**—to the international economic landscape. These TNCs reinforced the development project with new economic interests.

Transnational Corporations

Technically there have been TNCs at least since the mercantile groups of sixteenth-century Europe, and probably earlier. Nevertheless, the term—transnational corporation—came into common use after World War II and referred principally to manufacturing firms whose direct investments in a foreign nation produced consumer goods for the domestic market of that foreign nation. For example, General Motors made Chevrolets in Brazil to sell to Brazilians. The post–World War II TNCs were not looking for resource-based export possibilities nor were they primarily seeking cheap labor. These were principally U.S. oligopolies looking for the expansion of actual and potential markets for modern consumer goods by establishing production facilities in those markets.

The post–World War II uncertainties around decolonization in Africa, South Asia, and Southeast Asia made Europe, Latin America, and other politically stable and relatively prosperous sites attractive. Moreover, tariffs, quotas, and exchange controls in Latin America and the EEC obstructed exporting to those markets from the outside and increased incentives for TNC direct investment. The fast-growing East Asian economies were also desirable locations, but their closely regulated domestic markets, especially in Japan and Korea, restricted TNCs' freedom of action.

TNCs grew rapidly during the 1950s and 1960s, and in the mid-1970s, over half of world TNC investment was from the United States, although the proportion was beginning to decline. By 1971, foreign production of U.S. TNCs was almost four times the value of U.S. exports, and between 1957 and 1974, the proportion of total U.S. corporate profits from overseas operations rose from 8.6 to 26.9 percent. TNCs were almost exclusively large, capital-intensive firms, and of the nine largest manufacturing firms in the United States for which data are available, profits derived from foreign operations averaged well over 50 percent of total profits.[2]

Large-scale TNC investment in manufacturing between the 1950s and the mid-1970s shifted the composition of U.S. foreign direct foreign investment away from the older form of producing resource-based commodities (e.g., copper in Chile, bananas in Honduras, petroleum in Venezuela) for export to the metropolitan nations. This altered foreign firms' stakes in the local economies, and the interests of the post–World War II TNCs therefore contrasted sharply with such U.S. firms as Anaconda Copper, United Fruit, and Standard Oil. These extractive, export-oriented corporations have extremely narrow interests in the host nations, where vigorous domestic economic growth would have caused unwanted complications for the extractive corporations and raised the cost of doing business. In sharp contrast, foreign investors like General Electric, Ford Motors, Nestlé, Toyota, General Foods, Bayer, and Procter and Gamble, selling in the markets of their foreign hosts, were interested in expanding local markets for their products. Thus these TNCs were interested in LDC economic development as long as they were involved on favorable terms.

The Transformation of the International Economy

By the end of the 1960s, many observers recognized that the entire international economic system was undergoing a substantial change, but there was no consensus about the sources, implications, and direction of the changes. Three decades later, it is easier to see the two phases that characterized the reorganization of the international financial and trade regime. The first was the meltdown of the Dollar Exchange Standard in the late 1960s and early 1970s, and the second was the emergence of a new pattern of trade and finance. There is a fair amount of agreement on the list of forces that were driving these changes, but their relative importance in still hotly debated. The following interpretation differs from those that give more emphasis to the roles of such factors as technology, TNC initiatives, and deliberate U.S. government manipulations, but my interpretation is sufficiently comprehensive that it does not preclude inquiry into other causes.

The End of the Bretton Woods Payments System

Germany and Japan, jump-started by the Marshall Plan, rapidly became formidable competitors in international markets of manufactured products. South Korea's similar politically directed economy and Taiwan's brand of authoritarian politics also soon became serious market competitors. They were helped in this by millions upon millions in U.S. aid and privileged access to U.S. markets due to their being front-line nations in the Cold War.

The foreign penetration of U.S. manufacturing markets began in the 1960s and once started, increased quickly. U.S. imports of goods and services were less than 4 percent of GDP in the late 1940s, and while the proportion grew slowly through the next two decades, it rose sharply during the 1970s and 1980s, and imports equaled 12.7 percent of GDP by 1989. As a consequence of weakening international markets for U.S. manufactured goods, agricultural exports became a much more important component of total U.S. exports in the late 1970s and 1980s.

International competition in products such as textiles, apparel, and toys had been putting U.S. firms on the defensive for some time. This new international competition, however, was different in that it penetrated markets for heavy industrial products such as automobiles, steel, electronics, machinery, chemicals, and other sectors in which U.S. oligopolies had been preeminent in both domestic and international markets. One obvious response by U.S. firms to foreign competition was to raise barriers against foreign products. The protectionist impulse in the United States is by no means dead, but the U.S. business community is deeply divided on this issue. For examples in the U.S. auto industry, General Motors owns Saab and has acquired large stakes in Isuzu, Suzuki, Fiat, and Subaru. Ford Motor Company owns Jaguar, Volvo, and Land Rover and controls Mazda. Chrysler is now little more than an operating division of DaimlerChrysler, which owns a third of the Mitsubishi auto company. With this kind of interpenetration, the idea of protecting the U.S. market from foreign automobile manufacturers has lost much of its clarity. In addition, as I mentioned in chapter 2, many foreign companies, auto and other, now operate plants in the United States. This further complicates the design of protectionist legislation.

The U.S. government was further handicapped in an effort to protect domestic markets by already low barriers against imported manufactures and by its postwar record of pushing for freer multilateral international trade in manufactures—both legacies of the time when U.S. manufacturers had little international competition. Even so, there is good ol' arm twisting. A series of informal "voluntary" quotas ("Gentlemen's Agreements" and "Orderly Market Agreements") did slow the imports of foreign automobiles and textiles into the United States for a time. And there is political opportunism. President George W. Bush, contrary to his strong rhetorical support for free trade, imposed tariffs on the importation of steel in an effort to reward some constituencies and woo others. But pressures from the EU and the World Trade Organization (WTO) forced him to back down in 2005. If these restrictions had been effective in raising U.S. steel prices, it would have simply stimulated the importation of products, such as automobiles and various kinds of machinery that intensively use steel. Altogether, it is doubtful that trade protection will efficiently shield the U.S. economy against increasingly competitive international markets.

The new international competition continued to undercut the U.S. balance-of-trade position, and more than short run international trade and investment levels were at stake. Integral to its place as the economic and political leader of the capitalist world, the U.S. government spent millions of dollars every year on U.S. troops based mostly in Europe and Asia, on military assistance and foreign aid to friendly governments, on clandestine political operations against others, and on open warfare in Korea and Vietnam. Maintaining these large unilateral outflows required a positive balance of exports over imports, but the substantial surplus in the U.S. balance of merchandise trade practically disappeared in the late 1960s and became negative in the early 1970s.

By the late 1960s, what had been an early post–World War II crisis of an international dollar shortage changed into its opposite—a crisis of an international dollar glut. But the U.S. dollar was the international key currency and could not devalue, and none of the surplus nations was willing to appreciate its currency to rectify the dollar glut. The Bretton Woods agreements, made at a time when the United States was the principal surplus nation, had deliberately avoided formal provisions to pressure them to do so. The consequence was unsustainable balance-of-payments deficits that forced the United States to abrogate unilaterally the Bretton Woods convention. In 1971, the Nixon administration broke the connection between the U.S. dollar and gold and by default established a flexible exchange rate system, although one that still involved significant governmental intervention.

The Beginning of a New International Economy

International financial markets promptly devalued the dollar in 1971 and gave U.S. producers some measure of protection from imports, but the devaluation of the dollar had other, unforeseen results. Since the international price of oil was denominated in U.S. dollars, the devaluation of the dollar reduced the purchasing power of exports by oil-exporting nations. This contributed to galvanizing oil-exporting nations, especially those in the Middle East already angry about U.S. support for Israel, and it led to the 1973 temporary oil export boycott and quadrupling the price of oil. It was an extremely successful exercise of market power, and all individuals, corporations, and nations throughout the world with substantial oil deposits, whether or not members of OPEC, shared in the munificence.

Middle Eastern oil producers received large portions of the new bonanza, and these governments used some of the foreign exchange receipts to improve the standards of living of their citizens as well as to spend heavily on luxury goods, including sophisticated weapon systems. Nevertheless, they did not spend all of it and deposited millions and millions of dollars of the enhanced oil receipts ("petrodollars") in large, approved international banks.

Since banks' profits depend on their being able to lend funds at higher interest rates than they pay depositors, these huge new deposits posed a bit of a problem. The rise in oil prices that created the deposits also contributed to recessions in the industrialized nations, thus limiting the number of attractive lending opportunities and willing borrowers. In Africa, Asia, and especially Latin America, however, there were many willing borrowers. The oil price shock increased the costs of imported oil for energy-dependent nations, and at the same time, the resulting recessions dampened demand for LDC exports.

In a sense, then, it all fit together rather neatly. The rise in petroleum prices that weakened LDCs' export markets and raised their import costs also generated the apparent solution: petrodollars that banks needed to recycle as easy credit. And the commercial banks' initial terms were very easy; peddlers of bank credit pressed everyone in sight, independent of risk or record, to borrow as much as they could be talked into borrowing.

In 1979, OPEC's second major oil price hike was another blow to LDCs. Its effects, however, were soon dwarfed by the anti-inflationary policies of the U.S. administration of President Reagan, who was elected in 1980 as part of the generally conservative electoral tide that swept over industrialized nations' politics in the 1980s. The Reagan administration's anti-inflation policies in the early 1980s, coordinated with the Fed, succeeded in reducing inflation by driving U.S. unemployment rates to the highest levels since the Great Depression. Among other consequences, it further dampened the demand for LDC exports.

Monetary policy was an important weapon in the U.S. anti-inflation arsenal, and interest rates went to double-digit levels. Since interest rates on the bank loans to the LDCs were variable (that is, they rose and fell with current interest rates), the rising interest costs became impossible for a number of debtor governments to meet. So although oil prices began to decline in the early 1980s, the combination of weak export markets and record-breaking interest rates triggered the debt crisis. Mexico in 1982 was the first to declare openly that it could no longer pay even the interest charges on its foreign debt, and all of the Latin American nations (except Colombia) and most of the other heavily indebted LDCs soon followed. The debt crisis had arrived. The resulting credit crunch was eventually transmitted into bursting the speculative bubble within the United States, most dramatically in real estate investments and the crash of savings and loan institutions.

Many of the LDCs' creditors were large international banks, and the possibility of billions of dollars lent to LDCs turning into bad debts was said to threaten the survival of the banks and therefore the stability of the entire international financial system. This was the story that justified interventions by the metropolitan nations' governments, led by the United States, to save the banks from the consequences of their bad judgment. These governments designated the IMF as the chief collection agent for the big banks, and the alliance among big banks, big governments, and big international financial institutions constituted a formidable combination.

The principal and best-coordinated locus of official international financial power is Washington, D.C., headquarters for the IMF, the World Bank, the Inter-American Development Bank, and the U.S. government. These institutions, aptly dubbed the "Washington Consensus," had a clear idea of the reforms that they wished to promote in LDCs by using the leverage of the debt. In their agreements with the debtor nations, the Washington Consensus offered longer debt repayment schedules, some new loans, minor discounting of previous debt, and fixed (non-variable) interest rates in exchange for the governments' commitment to a series of reforms. I have summarized these prescriptions into the following four points with annotations to include some of the Washington Consensus' reasoning.[3]

1. Fiscal Discipline: There should be no government deficits over one percent of Gross National Product. Since taxes are disincentives for entrepreneurs, tax rates for upper bracket incomes should be no more than "moderate" and government deficit reductions should be achieved principally by restricting expenditures rather by than increasing revenues. Military expenditures, however, are "the ultimate prerogative of sovereign governments" and accordingly not targeted for reductions.

2. Deregulation: Government controls and subsidies should not distort the free play of market forces. This tenet explicitly included relaxing controls on interest rates, exchange rates, and foreign trade and invest-

ment. Deregulation also meant doing away with price controls, subsidized public services, and protections for labor unions.

3. Privatization: Since the production of goods and services is more efficient in private hands, governments should sell existing productive enterprises to private owners and refrain from establishing new ones.

4. Property Rights: They need to be secured and extended.

The Washington Consensus' reform package became known commonly as **Structural Adjustment Programs** (or SAPs), and it was very much in line with IMF's brand of free-market policies now called neoliberalism.[4] The prescriptions were also firmly in the IMF's tradition of applying a universal, one-size-fits-all formula for economic problems. The declared purpose of these measures was to produce strongly export-oriented economies that are internationally competitive. The IMF and World Bank touted this goal as the best way to foster long-run economic growth in LDCs. That is, they contended that the free-market mechanism is the most effective means to promote exports and that a strong export orientation is the most effective source of general economic growth.

While the actual relationships among unregulated markets, export promotion, and economic growth are murky at best, it is crystal clear and unambiguous that the policy prescriptions coincide precisely, perhaps uniquely, with what was necessary for LDC debt repayment to the large international banks. Downsizing governments releases resources for debt payments, and LDC governments could pay off the loans to the banks in hard currencies if and only if they were able to run substantial surpluses of exports over imports for extended periods.

By the beginning of the 1990s, the debts had not gone away, but the debt crisis had been tamed into a debt burden that was seen to be a problem of only the LDCs. Recent calls for debt relief might offer some genuine respite for of the world's poorest. But no matter how that debate is resolved, two legacies of the debt crisis and SAPs were that the LDCs had been more tightly integrated into the globalized economy, employers

were in a much stronger position than employees, and LDC governments' ability to act positively to shape their nations' economic futures
had been weakened. The point here is that these outcomes were carefully
engineered and not some putative "natural" result of globalizing market
relations.

The New International Economy

In the early 1980s, U.S. anti-inflation policy inadvertently stimulated the
continuing entry of imported goods and services and discouraged exports.
The Reagan administration's record peacetime federal government
deficit, together with its anti-inflation policy of double-digit interest rates,
encouraged huge foreign purchases of U.S. government bonds and other
domestic assets, and the United States became a net foreign debtor by the
mid-1980s. That is, for the first time since the nineteenth century, the
total of foreign investments in the United States was greater than what
U.S. investors owned in foreign countries. This inflow of foreign finance
increased the exchange rate of the U.S. dollar, lowered the dollar price of
imports in the United States, raised the foreign currency prices of U.S.
exports abroad, and thereby enhanced imports' competitiveness in U.S.
product markets and handicapped U.S. exports in foreign markets. This
is an example of the way that investment can affect export and import
balances, described in general terms in the previous chapter.

Imports, however, were not the only source of new foreign competition. As I described in chapter 2, the movement of foreign firms into the
United States ("transplants") substantially changed the competitive environment in major U.S. markets for manufactures. In response, U.S. firms
responded by cautiously adopting some shop floor reorganizations,
robotic production technologies, and such devices as "just-in-time" inventory control during the 1970s and 1980s. At the same time, the deregulation of financial dealings encouraged them to indulge in successive waves
of mergers and speculation—"paper entrepreneurialism"—which

included real estate ventures, LDC debt, and acquisitions financed by junk bonds.

U.S. corporations' efforts to reduce labor costs were one important response to heightened international competition. This included employers' forcing wage cuts and other concessions from employees, but firms went beyond reducing current workers' wages and increasingly sought labor with lower wages and benefits and without expensive labor protections or environmental restrictions. This is the time that large corporations began to increase the practice of peeling off heretofore in-house functions to independent contracting firms. This contracted outwork ranged from manufacturing components to keeping their accounts, managing financial investments, cleaning the buildings, and transporting their goods, thus paring their own workforces and shifting production to other firms frequently without unions and with lower labor costs.

Another tactic was to move operations within the United States, from highly unionized areas in the rustbelt (Great Lakes and New England) to the sunbelt (the U.S. South and Southwest) with little union strength. The most dramatic move, however, was to relocate labor-intensive phases of production abroad, first to Mexico but then to the Caribbean, other parts of Latin America, and especially to Southeast Asia. The very high proportion of young women workers has been a consistent aspect of this geographical dispersion of assembly production.

The initial, and by now almost classic, pattern was for a firm to export U.S.-made components to a foreign site for assembly and packaging—the most labor-intensive stages of the production process—and then import the assembled product back into the United States. Under special provisions of the customs code, the U.S.-made components are not subject to duty, and only the value added to them by foreign assembling is subject to duty. Since these are intra-firm transfers with prices set by the firms themselves (**transfer prices**), the value added is easily minimized for tax purposes, and up to a full third of international merchandise trade are intra-firm transfers between branches of the same company. Although U.S. businesses were not the principal innovators of the new international organization of production, the weight of the U.S. economy in the world was such that when they did become deeply involved in offshore production, what had been sporadic forays became the basis of a new international system of production.

Apparel and electronics products dominated foreign manufacture and assembly production in the 1970s, but continuing innovations in transportation, communication, and production technology increased the financial attractiveness of assembling a wider range of goods abroad. As the system became better tuned, flexible production processes enabled serving "niche" markets for more specialized goods with short product life cycles. The ability to reconfigure computer-controlled production processes cheaply and rapidly is the supply side of the story; the demand side reflected rising consumer prosperity in the metropolitan nations and an increasing concentration of income, which created larger markets for goods different from the standardized, mass-produced products of large-scale assembly lines. In addition, these affluent consumers were willing to pay for imported off-season fresh fruits, vegetables, and cut flowers.

The changes in production processes and markets encouraged greater use of foreign-origin components and promoted a variety of short-term outsourcing arrangements. While U.S. firms still own some foreign production sites, there is a considerable variation in ownership. Often there is no more than a contractual relationship with a local national or with an entrepreneur from elsewhere (e.g., a Taiwanese firm in Haiti). Benetton, Schwinn, the Gap, and Nike are only four well-known brand names of U.S. firms that do not own any production facilities, and they design and market goods produced entirely by foreign contractors. Wal-Mart and KMart, giant discount retailers, are increasingly contracting directly with foreign producers in a similar manner.

The same innovations in information and control technologies that have contributed to the geographical dispersion of production have at the same time heightened the cost advantages of large-scale operations in financing, communications, and marketing (including product design and brand name identification). And marketing, brand names, and logos are paramount. Just to keep a sense of proportion about the relative importance of production and marketing, when Nike reportedly paid $20 million to Michael Jordan to promote Nike, it was an amount greater than the annual wage bill of the Indonesian women making the shoes.

This, then, is an outline of the new international system of production, in which the division of labor is more and more defined by stages or components of production rather than by entire classes of products (for example, agricultural or manufacturing). In addition, the pattern is not a matter of skilled vs. unskilled labor. Off shore production continues to climb the skill ladder in such fields as software engineering, biotechnology, architectural design, and pharmaeutical testing. What began as the foreign assembly of a few products for U.S. markets became generalized into a complex web of geographically dispersed production in which worldwide pools of labor are systematically integrated into manufacturing primarily for the markets of the United States and other metropolitan nations. Although most international trade and investment continues to circulate among the most prosperous nations, the increased reach and fluidity of product and capital movements as well as the incorporation of LDCs into manufacturing represent a new international order with a novel dynamic.

As I have already noted, rise of the international order has been accompanied by a strong resurgence of faith in the free market. The other side of the coin is pervasive skepticism about collective (governmental) efforts to regulate the social order and ameliorate the effects of negative market outcomes. Within the United States, this new sensibility was enhanced politically by domestic U.S. corporations insisting that their international competitiveness was handicapped by worker safety rules, environmental regulations, and taxes needed to fund welfare and other social programs. On the international scene, the strong revival of enthusiasm for the free market is illustrated by three important recent changes.

The first involved a massive dismantling of institutions. From the 1920s to the 1970s, the command economy of the Soviet Union ruthlessly

"As I understand it, this is part of the transition to a free-market economy."

transformed a rural, backward, and war-torn society into an industrial nation with substantial education, health, and social welfare provisions and world-class cultural, scientific, and military establishments. And it did this within two generations, which included the terrible ravages of two world wars, an achievement that should be compared to the progress experienced in India or Brazil over the same time rather than with standards of life in already-industrialized economies. By the 1970s, however, it was clear that the Soviet command economy and authoritarian politics were ill suited for taking the next step: operating the economy along the lines of mass production and mass consumption. It is crucial to reiterate, however, that the exhaustion of the Soviet model was due to the command economy's unprecedented *success* in having created an industrial base, transportation and communication networks, monetized market economies, and workforces that to a substantial degree were literate, urban, healthy, and disciplined to modern work.

When the Soviet system became unglued between 1989 and 1991, the Russians were suddenly vulnerable to the ministrations of the IMF and the Clinton administration, which oversaw the dissolution of the Soviet institutions. The most charitable view of the pressures exerted on the prostrate Russian regime is that the foreign advisers saw an open, market economy as natural and that all that it would take to create a viable market system was the removal of all governmental interference. That is, the transformation was seen to be principally a negative process. The U.S. government and the IMF therefore ignored the social and cultural conditions necessary for the proper functioning of a modern market economy and disregarded the need to create regulatory institutions such as a strong judicial system, financial regulatory bodies like the U.S. Federal Reserve System and the Securities and Exchange Commission, and a fiscal structure capable of collecting taxes and disbursing public expenditures for national priorities.

Instead, the foreign advisers concentrated on privatization—distributing public assets among a new class of private owners. This emphasis was fully agreeable with those in a position to benefit from the fire sale of state-owned assets (often senior Communist Party members), and it was done in a rush through executive fiat in a manner that bypassed fledgling democratic institutions. As a result, the reforms created unstable conditions in finance, production, and marketing, which encourage corruption, speculation, and criminal activities more strongly than they do productive investment.

So what had been achieved at terrible human cost in Soviet industrialization is being squandered. Marshall Goldman, an eminent U.S. expert on Russia, reported that people on Moscow streets were saying, "Everything that the Communists told us about communism was a lie, but everything that they told us about capitalism was true." The massive inequalities, insecurities, loss of public services, and rapid decline in life expectancy in Russia have frightening implications for the world as a whole.[5]

The second illustration of free market enthusiasm, this one in institutional construction, was the creation of the World Trade Organization

(WTO), a new international organization to promote the expansion of free trade. The WTO was established in 1995 out of the Uruguay Round of GATT negotiations, and its purpose is to promote the free movement of goods and services among nations, in good part by policing government policies judged to be illegitimate trade restrictions. This function is quite similar to that of the International Trade Organization, proposed by the Bretton Woods conference more than sixty years ago but rejected by the U.S. Congress as conceding too much national sovereignty to a supranational organization. In the 1990s and first decade of the twenty-first century, however, the U.S. government has been the major supporter of the existence and authority of the WTO. Times do change!

The WTO has gained some notoriety for ruling against several efforts by national governments to restrict imports of goods made under conditions that violate protective standards for workers, the environment, and human rights. There is no question that some of these import restrictions were little more than special economic interests dressed up in the garb of universal human rights or ecological protections. But this is tricky stuff. There may be general agreement that, for example, clothes made by ten-year-olds chained to sewing machines do not have to be given free access to all markets, but any consensus pretty much dissolves beyond that. The next step at drawing the line on products involving severe human and ecological degradation is not clear, and the WTO has strongly preferred ruling against restrictions rather than attempting to draw meaningful lines. On the other hand, the WTO has been *extremely* cautious about confronting U.S.-sponsored embargoes currently against Cuba, North Korea, and Iran, and until 2003, against Libya and Iraq. These policies certainly sound like trade restrictions.

We have already mentioned the third example of free market convictions in the discussion of Structural Adjustment Programs. It is the expressed belief that private competitive markets are the most effective mechanism for improving the material welfare of people in Africa, Asia, and Latin America. The implosion of the Soviet Union and the end of the

Cold War meant that the strategic interests of the developed capitalist nations in LDCs have declined. As a consequence, the U.S. government's earlier foreign aid and tentative support for such social reforms as land and income redistribution in the LDCs have all but evaporated. In addition, new manufacturing TNCs have little immediate interest in LDCs other than as repositories of inexpensive but productive labor along with a reasonable infrastructure (transportation, communications, power, and utilities). To a large extent, the productive labor forces and the infrastructures are results of the previous state-led development efforts that neoliberals now represent as failures.

A striking example of this altered context is the marginalization of Africa, not needed now in Cold War competition and of little interest to TNCs. But Africa is only an extreme case in the general phenomenon. Metropolitan nations' official concern about the people of the poorer countries seems limited to their being sources of disease and of massive immigration to more prosperous regions.

Two Caveats

In all of the worldwide celebration of and movement toward free trade, there exist one major anomaly and one big worry. The anomaly is that along with the increasingly free flow of goods, services, and capital across borders, trading blocs are developing. These blocs, often called **common markets**, are groups of nations that arrange among themselves to give one another special commercial privileges denied to those outside the bloc.[6] For instance, they may have completely free trade within the bloc and a common set of restrictions for all outsiders, a practice that conflicts with general free trade principles. The EU, with twenty-five member nations and expanding into eastern and southern Europe, is the oldest and best integrated of the major trading blocs. They have even launched a common currency—the **euro**—although there is considerable foot dragging about fully adopting the new currency by some members, most notably Great Britain and Denmark.

The North American Free Trade Agreement (NAFTA)—among Canada, Mexico, and the United States—is definitely vigorous although established only in 1994.[7] One sign of its vitality is that discussions are under way to expand it to include all the nations in the Western Hemisphere (except Cuba, of course). The Asia-Pacific Economic Cooperation (APEC) is much less tightly organized than the EU or NAFTA, but it does have the potential of bringing together nineteen national economies. The Mercado Común del Cono Sur (MERCOSUR)—among Argentina, Brazil, Paraguay, and Uruguay (Chile is still holding out for an invitation from NAFTA)—is another notable initiative along these lines. In addition to these, there are two other common markets in Latin America and three in Africa, none as large or as well consolidated as those listed. The implications of such blocs for the movement toward general free trade are uncertain. Some argue that the accelerated freeing of trade within the blocs will hasten the general process of generalizing free trade throughout the world, and others maintain that blocs are political units that have a stake in sustaining and perhaps enhancing trade restrictions for outsiders.

Trading blocs are the anomaly; the big worry is how stable is this new system. In 1994, the very year that NAFTA was founded, the Mexican peso crashed as speculators got rid of billions of dollars' worth of pesos for other currencies. As in such runs, it was a self-fulfilling prophecy: you believe that the peso is going to devalue, so you sell pesos (borrowing them if you own none) in anticipation of the devaluation and thus contribute to forcing that devaluation. The billions of dollars of instant loans that the Clinton administration and the IMF poured into Mexico finally stemmed the peso's free fall, but the demonstrated power of speculative hot money movements, even in the absence of any economic crisis in Mexico, shook international financial markets. Three years later, a similar process occurred in Thailand and Indonesia. The outbreak soon turned into a contagion, adversely affecting most Southeast and East Asian economies, and the result was the Asian crisis of 1997. Recovery has been slow and uneven, and the vulnerability of the system to such panics has forced some serious rethinking about the dangers of an unregulated international economy, or at least an unregulated international financial system.

Some of this rethinking has been directed at the IMF, which has always been the subject of controversy since its founding. In the 1950s and 1960s, most criticism had come from LDC leaders and U.S. liberals who believed that the conditions the IMF demanded of borrowers were anti-development and anti-working people. In addition, the IMF was often accused of being an arm of U.S. foreign policy. For example, the IMF boycotted the Chile of President Salvador Allende but generously supported the brutal regime of General Augusto Pinochet who overthrew the democratically elected Allende. Conversely, the IMF lent Anastasio Somoza $66 million just before he was toppled by the Sandinista revolution but refused to deal with the Sandinista government.

Current criticisms of the IMF are different. Mounting evidence of IMF confusion and inappropriate policy prescriptions in Russia and during the Asian crisis made the IMF a target of serious censure. The IMF lent billions of dollars to Russia in the early 1990s with few safeguards, and lots of it simply disappeared. In 1997 and 1998, the IMF poured billions of dollars into Russia and Indonesia to keep the two currencies from devaluing. The result was merely to postpone the devaluations, allowing wealthy foreigners and locals to get their holdings out of Russian and Indonesian currencies and into hard currencies at a favorable price before the devaluation.

An intriguing aspect of the anti-IMF sentiment is that the most trenchant condemnations of the IMF have come not from long-time liberal and LDC critics but rather from conservative U.S. politicians and economists. (This is rather confusing to someone my age.) The IMF was designed to secure fixed exchange rates, and it has always had trouble dealing with the effects of international investment. In a world of flexible exchange rates and daily international movements of billions and billions of dollars, the IMF may have become an anachronism.

These criticisms are becoming more strident in higher circles of politics and economics, and although they stand in an uneasy relationship with the more populist protests against the WTO and related initiatives, both signal the possibility of some circumspect reforms in the next few years. These reforms presumably will guard the international financial system from the vicissitudes of massive movements of short-term speculative capital disrupting foreign trade and (long-term) investment.

A Final Note on the Place of the United States in the Global Economy

The first step in properly placing the United States in the new international economy is to observe the irony that the very economies whose international competitiveness contributed most to the creation of a new economic order have done quite poorly in the new order when it arrived. Even taking into account the travails of the unification of West Germany and East Germany after the fall of the Berlin Wall, the German economy has been performing very sluggishly. The slowness of the Japanese economy's recovery from extended recession has exposed the extreme weakness of its financial system. In the 1970s and 1980s, academics and pundits touted the need for all to emulate Japanese economic practices, and suddenly the Japanese prime minister had to maintain a straight face while President Clinton advised him on proper economic policy. Economic distress in South Korea in the late 1990s led to its practically being put into receivership by the IMF, which forced Korea to open its economy to TNC investment.

This successful adaptation leads to the second observation. It seems as though every quarter of the last ten to fifteen years we heard the announcement that the United States had again an unprecedented, record-setting balance-of-trade deficit. The recent economic slowdown reduced the deficit a bit, but with the gradual recovery, the deficit is once again breaking records. These deficits are larger than the deficits of the 1960s and 1970s that were not sustainable and that finally led to the destruction of the Bretton Woods system.

In the last few years, any discussion of the U.S. trade deficit includes talk about China. And there is good reason. Although the United States still trades more with Canada than any other nation, our deficit with China is the biggest: we import six times more from China than we export to China. It is important to understand that the magnitude of that deficit is somewhat exaggerated by how such things are counted. For example, let's say that all the components of a computer are produced in South Korea, then they are shipped to China to be assembled, and the new computer is then sold in the United States. This practice is common among Japanese, Korean, and even Taiwanese firms. The problem is that our bean counters (like all customs officials) regard the total value of that computer to be imported from China, even though three quarters of the value was actually produced in South Korea. That is, only one quarter of the value added in the computer should be attributed to China in this example, and current statistical procedures would have inflated China's contribution to our imports by a factor of three. This does not affect the size of the U.S. trade deficit, only its sources.

So while the magnitude of the trade deficit with China may be overblown, it is still very real. Some of this deficit is caused by the Chinese government's deliberate policy of keeping the value of their currency (yuan) at a level below what it would be if it were genuinely to float. This action keeps the price of Chinese exports in foreign currencies lower than they would otherwise be and discourages imports. The Chinese government has been under strong international pressure to relent in this practice, and in the second half of 2005, the Chinese government allowed the yuan to creep up 3.3 percent. While not a stunning change, it sounds likely that more will be forthcoming.

One of the most interesting recent developments is that China is developing a substantial labor shortage. I know "Chinese labor shortage" sounds like an oxymoron, but China has experienced such rapid and sustained growth in export-oriented employment that employers are beginning to run into shortages and having to raise wages and improve working conditions. On the supply side, there are a number of factors constraining the pool of able and willing workers. The Chinese government's efforts to improve the lives of the rural poor in inland and western provinces have had some success and thus dampened young people's eagerness to migrate to factory jobs. And there are fewer 15- to 25-year-olds, due in good part to China's one-child policy that began affecting family sizes a little more than twenty years ago. Finally, more young people than ever are attending college rather than joining a factory work force.

These two pressures—the slowly rising value of the yuan and rising wages—are causing rising production costs and export prices in foreign markets and pulling down profit margins that are already low due to the bargaining power of the big retailers like Target and Wal-Mart that shop the world. Chinese firms are responding to these changes in two principal ways. One is to go to lower-wage areas, and Vietnam is frequently mentioned in this regard. The second is to shift production in the direction of up-market products where profit margins are greater. In apparel, this has meant supplying The Gap and Liz Claiborne rather than Wal-Mart, or shifting from shoes made of synthetic materials to high-quality leather shoes. In addition, it means going more aggressively into new export products like electronics, automobiles, and other sophisticated products that have higher profit margins.

If this trend continues, China will be competing with South Korea and southern Europe more and more instead of Thailand and Indonesia. This process would be replicating the experience of post–World War II Japan and South Korea, which made the transition from exporting cheap apparel, toys, and sporting equipment to exporting a wide range of quality merchandise aimed at prosperous customers. A significant expansion of China's domestic markets would require seismic shifts in the distribution of income and in the provision of social services (e.g., health and education) that is considerably riskier politically than working up the export food chain.

The U.S. balance-of-trade deficit is the quintessential expression of the United States' role in the global economy; that role is as a consumer, or perhaps *the* consumer. No one competes with our ability to consume. As the distribution of income in the United States becomes more unequal, consumer markets become more segmented in a number of ways, including the source of imports. On the one hand, you see an explosion of advertisements in such media the *New York Times Sunday Magazine* for high-end glitz made in France, Germany, Italy, and Japan, and on the other, you see discount stores filled with merchandise made in the world's poorest regions. And across the board, credit card debt is at an all-time high. The market for consumer goods may be segmented, but as a nation, we are ace consumers. Access or the denial of access to U.S. markets continues to be a potent tool of U.S. foreign policy.

Consuming more than one produces is good work if you can get it, but how can we get away with it? Why is there no stern deity to punish us for all this hedonism?[8] In more concrete terms, why have flexible exchange rates not worked to depreciate the value of the U.S. dollar, curtailing our consumption of foreign-produced goods by raising their prices in U.S. dollars? In addition, a currency depreciation lowers the prices of our exports in foreign currencies, and thus puts the squeeze on our consumption of domestically produced goods by giving U.S. producers more incentive to send products abroad rather than selling them at home.

Well, some devaluation has happened. From early 2003 to the end of 2004, the price of the U.S. dollar fell roughly one third in respect to the euro and about 15 percent in respect to the Japanese yen. By the end of 2005, however, the dollar had regained about half of its loss in respect to the euro and all of the loss in respect to the yen. The secret to the entire process is that foreign purchases of U.S. financial and real assets continue to contribute to the strength of the dollar and helps our continuing consumption of both foreign and domestic goods in profusion. When foreigners make money catering to our consumption habit, they turn around and invest their profits in the U.S. economy. This inflow of investment keeps the dollar strong in relation to other currencies and subsidizes our consumption. The U.S. dollar and the U.S. economy are safe and profitable havens for investing. In its starkest form, foreign owners who make profits selling in the U.S. market can plow their profits right back into the United States and keep their assets safe from the workers who make the goods that are so attractive to us. It's rather neat.

The obvious concern is whether it can last. How stable are these arrangements? Probably not all that solid, but as I have noted, there is some chance of new initiatives that would make the system more robust. And there is no likelihood, given the current patterns of international power, that any new arrangements are going to be severely against U.S. interests in consuming.

Getting away from the cold, calculating type of analysis, there is a second question. Not all foreign investment goes into U.S. public and private debt (i.e., loans). Some of it also buys real assets—U.S. firms and real estate. Chrysler Motors, Rockefeller Center, Universal Studios, Ben and Jerry's ice cream, Snapple drinks, Firestone/Bridgestone tire company, Smith & Wesson guns, Stonyfield Farm dairy products, Stop & Shop grocery stores, and a number of landmark hotels and banks are highly visible examples.

Even among those who understand and value how foreigners' purchase of U.S. assets supports their consumption habits, many are anxious about this. If these foreigners become our employers, they are going to do things differently, right? What is it going to be like working for foreigners?

Not to worry. There is a lot of hype about the ways in which the new international order is fostering worldwide cultural homogeneity, a discourse that freely uses expressions like "McDonaldization" or "Disneyfication." David Rothkopf, in a provocative article titled "In Praise of Cultural Imperialism," puts an interesting spin on these claims. He argues that the cultural homogenization is indeed happening; it is a culture based on a tolerance for diversity; it is the triumph of U.S. cultural values; and it is occurring from the top down. In his view, and he was the

director of Kissinger Associates and thereby in a good position to know, the new internationalization is producing a coherent global elite that depends less and less on national governments (and thus on any national citizenry). In the article, he approvingly describes this denationalized elite:

> Business leaders in Buenos Aires, Frankfurt, Hong Kong, Johannesburg, Istanbul, Los Angeles, Mexico City, Moscow, New Delhi, New York, Paris, Rome, Santiago, Seoul, Singapore, Tel Aviv, and Tokyo all read the same newspapers, wear the same suits, drive the same cars, eat the same food, fly the same airlines, stay in the same hotels, and listen to the same music. [This integrated elite also includes] international bureaucrats . . . [who] coordinate policy . . . on global issues such as trade, the environment, health, development, and crisis management.[9]

Now that you have read this book, you are in a position to recognize that the cultural values Rothkopf is touting are less U.S. national values than they are functional elements of a competitive capitalist market. Remember the competitive market axiom from chapter 2: "You give me a good price for quality merchandise/work, and I do not care about your race, gender, religion, sexual orientation, national origin, or whatever." And this is not voluntary goodwill, because in fully competitive market environments, any employer with a strong "taste for discrimination" would be driven out of the market or at best be limited to a narrow niche.

The outcome of competitive capitalism with a worldwide labor surplus is that capital (i.e., employers) is in the saddle, and labor (i.e., workers) is on the defensive. In line with classical liberalism, neoliberals in the United States and abroad represent the market as the realm of freedom and government policy as the realm of coercion. Since free markets mean freedom for capital to operate without considering anything other than private gain, market freedoms are indeed liberating for those whose wealth and exercise of power had been constrained by government policy.

On the other hand, free markets are debilitating for those whose standards of living depended on governments' enforcement of protections and rights. The consequence is increasingly polarized societies. The hold of the neoliberal narrative, however, does appear to be weakening, especially in Latin America and even in the United States.

Notes

1. The U.S. Congress even blocked U.S. membership in the League of Nations, which was U.S. President Woodrow Wilson's vision.

2. The data from this and the following paragraphs are mostly from *Survey of Current Business* (1958) 38(9), (1976) 56(8), and (1994) 74(1) and from *U.S. Commodity Exports and Imports as Related to Output, 1960 & 1959* (Washington, D.C.: U.S. Department of Commerce, Government Printing Office, 1962) and *U.S. Commodity Exports and Imports as Related to Output, 1976 & 1975.* (Washington, D.C.: U.S. Department of Commerce, Government Printing Office, 1980).

3. Williamson, John, "What Washington Means by Policy Reform," in J. Williamson (ed.), *Latin American Adjustment: How Much Has Happened?* (Washington, D.C.: Institute for International Economics, 1990), pp. 7–17, produced a widely accepted ten-point summary of the mid-1980s Washington Consensus prescriptions. I have in turn summarized them into four points. The quotation in the first point is from page 11.

4. The terms are rather confusing. In the 1980s lexicon, "reform" essentially means undoing the regulations and protections called reforms in previous decades. "Structural," as in Structural Adjustment, refers to free-market reforms, while until the 1980s, the term was identified with opposition to free-market policies. Neoliberalism is occasionally called neoconvervatism. What can I say?

5. Cuba has the potential for a similar disaster. If the same institutional "reforms" were wreaked on Cuba, as many prominent in U.S. politics would have it, the Cuban Revolution's unusual degree of income equality and world-class health and education systems would be out the window.

6. These common markets should not be confused with two international organizations often in the news. The Organization for Economic Cooperation and Development (OECD) is comprised of thirty-one of the world's richest nations for the purposes of coordinating policies and fostering mutually beneficial agreements on a range of issues. The Group of Seven (G-7) is a loosely knit club of seven of the largest economic powers with pretty much the same agenda as the OECD. With the admission of Russia in 1997, the G-7 became the G-8. China may be admitted before long.

7. NAFTA formally began on January 1, 1994, which is the same day that the Zapatistas in Chiapas of southern Mexico declared themselves to the world and began the process of "liberating" parts of Chiapas. The timing was not accidental.

8. Environmental destruction may be the comeuppance, but as the saying goes, what have the future generations ever done for us?

9. David Rothkopf, "In Praise of Cultural Imperialism?" *Foreign Policy* 107 (1007): 44–45.

Appendix A

Input-Output Economics

able A.1 is an input-output table for the United States in 1997. Although now and then, you see references to "input-output theory," it really is simply a particular array of economic data. In order to get a grip on what the data mean, look down the left column at "Manufactured Products" in the fourth row. The 51.5 in the first column of that row means that in 1997, manufacturing firms sold $51.5 billion of manufactured goods to firms in agriculture, forestry, and fishing. The agriculture, forestry, and fishing firms used these goods as inputs in their own production, and chemical fertilizers and herbicides are reasonable examples. The $15.1 billion in the next column is the value of the goods that firms in the manufacturing sector sold to mining firms and includes dynamite and lightbulbs for miners' helmets. The $280.6 billion in the

TABLE A.1 Input-Output Table for the United States, 1997 (billions of dollars)

	Agriculture, Forestry, and Fishing	Mining	Construction	Manufactured Products	Transportation, Communications, and Utilities	Wholesale and Retail Trade	Finance, Insurance, and Real Estate	Services	Other	Total Intermediate Uses	Final Uses (C + I + G + X − M = GDP)	Total Output
Agriculture, forestry, fishing	75.1	0.0	5.41	149.2	0.1	1.6	10.1	11.4	0.5	253.5	41.6	295.1
Mining	0.4	32.6	6.8	114.6	62.1	0.0	0.0	0.0	2.9	219.4	−55.6	163.8
Construction	3.4	4.7	0.9	27.3	44.4	11.6	71.5	27.1	24.6	215.6	728.8	944.3
Manufactured products	51.5	15.1	280.6	1,372.5	76.9	68.2	19.5	321.5	18.2	2,224.1	1,583.1	3,807.1
Transportation, communications, and utilities	12.6	12.8	23.3	177.4	189.9	66.5	49.8	115.8	20.7	668.8	562.6	1,231.4
Wholesale and retail trade	14.7	3.8	75.4	233.9	17.5	31.5	4.8	64.5	2.7	448.9	1,050.3	1,499.2
Finance, insurance, and real estate	21.5	28.7	15.3	68.3	36.9	101.4	384.1	223.0	7.0	886.1	1,423.5	2,309.6
Services	8.2	5.8	91.6	229.5	131.4	200.5	172.7	472.9	11.7	1,324.2	2,066.0	3,390.2
Other	0.2	0.0	1.0	13.2	3.0	10.7	24.4	23.6	2.8	78.9	984.3	1,063.3
Total intermediate inputs	187.7	105.1	500.3	2,406.6	585.1	499.0	744.3	1,264.8	92.6	6,385.6		

Source: *Survey of Current Business* (January 2001), p. 9.

next column—manufactured goods sold to construction firms—includes nails, milled lumber, and cement. The fourth column shows the value of the goods that manufacturing firms sold to other manufacturing firms for use in further production—steel, rubber, plastic, and engines to a company making the big cranes that load and unload container ships.

Go on across the row, and each column entry represents input sales by manufacturing firms to firms in another sector. The third from last entry is in the column for "Total Intermediate Uses." This is the sum of the previous entries in that row. The next column, "Final Uses," is our old final user friends $C + I + G + X - M$. Here we are talking about automobiles for households (C), tractors for farmers (I), asphalt for town governments (G), and automatic rifles for the Colombian army (X), all netted by the value of imports (M). The figures in the last column are simply the sum of the previous two columns.

Another kind of exercise is to trace a particular product bouncing around various sectors as it goes through its various stages of production. Using the familiar wheat-flour-bread example, the wheat that the farmers sold to the miller is included in the $149.2 billion that agriculture, forestry, and fishing firms sold to manufacturing firms. When the miller sold the flour to the baker, this is part of the $1,372.5 billion sold by manufacturing firms to other manufacturing firms. The baker's sale of the bread to the supermarket, then, is in the $68.2 billion that manufacturing firms sold to retail firms (here, supermarkets). At last, the final sale was from the supermarket to the household, and that is included in the $1,050.3 billion sold by wholesale and retail firms as consumption goods.

Now that you have some sense of how the table is constructed, you are ready to look down the columns. The numbers in each column show the value of goods and services *bought* by firms in each sector from other firms for use in further production.

This table combines all production into nine sectorial categories, and at that level of aggregation, it is not very useful except for explaining general input-output principles. The table is available in over 300 categories of goods and services, and this level of detail enables some interesting work. For instance, if you want to double the production of a certain type of tank for desert warfare, you can look down the tank column (a subcategory of manufacturing) and figure out how much more in inputs from other sectors will be required to produce those additional tanks. Of course, once you determine what additional inputs are needed from other sectors, you will have to look down the columns of each of those sectors to determine what additional inputs are needed for those additional inputs, and so on. Fortunately, there is a shortcut procedure from linear algebra that provides the calculations fairly easily.

Retreating a bit from the technical properties, the input-output table is a road map of the U.S. economy, and its level of aggregation is between that of microeconomics and macroeconomics. Even though the difficulty of compiling the table always makes it a few years late, see how useful such a map would be for an economic planner? That usefulness actually resulted in the government suspending the compilation of input-output tables in the 1950s, because some in the U.S. Congress accused it of being "a recipe for push-button planning" and antithetical to free market capitalism. The founder of input-output economics, Wassily Leontief, was a professor at Harvard, but his name probably did not allay fears of a communist conspiracy.

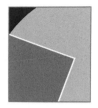

Appendix B

Websites of Related Interest

Here is a short list of websites that you may consult for additional information and understanding about economic affairs. I have used all of them, so I can recommend them for their accuracy and ease of use. On the other hand, it would be difficult to characterize the prose of all but a couple of these sites as gracious and spirited. Use at your own risk.

U.S. Government Data

www.census.gov/prod/www/statistical-abstract.html
The Statistical Abstract of the United States is the most comprehensive compilation of general data. Since the tables appear to have been scanned into the website, they can be difficult to read, and because the data are

assembled annually, they are not current. Nevertheless, The Statistical Abstract is a good place to begin looking for economic information, because each one contains excellent guides to data sources.

http://www.bea.gov/

The home page of the U.S. Department of Commerce, Bureau of Economic Analysis offers the most complete and current economic information, domestic and international. The *Survey of Current Business* is their monthly publication that can be accessed through a link on the left of the BEA home page. Each Survey includes valuable articles on different aspects of U.S. economic activity as well as a standard set of tables of current and historical data.

http://www.federalreserve.gov/

This is the home page of the Board of Governors of the Federal Reserve System, and it has a wide range of current data and analyses that are easy to access. One of the useful features of this website is that it can connect you to all twelve regional Federal Reserve banks. In the search window (on the left), type in "district banks." You will be taken to a screen of FAQs (frequently asked questions). The first one is this: FRB: FAQs: Federal Reserve Banks. Click on that link, and the third question down in the next page is "How many Federal Reserve Banks are there, and where are they located?" This link will take you to a list of links to the regional banks. My favorites are the analyses available from the Boston and Chicago banks, but you should poke around the one in your area for good information about your region and analyses of local and national issues.

http://www.bls.gov/

This is the website of the U.S. Department of Labor, Bureau of Labor Statistics. There are a lot of data there with a particular focus on the characteristics of the U.S. labor force. It is also the principal source of information about the Consumer Price Index. The site can be confusing to use.

http://minneapolisfed.org/research/data/us/
I recommend this site of the Minneapolis Federal Reserve Bank for a website with clear labels and links that has a good exposition of the Consumer Price Index and other financial data.

Business News and Views

The Economist and *The Wall Street Journal* require subscriptions to access their online editions. *Business Week* (www.businessweek.com), *Forbes Magazine* (www.forbes.com), and *The New York Times* (www.nytimes.com) allow limited access to current stories at no cost. All three are good, but *The New York Times* business section is my favorite; it is clear, timely, and often irreverent.

www.dollars&sense.org
This is the online version of the magazine *Dollars and Sense* written and published by a group of heterodox economists skeptical about the discipline of economics and the economic system. They offer well-thought-out and refreshingly lively arguments about how our economy functions.

www.thenation.com
The website of the *The Nation* magazine has a subtitle: "Unconventional Wisdom since 1865." That is an accurate description of the magazine and the website, which does not respect artificial distinctions between "politics" and "economics." It also has interesting and provocative coverage of cultural trends. Closely associated with *The Nation*, Tom Engelhardt produces a free e-mail newsletter from tomdispatch@nationinstitute.org as "a regular antidote to the mainstream media." It's worth looking at.

International

http://worldbank.org
The World Bank home page is an interesting and well-designed site. Hit "Data & Research" at the top of the page for a rich variety of data and analyses.

http://www.imf.org
The IMF home page contains a large number of easily navigated links to current issues and international financial data.

http://jolis.worldbankimflib.org/
This is the site of IMF-World Bank Joint Library. Just hit the JOLIS link, and you can search the catalogue.

http://www.imfsite.org
The Hoover Institution—a conservative think tank on the Stanford University campus—offers an extensive and critical study of the IMF.

http://www.odci.gov/cia/publications/factbook
The CIA *World Factbook* is a useful source of once-over-lightly information about individual nations. My favorite is the second link—Reference Maps.

Index

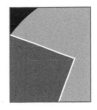

About the Author

Frederick S. Weaver is professor emeritus of economics and history at Hampshire College, and his most recent books are *Global and Local: Revisioning the Area Studies Debate* (2003) and *Latin America in the World Economy: Mercantile Colonialism to Global Capitalism* (2000). He has taught introductory economics at five colleges and universities—public and private, large and small, high-wage and low-wage, lively and grim.